THE REAL APPEAL OF THE BIBLE . . .

lies in the fact that it is the richest collection of observations on life ever bound between two covers. It is filled with drama and melodrama, blood and thunder, intrigue and hate, greed and lust; it throbs with life, bizarre and beautiful, sublime and ridiculous.

This fresh approach to the Bible rescues the Old Book from the contempt bred by familiarity. It reaffirms its value as an illuminating portrait of man's human nature as well as his Divine aspirations.

Other **BALLANTINE/EPIPHANY** *titles*

IS *THAT* IN THE BIBLE?

Dr. Charles Francis Potter
A.M., S.T.M., LITT. D.

BALLANTINE BOOKS • NEW YORK

Contents

Acknowledgments

Acknowledgments are hereby duly and gratefully made to the following firms for permission to quote passages herein from the copyrighted books indicated below.

Edwin S. Gorham, New York, The Book of the Prophet Ezekiel, by H. A. Redpath in Westminster Commentaries.

Harper & Brothers, New York, The Holy Bible, A New Translation, by James Moffatt.

The International Council of Religious Education, Chicago, The American Standard Edition of the Revised Bible.

The Macmillan Company, New York, Folk-lore in the Old Testament, by James Frazer.

Oxford University Press, London and New York, Jeremiah, by A. S. Peake in the New Century Bible series; and the Book of Jubilees in The Apocrypha and Pseudepigrapha of the Old Testament in English, by R. H. Charles.

Charles Scribner's Sons, New York, Commentaries on Deuteronomy, by S. R. Driver, Ecclesiastes, by G. A. Barton, and St. Matthew, by W. C. Allen, all in the International Critical Commentary series; and Hastings' Dictionary of the Bible.

Abbreviations

IN THIS BOOK the Bible passages are quoted from the King James Authorized Version unless otherwise noted. When referred to for purposes of comparison, this version is abbreviated "AV." The initials "RV" refer to the American Standard Revised Version. "Moffatt" is used to designate the modern English translation by Dr. James Moffatt; "m" or "margin" indicates the marginal explanatory notes in either the AV or the RV.

Foreword

MOST PEOPLE take the Bible too religiously. It has been looked upon as a basis for theology, a revelation of a plan of salvation, a source book for expository sermons, a manual for devotional reading, and a collection of "golden texts" for Sunday-school lessons.

Others have looked upon it in too academic a fashion, considering it either as a composite of J, E, D, P, and Q documents, or as a sample of early seventeenth-century English literature.

Its real appeal today lies in neither of these points of view. Theology is rapidly waning; documentary analysis was a temporary crossword puzzle craze among theological seminary professors; and the "Bible as literature" idea was mainly a device to retain Bible study in college curricula where it had originally been installed for the purpose of saving student souls.

In spite of the fact that the religious and literary aspects of the Bible seem to be losing their appeal, the Bible itself continues to be the world's best seller simply because no other book even approaches it in vital human interest.

It is this "human-interest" approach which is emphasized in *Is That in the Bible?* Herein are recognized many matters which have escaped popular notice because the theologians, who have set themselves up as interpreters of the Bible, have concentrated attention on certain parts to the neglect of others.

The majority of the lay public who study the Bible do so in the Sunday schools, where they study, not the Bible itself but the "quarterlies" and other lesson-helps. The uniform international Sunday-school lessons are selected by a committee and, since all pupils, young or old, study the same lesson on a given Sunday, there can be nothing chosen which children should not read or could not understand. The "proper" passages, which are moral and orthodox or can be made to seem so, are soon exhausted, and then the cycle starts all over again.

David and Goliath, the Crossing of the Red Sea, the Feeding of the Five Thousand, and the Healing of the Man Born Blind come around again and again. But there are interesting sections of the Bible which have never yet been given as a Sunday-school lesson and of which, therefore, many are unaware. Thus has standardization mutilated the Bible for us.

This present book is intended for those who are more interested in human life than in divine theology, and who appreciate an amusing situation or a touch of human nature, even if it is in the Bible.

And the Bible is the richest collection of human "case histories" and observations on life that was ever bound between two covers. It is full of drama and melodrama, of blood and thunder, of intrigue and hate, of greed and hot lust. It throbs with life, bizarre and beautiful, sublime and ridiculous.

When one first reads the Old Testament in the Hebrew, he is astonished at its roughness, its saltiness, and its Rabelaisian humor, which is so successfully concealed, for the most part, in the English versions.

There has not yet appeared an unexpurgated version of the Bible in English.

The Bible, to be appreciated, must be taken unadulterated and undiluted by theology. Most books about it are as tiresome as the Bible itself is interesting. They are tiresome because they are written to prove some dogma or doctrine. Once it may have seemed important whether there were two Isaiahs or three. Now few people care if there were thirteen.

This book in hand does not attempt to prove anything. Theology has been purposely left out, both the fundamentalistic plan-of-salvation type and the hypercritical modernistic variety.

We need to find a fresh way of stating Bible episodes whose meaning has been blurred by much quotation, to rescue the Old Book from the contempt bred by familiarity, and to rediscover to the young people of today the great volume, of which they are often so woefully ignorant.

Centuries ago the Bible was unknown by the common people because it was written in Latin and kept chained in monastic libraries.

When it was translated into the vernacular and distributed broadcast to the people, it became a part of their life. They read it eagerly, all of it, and rejoiced to discover the rich human stuff therein. They named their children after its heroes and heroines, and colored their daily conversation with its phrases.

Today many avoid the Bible because they associate it with a religion with which they do not agree. They think of it as a book for pious and fanatic religionists.

Once again the time has come to insist that the church has no right to monopolize the Bible. It is too great a book to be kept in theological chains. It is so universal in its appeal that it holds great interest even for those who do not consider themselves religious and who may never go near a church.

CHARLES FRANCIS POTTER

I

Pertaining to the Household

1. Where in the Bible does it tell how a man wipes dishes?
2. What women sewed pillows on elbows for soul-traps?
3. Whose steps were washed with butter?
4. When did women give up their brass mirrors to make a bathtub for men?
5. What woman "opened a bottle of milk"?
6. Who had ten housekeepers and put them all in prison for life?
7. Whose dishes were all of gold?
8. What verse mentions the oven, frying pan, and griddle?
9. Who was too vile to be cleansed even with lye and soap?
10. Who was called a half-baked pancake?
11. Who said, "A little leaven leaveneth the whole lump"?
12. Who used meal to counteract poison?
13. Who stole shovels and spoons from the Hebrews?
14. Who contemplated a bath in snow-water?
15. What treatment for the sick is recommended in the New Testament?
16. Who purified drinking water with salt?
17. To whom did God give a formula for compounding an oil for furniture?
18. Where is the only place grease is mentioned in the Bible?

19. What was the first cellar mentioned in the Bible used for?

20. Where is described a bed too short and a quilt too narrow?

21. Who gave a party for thirty people in a parlor?

22. Whose bedrooms were paved with red, white, blue, and black marble?

23. Where is soap mentioned?

24. Who asked a visiting preacher not to lie to her?

25. Why do some devout people eat cold food on the Sabbath?

26. Who broke three hundred pitchers?

27. Who were complained of because they did not wash their hands before meals?

28. Who slept on an iron bedstead over thirteen feet long?

29. What woman had a very great store of spices?

30. What girl was trapped by her cooking?

31. Who told a woman to borrow dishes from her neighbors?

32. What man's style of housekeeping took the spirit out of a woman?

ANSWERS TO QUESTIONS
PERTAINING TO THE HOUSEHOLD

1. Where in the Bible does it tell how a man wipes dishes?

Second Kings 21:13.—". . . and I will wipe Jerusalem as a man wipeth a dish, wiping it, and turning it upside down." The margin gives the literal meaning of the Hebrew as, "he wipeth and turneth it upon the face thereof."

2. What woman sewed pillows on elbows for soul-traps?

Superstitious women of Ezekiel's day, Ezekiel 13:18–23 RV.—". . . Woe to the women that sew pillows upon all el-

bows, . . . to hunt souls! Will ye hunt the souls of my people, and save souls alive for yourselves? . . . Wherefore thus
saith the Lord Jehovah: Behold, I am against your pillows,
wherewith ye there hunt the souls to make them fly, and I
will tear them from your arms; and I will let the souls go,
even the souls that ye hunt to make them fly, . . . Therefore,
ye shall no more see false visions, nor divine divinations:
and I will deliver my people out of your hand; . . ."

Some translators prefer "fillets" to "pillows" and "armholes" to "elbows." Frazer, in Folk-lore in the Old Testament, Volume 2, page 511, comments on this passage as
follows: "The nefarious practices of these women, which
the prophet denounces, apparently consisted in attempts to
catch stray souls in fillets and cloths, and so to kill some people by keeping their souls in durance vile, and to save the
lives of others, probably of sick people, by capturing their
vagabond souls and restoring them to their bodies. Similar
devices have been and still are adopted for the same purpose
by sorcerers and witches in many parts of the world." Frazer
then gives numerous interesting examples.

3. Whose steps were washed with butter?

Job's, Job 29:6.—"When I washed my steps with butter,
and the rock poured me out rivers of oil;" This was a sign
of plenty.

4. When did women give up their brass mirrors to make a bathtub for men?

At the time of the furnishing of the tabernacle, Exodus
38:8 and 40:30–31 RV.—"And he made the laver of brass,
and the base thereof of brass, of the mirrors of the minister-
ing women. . . . And he set the laver between the tent of
meeting and the altar, and put water therein, wherewith to
wash. And Moses and Aaron and his sons washed their hands
and their feet thereat;"

5. What woman "opened a bottle of milk"?

Jael, Judges 4:19.—". . . And she [Jael] opened a bottle
of milk, and gave him drink, and covered him." The bottles
of those days were leather bags made from skins.

6. Who had ten housekeepers and put them all in prison for life?

David, Second Samuel 20:3.—"And David came to his
house at Jerusalem; and the king took the ten women his

concubines, whom he had left to keep the house, and put them in ward, and fed them, but went not in unto them. So they were shut up unto the day of their death, living in widowhood." The reason for his doing so may be found in chapter 16:20–23.

7. Whose dishes were all of gold?

Solomon's, First Kings 10:21.—"And all king Solomon's drinking vessels were of gold, and all the vessels of the house of the forest of Lebanon were of pure gold; . . ."

8. What verse mentions the oven, frying pan, and griddle?

Leviticus 7:9.—"And all the meat offering that is baken in the oven, and all that is dressed in the fryingpan, and in the pan, shall be the priest's that offereth it." For the last utensil mentioned, the marginal note has "on the flat plate, or slice"; the RV has "baking pan"; but Moffatt has "griddle," which is probably correct, as the Hebrew word, "machabath," meant "thin plate."

9. Who was too vile to be cleansed even with lye and soap?

Israel, Jeremiah 2:22 RV.—"For though thou wash thee with lye, and take thee much soap, yet thine iniquity is marked before me, saith the Lord Jehovah." AV has "wash thee with nitre, and take thee much sope," Jeremiah is referring to the nation's idolatry and wickedness.

10. Who was called a half-baked pancake?

Ephraim, the Hebrew people personified, Hosea 7:8.— ". . . Ephraim is a cake not turned."

11. Who said, "A little leaven leaveneth the whole lump"?

Paul, in First Corinthians 5:6 and Galatians 5:9.

12. Who used meal to counteract poison?

Elisha, Second Kings 4:40–41.—". . . And it came to pass, as they were eating of the pottage, that they cried out, and said, O thou man of God, there is death in the pot. And they could not eat thereof. But he said, Then bring meal. And he cast it into the pot; and he said, Pour out for the people, that they may eat. And there was no harm in the pot."

13. Who stole shovels and spoons from the Hebrews?

The Chaldeans, Second Kings 25:13–14.—"And the pillars of brass . . . did the Chaldees break in pieces, and carried the brass of them to Babylon. And the pots, and the shovels, and the snuffers, and the spoons, . . . took they away."

14. Who contemplated a bath in snow-water?

Job, Job 9:30.—"If I wash myself with snow water, and make my hands never so clean;"

15. What treatment for the sick is recommended in the New Testament?

Anointing with oil and praying, James 5:14–15.—"Is any sick among you? let him call for the elders of the church; and let them pray over him, anointing him with oil in the name of the Lord: And the prayer of faith shall save the sick, and the Lord shall raise him up; . . ."

16. Who purified drinking water with salt?

Elisha, Second Kings 2:20–22.—"And he [Elisha] said, Bring me a new cruse, and put salt therein. And they brought it to him. And he went forth unto the spring of the waters, and cast the salt in there, . . . So the waters were healed. . . ."

17. To whom did God give a formula for compounding an oil for furniture?

Moses, Exodus 30:22–28.—"Moreover the Lord spake unto Moses, saying, Take thou also unto thee principal spices, of pure myrrh five hundred shekels, and of sweet cinnamon half so much, . . . and of sweet calamus two hundred and fifty shekels, and of cassia five hundred shekels, . . . and of oil olive an hin: And thou shalt make it an oil of holy ointment, an ointment compound after the art of the apothecary: . . . And thou shalt anoint the tabernacle of the congregation therewith, and the ark of the testimony, And the table and all his vessels, and the candlestick and his vessels, and the altar of incense, . . ."

18. Where is the only place grease is mentioned in the Bible?

Psalm 119:70.—"Their heart is as fat as grease; but I delight in thy law."

19. What was the first cellar mentioned in the Bible used for?

Wine, First Chronicles 27:27.—". . . over the increase of

the vineyards for the wine cellars was Zabdi the Shiphmite."

20. Where is described a bed too short and a quilt too narrow?

Isaiah 28:20.—"For the bed is shorter than that a man can stretch himself on it: and the covering narrower than that he can wrap himself in it."

21. Who gave a party for thirty people in a parlor?

Samuel, First Samuel 9:22–24.—"And Samuel took Saul and his servant, and brought them into the parlour, and made them sit in the chiefest place among them that were bidden, which were about thirty persons. And Samuel said unto the cook, Bring the portion which I gave thee, of which I said unto thee, Set it by thee. And the cook took up the shoulder, and that which was upon it, and set it before Saul. And Samuel said, Behold that which is left! Set it before thee, and eat: for unto this time hath it been kept for thee since I said, I have invited the people. . . ."

22. Whose bedrooms were paved with red, white, blue, and black marble?

Ahasuerus' (Xerxes'), Esther 1:6.—". . . the beds were of gold and silver, upon a pavement of red, and blue, and white, and black, marble."

23. Where is soap mentioned?

Jeremiah 2:22 and Malachi 3:2 RV.—". . . and take thee much soap," ". . . for he is like a refiner's fire, and like fullers' soap:"

24. Who asked a visiting preacher not to lie to her?

The woman of Shunem, Second Kings 4:8–17.—"And it fell on a day, that Elisha passed to Shunem, where was a great woman; and she constrained him to eat bread. And so it was, that as oft as he passed by, he turned in thither to eat bread. . . . And he said, About this season, according to the time of life, thou shalt embrace a son. And she said, Nay, my lord, thou man of God, do not lie unto thine handmaid. And the woman conceived, and bare a son at that season that Elisha had said unto her, . . ."

25. Why do some devout people eat cold food on the Sabbath?

Because the law of Moses forbids kindling a fire on the

Sabbath, Exodus 35:3.—"Ye shall kindle no fire throughout your habitations upon the Sabbath day."

26. Who broke three hundred pitchers?

Gideon and his men, Judges 7:16, 19.—"And he divided the three hundred men into three companies, and he put a trumpet in every man's hand, with empty pitchers, and lamps within the pitchers. . . . So Gideon, and the three hundred men that were with him, came unto the outside of the camp . . . and they blew the trumpets, and brake the pitchers that were in their hands."

27. Who were complained of because they did not wash their hands before meals?

Jesus' disciples, Matthew 15:1–2.—"Then came to Jesus scribes and Pharisees, . . . saying, Why do thy disciples transgress the tradition of the elders? for they wash not their hands when they eat bread." Mark 7:5.—". . . but eat bread with unwashen hands?"

28. Who slept on an iron bedstead over thirteen feet long?

Og, King of Bashan, Deuteronomy 3:11.—"For only Og king of Bashan remained of the remnant of the giants; behold, his bedstead was a bedstead of iron; is it not in Rabbath of the children of Ammon? nine cubits was the length thereof, and four cubits the breadth of it, after the cubit of a man." The common measures of the early Jews are easy to remember, for they are all taken from a man's hand and forearm, literally the handiest sort of measure. Four fingers made one palm; three palms, one span; two spans, one cubit. The finger's breadth was ¾ of an inch; the palm, three inches; the span, nine inches; and the cubit, eighteen inches. The span was the distance from the tip of the thumb to the tip of the little finger when the hand was stretched to its limit. The cubit (Latin, *cubitus*, elbow) was the distance from the elbow to the tip of the middle finger. A bedstead nine cubits long would then be thirteen and a half feet long.

29. What woman had a very great store of spices?

The Queen of Sheba, First Kings 10:10.—"And she gave the king . . . of spices very great store, . . . there came no more such abundance of spices as these which the queen of Sheba gave to king Solomon."

30. What girl was trapped by her cooking?

Tamar, Second Samuel 13:6–14.—"So Amnon lay down, and made himself sick: and when the king was come to see him, Amnon said unto the king, I pray thee, let Tamar my sister come, and make me a couple of cakes in my sight, that I may eat at her hand. . . . And when she had brought them unto him to eat, he took hold of her, and said unto her, Come lie with me, my sister. And she answered him, Nay, my brother, do not force me: . . . Howbeit he would not hearken unto her voice: but, being stronger than she, forced her, and lay with her."

31. Who told a woman to borrow dishes from her neighbors?

Elisha, Second Kings 4:3.—"Then he [Elisha] said, Go, borrow thee vessels abroad of all thy neighbours, even empty vessels; borrow not a few."

32. What man's style of housekeeping took the spirit out of a woman?

Solomon's, First Kings 10:4–5.—"And when the queen of Sheba had seen all Solomon's wisdom, and the house he had built, And the meat of his table, and the sitting of his servants, and the attendance of his ministers, and their apparel, and his cupbearers, . . . there was no more spirit in her." The margin has "butlers" for "cupbearers."

II

Clothing and Fashions

1. What Bible characters practised nudism?
2. Where is manicuring commanded for a bride?
3. Where is wearing pearls prohibited?
4. To what superstitious uses were kerchiefs put?
5. What men wore "goodly bonnets of fine linen"?
6. What two materials were forbidden in the same garment?
7. Where are trimmed beards prohibited?
8. Who had camel's-hair clothes?
9. What two apostles warned women not to braid their hair?
10. With what kind of fruit was the high-priest's garment decorated?
11. Who inherited Elijah's mantle?
12. What man wore bracelets?
13. What prophet was a hairy man and wore a leather belt?
14. Who tore his new clothes into twelve pieces?
15. Who gave a priest a suit of clothes every year?
16. Who admired a princess's feet in sandals?
17. Where are sealskin shoes mentioned?
18. Are hats ever mentioned in the Bible?
19. Where are described colored garments embroidered on both sides?

20. What boy had a variegated coat?

21. Who wore a checkered coat?

22. Who had a seamless coat?

23. What woman made her little son a coat every year?

24. What woman made a pair of kid gloves for her son?

25. Who sewed leaves together to make aprons?

26. Who fled naked when Jesus was arrested?

27. Who lay naked all day and night?

28. Where are women praised for their long hair?

29. Who condemned imported clothes?

30. Who took off his shoe to bind a contract?

31. Where is coral mentioned?

32. Where are described the shortest skirts in the Bible?

33. Whose shoes lasted forty years without wearing out?

34. What women had "changeable suits of apparel"?

35. Who sold the needy for a pair of shoes?

36. Who had reeds wrapped round his head?

37. What was the first change of style in clothing?

38. Who wore a complete linen ensemble—coat, trousers, belt, and hat?

39. What were crisping pins?

40. What were wimples?

41. Where is it stated that a man should be ashamed to wear long hair?

42. Aprons from what man's body were used to cure the sick?

43. What men were not permitted to wear any garment which made them sweat?

ANSWERS TO QUESTIONS ABOUT
CLOTHING AND FASHIONS

1. What Bible characters practised nudism?

Adam, Eve, Saul, Isaiah, and Simon Peter.

Adam and Eve, Genesis 2:25.—"And they were both naked, the man and his wife, and were not ashamed."

Saul, First Samuel 19:24.—"And he stripped off his clothes also, and prophesied before Samuel in like manner, and lay down naked all that day and all that night. Wherefore they say, Is Saul also among the prophets?"

Isaiah, Isaiah 20:3–4.—"And the Lord said, Like as my servant Isaiah hath walked naked and barefoot three years for a sign and wonder upon Egypt and upon Ethiopia; So shall the king of Assyria lead away the Egyptians prisoners, and the Ethiopians captives, young and old, naked and barefoot, even with their buttocks uncovered, to the shame of Egypt."

Simon Peter, John 21:7.—". . . Now when Simon Peter heard that it was the Lord, he girt his fisher's coat unto him, (for he was naked,) and did cast himself into the sea."

For related cases of partial or temporary nudity, see Genesis 9:21–23, Exodus 32:25, Second Samuel 6:14–23, Second Chronicles 28:15–19, Job 24:7–10, Hosea 2:3, Micah 1:8, Mark 14:52.

2. Where is manicuring commanded for a bride?

Deuteronomy 21:11–12.—"And seest among the captives a beautiful woman, and hast a desire unto her, that thou wouldest have her to thy wife; Then thou shalt bring her home to thine house; and she shall shave her head, and pare her nails;" The word translated "pare" means in the Hebrew, "make" or "dress."

3. Where is wearing pearls prohibited?

First Timothy 2:9.—". . . that women adorn themselves . . . not with . . . pearls, . . ."

4. To what superstitious uses were kerchiefs put?

To "hunt souls," a form of divination, Ezekiel 13:18.—

". . . Woe to the women that . . . make kerchiefs upon the head of every stature to hunt souls! . . ." The cloth was supposed to form a sort of trap or net in which the soul might be caught. A somewhat similar use is recorded in the New Testament, where the kerchiefs were supposed by some magic to cure diseases by driving out or trapping evil spirits, Acts 19:11–12.—"And God wrought special miracles by the hands of Paul: So that from his body were brought unto the sick handkerchiefs or aprons, and the diseases departed from them, and the evil spirits went out of them."

5. *What men wore "goodly bonnets of fine linen"?*

Aaron and his sons, Exodus 39:27–29 RV.—"And they made the coats of fine linen of woven work for Aaron, and for his sons, and the mitre [margin, "turban"] of fine linen, and the goodly head-tires of fine linen, and the linen breeches of fine twined linen, and the girdle of fine twined linen, and blue, and purple, and scarlet, the work of the embroiderer; as Jehovah commanded Moses."

6. *What two materials were forbidden in the same garment?*

Woolen and linen, Deuteronomy 22:11.—"Thou shalt not wear a garment of divers sorts, as of woollen and linen together." Pioneer Americans transgressed this commandment when they wore "linsey-woolsey" clothes.

7. *Where are trimmed beards prohibited?*

Leviticus 19:27.—"Ye shall not round the corners of your heads, neither shalt thou mar the corners of thy beard."

8. *Who had camel's-hair clothes?*

John the Baptist, Matthew 3:4.—"And the same John had his raiment of camel's hair, . . ."

9. *What two apostles warned women not to braid their hair?*

Paul and Peter, First Timothy 2:9 RV.—"In like manner, that women adorn themselves in modest apparel, with shamefastness and sobriety; not with braided hair, . . ." First Peter 3:3 RV.—"Whose adorning let it not be the outward adorning of braiding the hair, . . ."

10. *With what kind of fruit was the high-priest's garment decorated?*

Pomegranates, Exodus 28:33.——"And beneath upon the hem of it thou shalt make pomegranates of blue, and of purple, and of scarlet, round about the hem thereof; . . ."

11. Who inherited Elijah's mantle?

Elisha, Second Kings 2:12–13.—"And Elisha . . . took hold of his own clothes, and rent them in two pieces. And he took the mantle of Elijah that fell from him, . . ." See also First Kings 19:19.

12. What man wore bracelets?

Saul, Second Samuel 1:10.—". . . and I took the crown that was upon his [Saul's] head, and the bracelet that was on his arm, and have brought them hither unto my lord."

13. What prophet was a hairy man and wore a leather belt?

Elijah, Second Kings 1:8.—"And they answered him, He was an hairy man, and girt with a girdle of leather about his loins. And he said, It is Elijah the Tishbite."

14. Who tore his new clothes into twelve pieces?

Ahijah, First Kings 11:30.—"And Ahijah caught the new garment that was on him, and rent it in twelve pieces:"

15. Who gave a priest a suit of clothes every year?

Micah, Judges 17:10.—"And Micah said unto him, Dwell with me, and be unto me a father and a priest, and I will give thee ten shekels of silver by the year, and a suit of apparel, and thy victuals. So the Levite went in."

16. Who admired a princess's feet in sandals?

Solomon, Song of Solomon 7:1 RV.—"How beautiful are thy feet in sandals, O prince's daughter! . . ."

17. Where are sealskin shoes mentioned?

Ezekiel 16:10 RV.—"I clothed thee also with broidered work, and shod thee with sealskin, . . ." The margin gives, "porpoise-skin," and the AV has, "badgers' skin."

18. Are hats ever mentioned in the Bible?

Yes, Daniel 3:21.—"Then these men were bound in their coats, their hosen, and their hats, . . ." The margin has, "turbans."

19. Where are described colored garments embroidered on both sides?

Judges 5:30 RV.—". . . have they not divided the spoil? . . . To Sisera a spoil of dyed garments, A spoil of dyed garments embroidered, Of dyed garments embroidered on both sides, on the necks of the spoil?"

20. What boy had a variegated coat?

Joseph, Genesis 37:3.—"Now Israel loved Joseph more than all his children, . . . and he made him a coat of many colours." AV margin has "pieces" instead of "colours," and RV margin has instead of "a coat of many colours," "a long garment with sleeves."

21. Who wore a checkered coat?

Aaron, Exodus 28:2, 4 RV.—"And thou shalt make holy garments for Aaron thy brother, for glory and for beauty. . . . And these are the garments which they shall make: a breastplate, and an ephod, and a robe, and a coat of checker work, a mitre, and a girdle: . . ."
Verse 29 says that the coat was "in checker work of fine linen," but the translators put "or silk" in the margin. Fancy, or even bizarre, garments have been characteristic of priests, from medicine men to bishops.

22. Who had a seamless coat?

Jesus, John 19:23.—"Then the soldiers, when they had crucified Jesus, took his garments, and made four parts, to every soldier a part; and also his coat: now the coat was without seam, woven from the top throughout."

23. What woman made her little son a coat every year?

Hannah, First Samuel 2:19.—"Moreover his mother made him a little coat, and brought it to him from year to year, when she came up with her husband to offer the yearly sacrifice."

24. What woman made a pair of kid gloves for her son?

Rebekah, Genesis 27:15–16 RV.—"And Rebekah took the goodly garments of Esau her elder son, which were with her in the house, and put them upon Jacob her younger son; and she put the skins of the kids of the goats upon his hands, . . ."

25. Who sewed leaves together to make aprons?

Adam and Eve, Genesis 3:7.—"And the eyes of both of them were opened, and they knew that they were naked;

and they sewed fig leaves together, and made themselves aprons."

26. Who fled naked when Jesus was arrested?

"A certain young man," perhaps Mark himself, Mark 14:51–52.—"And there followed him a certain young man, having a linen cloth cast about his naked body; and the young men laid hold on him: And he left the linen cloth, and fled from them naked."

27. Who lay naked all day and night?

David, First Samuel 19:24.—"And he [Saul] stripped off his clothes . . . and lay down naked all that day and all that night."

28. Where are women praised for their long hair?

First Corinthians 11:15.—"But if a woman have long hair, it is a glory to her: . . ,"

29. Who condemned imported clothes?

Zephaniah, Zephaniah 1:8 RV.—"And it shall come to pass . . . that I will punish the princes, and the king's sons, and all such as are clothed with foreign apparel."

30. Who took off his shoe to bind a contract?

Boaz, Ruth 4:7–9.—"Now this was the manner in former time in Israel concerning redeeming and concerning changing, for to confirm all things; a man plucked off his shoe, and gave it to his neighbour: and this was a testimony in Israel. Therefore the kinsman said unto Boaz, Buy it for thee. So he drew off his shoe. And Boaz said unto the elders, and unto all the people, Ye are witnesses this day, that I have bought all that was Elimelech's, and all that was Chilion's and Mahlon's, of the hand of Naomi."

31. Where is coral mentioned?

Job 28:18.—"No mention shall be made of coral, or of pearls: for the price of wisdom is above rubies."

Also Ezekiel 27:16.—"Syria was thy merchant by reason of the multitude of the wares of thy making: they occupied in thy fairs with emeralds, purple, and broidered work, and fine linen, and coral, and agate."

32. Where are described the shortest skirts in the Bible?

First Chronicles 19:4.—"Wherefore Hanun took David's

servants, and shaved them, and cut off their garments in the midst hard by their buttocks, and sent them away."

33. Whose shoes lasted forty years without wearing out?

Those of the children of Israel in the wilderness, Deuteronomy 29:5.—"And I have led you forty years in the wilderness: your clothes are not waxen old upon you, and thy shoe is not waxen old upon thy foot."

34. What women had "changeable suits of apparel"?

The daughters of Zion, Isaiah 3:16–22.—"Moreover the Lord saith, Because the daughters of Zion are haughty, and walk with stretched forth necks and wanton eyes, walking and mincing as they go, . . . In that day the Lord will take away . . . the changeable suits of apparel, and the mantles, and the wimples, and the crisping pins, . . ."

35. Who sold the needy for a pair of shoes?

Israel (the Hebrew nation, northern kingdom, personified), Amos 2:6.—"Thus saith the Lord; For three trangressions of Israel, and for four, I will not turn away the punishment thereof; because they sold the righteous for silver, and the poor for a pair of shoes;"

36. Who had reeds wrapped round his head?

Jonah, Jonah 2:5.—"The waters compassed me about, even to the soul: the depth closed me round about, the weeds were wrapped about my head."

37. What was the first change of style in clothing?

From aprons to coats, Genesis 3:7 and 3:21.—". . . and they sewed fig leaves together, and made themselves aprons." "Unto Adam also and to his wife did the Lord God make coats of skins, and clothed them."

38. Who wore a complete linen ensemble—coat, trousers, belt, and hat?

Aaron, Leviticus 16:3–4.—"Thus shall Aaron come into the holy place: . . . He shall put on the holy linen coat, and he shall have the linen breeches upon his flesh, and shall be girded with a linen girdle, and with the linen mitre shall he be attired: these are holy garments; . . ." For "mitre" the RV margin has "turban."

39. What were crisping pins?

They are mentioned among the costume accessories of the fashionable women of Isaiah's day, especially Isaiah 3:22. The Hebrew word is "charitim" which is translated in the AV as crisping-pins. A crisping-pin is a crimping-pin, for curling the hair, a sort of primitive attempt at a permanent wave. But the RV has "satchels," which is much nearer the meaning of "charitim," which means "bags" and is so translated even by the AV where it occurs again in Second Kings 5:23.

40. What were wimples?

Wimples are in the same list as the above, Isaiah 3:22. The Hebrew word, "mitpachath" meant large veils of muslin or lace covering the head and neck. The same word is used in Ruth 3:15 and is there translated "vail."

41. Where is it stated that a man should be ashamed to wear long hair?

First Corinthians 11:14.—"Doth not even nature itself teach you, that, if a man have long hair, it is a shame unto him?"

42. Aprons from what man's body were used to cure the sick?

From Paul's, Acts 19:11–12.—"And God wrought special miracles by the hands of Paul: So that from his body were brought unto the sick handkerchiefs or aprons, and the diseases departed from them, . . ."

43. What men were not permitted to wear any garment which made them sweat?

The priests, Ezekiel 44:15–18.—"But the priests the Levites, the sons of Zadok, . . . when they enter in at the gates of the inner court, they shall be clothed with linen garments; and no wool shall come upon them, whiles they minister in the gates of the inner court, and within. They shall have linen bonnets upon their heads, and shall have linen breeches upon their loins; they shall not gird themselves with any thing that causeth sweat." Sweat was looked on as a form of uncleanness.

III

Concerning Food

1. Who sent a king pistachio nuts?

2. Who ate veal cooked by a witch?

3. Who fed seventy kings under his table?

4. Who is the only Bible writer to mention the stomach?

5. Where are "cracknels" mentioned?

6. What is the only place where garlic, onions, melons, and leeks are mentioned?

7. What Hebrew served a quick lunch under a tree?

8. Who ate her own son?

9. Why did God threaten to feed meat to the Israelites until it came out their nostrils?

10. Who placed "hot bread" before the Lord?

11. What woman gave David one hundred bunches of raisins?

12. Where are raisins and apples prescribed for the lovesick?

13. What nation was fond of raisin cakes?

14. Who said, "Is there any taste in the white of an egg?"

15. Who went forty days on the strength of two meals?

16. Who were the Hebrew confectioners?

17. Who served boiled beef to a crowd?

18. Who tells of a "garden of nuts"?

19. What king was put on a diet for life?

20. Who fed one hundred prophets in a cave?

21. What woman was preparing her last meal when asked to have the preacher to dinner?

22. Who cooked and ate a fish out-of-doors?

23. When did four vegetarians win a young men's beauty contest?

24. What hungry man cursed a fruitless fig tree?

25. What whole nation was made sick by a quail dinner?

26. Where does it tell about a shore dinner for eight persons?

27. Who fed on wind?

28. What food were Hebrews allowed to sell to foreigners but not permitted to eat themselves?

29. Who had food from heaven and didn't like it?

30. Who prophesied that men would eat the flesh of their own arms?

31. In what two places are cucumbers mentioned?

32. Who brought whom "full ears of corn in the husk"?

33. How many kinds of cheese are mentioned in the Bible?

34. How many people were given a fish dinner from two fishes?

35. Who had free fresh fish for food frequently?

36. What father and son disagreed about the value of fasting?

37. Where were idolatrous cookies made?

38. What king became herbivorous?

39. When were clean teeth a sign of famine?

40. Of what insectivorous man was it said that none greater was ever born?

41. Why were the Hebrews forbidden to eat camel meat?

42. Why were the Hebrews forbidden to eat pork?

43. With what food did a serpent tempt a woman?

44. What prophet was fed by birds?

45. When was "doves' dung" sold for food?

46. What widow ate parched corn?

47. Who ate a little book and got indigestion?

48. Who ate a book and found it sweet?

ANSWERS TO QUESTIONS
CONCERNING FOOD

1. Who sent a king pistachio nuts?

Israel, Genesis 43:11, RVm.—"And their father Israel said to them, . . . carry down the man a present, a little balm, and a little honey, spicery and myrrh, nuts, and almonds;" The margin gives "pistachio nuts" which is the correct translation of the Hebrew word used.

2. Who ate veal cooked by a witch?

Saul, First Samuel 28. The whole chapter is the story of Saul's remarkable interview with the Witch of Endor, and ends with: "And the woman had a fat calf in the house; and she hasted, and killed it, and took flour, and kneaded it, and did bake unleavened bread thereof: And she brought it before Saul, and before his servants, and they did eat. . . ."

3. Who fed seventy kings under his table?

Adoni-bezek, Judges 1:7.—"And Adoni-bezek said, Three-score and ten kings . . . gathered their meat under my table. . . ."

4. Who is the only Bible writer to mention the stomach?

Paul, First Timothy 5:23.—". . . use a little wine for thy stomach's sake and thine often infirmities." But "stomacher" is used in Isiah 3:24, and "belly" many times.

5. Where are "cracknels" mentioned?

First Kings 14:3.—"And take with thee ten loaves, and

cracknels, and a cruse of honey, and go to him: . . ." RV has "cakes."

6. What is the only place where garlic, onions, melons, and leeks are mentioned?

Numbers 11:5.—". . . and the melons, and the leeks, and the onions, and the garlick:"

7. What Hebrew served a quick lunch under a tree?

Abraham, Genesis 18:6–8.—"And Abraham hastened into the tent unto Sarah, and said, Make ready quickly three measures of fine meal, knead it, and make cakes upon the hearth. And Abraham ran unto the herd, and fetcht a calf tender and good; and gave it unto a young man; and he hasted to dress it. And he took butter, and milk, and the calf which he had dressed, and set it before them; and he stood by them under the tree, and they did eat."
The "them" refers to three strangers of verse 2.

8. Who ate her own son?

A woman of Samaria, Second Kings 6:29.—"So we boiled my son and did eat him: . . ." See also Lamentations 4:10. —"The hands of the pitiful women have sodden their own children: they were their meat . . ." The word "sodden" is the past participle of the verb "seethe," meaning to boil.

9. Why did God threaten to feed meat to the Israelites until it came out their nostrils?

Because they had tired of manna and had wept for meat. Numbers 11:18–20.—". . . for ye have wept in the ears of the Lord, saying, Who shall give us flesh to eat? for it was well with us in Egypt: therefore the Lord will give you flesh, and ye shall eat. Ye shall not eat one day, nor two days, nor five days, neither ten days, nor twenty days; But even a whole month, until it come out at your nostrils, and it be loathsome unto you: . . ."

10. Who placed "hot bread" before the Lord?

Ahimelech, First Samuel 21:6.—"So the priest [Ahimelech, see verse 1] gave him hallowed bread: for there was no bread there but the shewbread, that was taken from before the Lord, to put hot bread in the day when it was taken away."
The meaning is clearer in Moffatt's translation: "So the priest gave him consecrated bread, for the only bread there

was Presence-bread which had been removed from the presence of the Eternal to let hot bread be placed there the same day."

11. What woman gave David one hundred bunches of raisins?

Abigail, First Samuel 25:18.—"Then Abigail made haste, and took two hundred loaves, and two bottles of wine, and five sheep ready dressed, and five measures of parched corn, and an hundred clusters of raisins, and two hundred cakes of figs, and laid them on asses." She took them to David. (The intervening verses of the King James Authorized Version cannot be printed here without risking trouble with the postal authorities.) He accepted the raisins and other gifts, for verse 35 states, "So David received of her hand that which she had brought him, and said unto her, Go up in peace to thine house; see, I have hearkened to thy voice, and have accepted thy person." As for accepting her person as well as her present, he did that by making her his wife a few days later, for in the interval (verse 38) "the Lord smote Nabal, that he died." There was the problem, also, of David's wife, Michal, but the narrator states (verse 44) that Saul had already given Michal his daughter, David's wife, to another man. And meanwhile the impressionable David had taken to wife (verse 43) still another damsel, "Ahinoam."

12. Where are raisins and apples prescribed for the love-sick?

Song of Solomon 2:5.—"Stay me with flagons, comfort me with apples: for I am sick of love" is the AV and more familiar translation, but the RV has: "Stay ye me with raisins, refresh me with apples; for I am sick from love." If raisins were supposed to be a cure for the love-sick, they apparently did not work very well in David's case.

13. What nation was fond of raisin cakes?

The Israelites, Hosea 3:1, RV.—"And Jehovah said unto me, Go again, love a woman beloved of her friend, and an adulteress, even as Jehovah loveth the Children of Israel, though they turn unto other gods, and love cakes of raisins."

14. Who said, "Is there any taste in the white of an egg?"

Job, Job 6:6.—"Can that which is unsavoury be eaten without salt? or is there any taste in the white of an egg?"

15. Who went forty days on the strength of two meals?

Elijah, First Kings 19:7–8.—"And the angel of the Lord came again the second time, and touched him, and said, Arise and eat; because the journey is too great for thee. And he arose, and did eat and drink, and went in the strength of that meat forty days and forty nights unto Horeb the mount of God."

16. Who were the Hebrew confectioners?

Some of the sons of the priests, First Chronicles 9:30.— "And some of the sons of the priests prepared the confection of the spices."

17. Who served boiled beef to a crowd?

Elisha, First Kings 19:21.—"And he [Elisha] returned back from him, [Elijah] and took a yoke of oxen, and slew them, and boiled their flesh with the instruments of the oxen, and gave unto the people, and they did eat. . . ." Evidently by "instruments" is meant the yokes which he used as fuel.

18. Who tells of a "garden of nuts"?

Solomon, if he wrote the Song of Solomon 6:11.—"I went down into the garden of nuts to see the fruits of the valley, . . ." The Hebrew word used here means "walnuts."

19. What king was put on a diet for life?

Jehoiachin, Jeremiah 52:34.—"And for his diet, there was a continual diet given him of the king of Babylon, every day a portion until the day of his death, all the days of his life."

20. Who fed one hundred prophets in a cave?

Obadiah, First Kings 18:4.—"For it was so, when Jezebel cut off the prophets of the Lord, that Obadiah took an hundred prophets, and hid them by fifty in a cave, and fed them with bread and water."

21. What woman was preparing her last meal when asked to have the preacher to dinner?

The Widow of Zarephath, First Kings 17:10–12.—"So he [Elijah] arose and went to Zarephath. And when he came to the gate of the city, behold, the widow woman was there gathering of sticks: and he called to her, and said,

Fetch me, I pray thee, a little water in a vessel, that I may drink. And as she was going to fetch it, he called to her, and said, Bring me, I pray thee, a morsel of bread in thine hand. And she said, As the Lord thy God liveth, I have not a cake, but, an handful of meal in a barrel, and a little oil in a cruse: and, behold, I am gathering two sticks, that I may go in and dress it for me and my son, that we may eat it, and die."

22. Who cooked and ate a fish out-of-doors?

Jesus, John 21:9–15.—"As soon then as they were come to land, they saw a fire of coals there, and fish laid thereon, and bread. . . . Jesus saith unto them, Come and dine. . . . So when they had dined . . ."

23. When did four vegetarians win a young men's beauty contest?

Daniel 1:11–16.—"Then said Daniel to Melzar, whom the prince of the eunuchs had set over Daniel, Hananiah, Mishael, and Azariah, Prove thy servants, I beseech thee, ten days; and let them give us pulse to eat, and water to drink. Then let our countenances be looked upon before thee, and the countenance of the children that eat the portion of the king's meat: and as thou seest, deal with thy servants . . . And at the end of ten days their countenances appeared fairer and fatter in flesh than all the children which did eat the portion of the king's meat. Thus Melzar took away the portion of their meat, and the wine that they should drink; and gave them pulse." Moffatt translates "pulse" as "vegetables."

24. What hungry man cursed a fruitless fig tree?

Jesus, Mark 11:12–14.—"And on the morrow, when they were come from Bethany, he [Jesus] was hungry: And seeing a fig tree afar off having leaves, he came, if haply he might find any thing thereon: and when he came to it, he found nothing but leaves; for the time of figs was not yet. And Jesus answered and said unto it, No man eat fruit of thee hereafter forever. And his disciples heard it." Matthew adds (Matthew 21:19): "And presently the fig tree withered away."

25. What whole nation was made sick by a quail dinner?

The Israelites, Numbers 11:32–33.—"And the people . . . gathered the quails: . . . And while the flesh was yet be-

tween their teeth, ere it was chewed, the wrath of the Lord
was kindled against the people, and the Lord smote the
people with a very great plague."

26. Where does it tell about a shore dinner for eight per-
        sons?

John 21:2, 13.—"There were together Simon Peter, and
Thomas called Didymus, and Nathanael of Cana in Galilee,
and the sons of Zebedee, and two other of his disciples. . . .
Jesus then cometh, and taketh bread, and giveth them, and
fish likewise." The eight are accounted for by including
Jesus and remembering that there were two sons of Zebedee.
The meal took place on the shore, as verse 9 reveals.

27. Who fed on wind?

Ephraim (the Hebrew people personified), Hosea 12:1.
—"Ephraim feedeth on wind, and followeth after the east
wind: he daily increaseth lies and desolation; . . ." The
meaning of feeding on wind was evidently much like that
of our slang phrase, "hot air."

28. What food were Hebrews allowed to sell to foreigners
        but not permitted to eat themselves?

That which died of itself, Deuteronomy 14:21.—"Ye shall
not eat of any thing that dieth of itself: thou shalt give it
unto the stranger that is within thy gates, that he may eat
it; or thou mayest sell it unto an alien: for thou art an
holy people unto the Lord thy God. . . ."

29. Who had food from heaven and didn't like it?

The Israelites, Numbers 11:9, 4, 6.—"And when the dew
fell upon the camp in the night, the manna fell upon it
. . . and the children of Israel also wept again, and said,
Who shall give us flesh to eat? . . . But now our soul is
dried away: there is nothing at all, beside this manna, before our eyes."

30. Who prophesied that men would eat the flesh of their
        own arms?

Isaiah, Isaiah 9:20.—". . . they shall eat every man the
flesh of his own arm."

31. In what two places are cucumbers mentioned?

Numbers 11:5.—". . . the cucumbers, and the melons, . . ." and Isaiah 1:8, ". . . as a lodge in a garden of cucumbers, . . ."

32. Who brought whom "full ears of corn in the husk"?

A man from Baal-shalisha brought them to Elisha, Second Kings 4:42.—"And there came a man from Baal-shalisha, and brought the man of God bread of the first-fruits, twenty loaves of barley, and full ears of corn in the husk thereof. . . ."

In the United States, "corn in the husk" means Indian corn, or maize, but this was not known in Palestine. Corn is mentioned many times in the Bible, but evidently meant several kinds of grain. Moffatt translates this passage as, "fresh vegetables in a basket."

33. How many kinds of cheese are mentioned in the Bible?

Three, First Samuel 17:18, Second Samuel 17:29, and Job 10:10.—These are three different Hebrew words, and are translated, "cheeses," "cheese of the herd," and "curdled cheese."

34. How many people were given a fish dinner from two fishes?

This is known as The Miracle of the Feeding of the Five Thousand, but the text explicitly states that that figure did not include the women and children. Matthew 14:15–21.— "And they say unto him, We have here but five loaves and two fishes. . . . And they did all eat, and were filled. . . . And they that had eaten were about five thousand men, beside women and children."

35. Who had free fresh fish for food frequently?

The Israelites in Egypt, Numbers 11:5.—"We remember the fish, which we did eat in Egypt freely; . . ."

36. What father and son disagreed about the value of fasting?

Saul and Jonathan, First Samuel 14:24, 29, 30.—". . . for Saul had adjured the people, saying, Cursed be the man that eateth any food until evening, that I may be avenged on mine enemies . . . Then said Jonathan, My father hath troubled the land: see, I pray you, how mine eyes have been enlightened, because I tasted a little of this honey. How much more, if haply the people had eaten freely to-day of the spoil of their enemies which they found? . . ."

37. Where were idolatrous cookies made?

In the cities of Judah and the streets of Jerusalem, Jeremiah 7:17, 18.—"Seest thou not what they do in the cities of Judah and the streets of Jerusalem? The children gather wood, and the fathers kindle the fire, and the women knead their dough, to make cakes to the queen of heaven, and to pour out drink offerings unto other gods, that they may provoke me to anger?"

38. What king became herbivorous?

Nebuchadnezzar, Daniel 4:33.—"The same hour was the thing fulfilled upon Nebuchadnezzar: and he was driven from men, and did eat grass as oxen, . . ."

39. When were clean teeth a sign of famine?

Amos 4:6.—"And I also have given you cleanness of teeth in all your cities, and want of bread in all your places: . . ."

40. Of what insectivorous man was it said that none greater was ever born?

John the Baptist, Matthew 3:4.—"And this same John had his raiment of camel's hair, . . . and his meat was locusts and wild honey." Matthew 11:11.—"Verily I say unto you, Among them that are born of women there hath not risen a greater than John the Baptist: . . ."

41. Why were the Hebrews forbidden to eat camel meat?

The Hebrews were permitted to eat only those cud-chewing animals which were also cloven-hoofed. Leviticus 11:4.—". . . the camel, because he cheweth the cud, but divideth not the hoof; he is unclean unto you."

42. Why were the Hebrews forbidden to eat pork?

The eating of pork was prohibited because (Leviticus 11:7) ". . . the swine, though he divide the hoof, . . . yet he cheweth not the cud; . . ." This is probably a late explanation of an ancient taboo, as was probably the case with the camel also.

43. With what food did a serpent tempt a woman?

The fruit of the tree of the knowledge of good and evil, Genesis 2:17; 3:4, 6.—"But of the tree of the knowledge of good and evil, thou shalt not eat of it: for in the day that thou eatest thereof thou shalt surely die. . . . And the serpent said unto the woman, Ye shall not surely die: . . . And when the woman saw that the tree was good for food, and that it was pleasant to the eyes, and a tree to be desired to make one wise, she took of the fruit thereof, and did eat, and gave also unto her husband with her; and he did eat." This fruit has popularly been interpreted as apples, but there is a clew in verse 7 that it may have been figs, for immediately that they ate, their eyes were opened; they became conscious of their nakedness, and made themselves aprons of fig-leaves.

44. What prophet was fed by birds?

Elijah, First Kings 17:6.—"And the ravens brought him [Elijah] bread and flesh in the morning, and bread and flesh in the evening; . . ."

45. When was "doves' dung" sold for food?

In time of famine, Second Kings 6:25.—"And there was a great famine in Samaria: and, behold, they besieged it, until an ass's head was sold for fourscore pieces of silver, and the fourth part of a cab of dove's dung for five pieces of silver." Roasted chick peas were popularly called "dove's dung."

46. What widow ate parched corn?

Ruth, Ruth 2:14.—". . . And she [Ruth] sat beside the reapers: and he [Boaz] reached her parched corn, and she did eat, and was sufficed, and left." Ruth 1:1–5 reveals that Ruth was a widow.

47. Who ate a little book and got indigestion?

The author of Revelation 10:10.—"And I took the little book out of the angel's hand, and ate it up; . . . and as soon as I had eaten it, my belly was bitter."

48. Who ate a book and found it sweet?

Ezekiel, Ezekiel 2:9 and 3:3.—"And when I looked, behold, an hand was sent unto me; and, lo, a roll of a book was therein; . . . Then did I eat it; and it was in my mouth as honey for sweetness."

IV

Relating to Sex

1. By what man did 78 women have 88 children?

2. Where is there a definite commandment against the wearing of men's clothes by women or the wearing of women's clothes by men?

3. Who was killed for practising birth control?

4. Under what kings did the Hebrews practise phallic worship?

5. What woman preacher taught fornication?

6. What woman made golden images of men and then made love to the images?

7. Who put on make-up to "vamp" a soldier?

8. Who warned his son to beware of a woman's eyelids?

9. What king's women were perfumed for a year before they came to him?

10. What prophet said that the hire of a harlot would be "holiness to the Lord" and would be used to purchase food and clothing for the Lord's people?

11. Who kissed a beautiful young girl and then wept?

12. Who loved a girl much and hated her more as soon as he got her?

13. Who advised a harlot to take a harp and sing around the city?

14. Who killed his brother for humbling his sister?

15. The men of what city were struck blind because they

tried to have sexual relations with celestial beings?

16. What chapter describes the salesmanship of professional prostitutes?

17. Where is a "single standard" of sexual immorality for men and women defended?

18. Who was struck barren for rebuking her husband for indecent exposure?

19. Who "neighed after his neighbor's wife"?

20. What woman fell in love with young men from their portraits?

21. Who bought an adulteress for silver and grain?

22. What woman tried to seduce a handsome young slave?

23. What two prophets committed adultery and were roasted in the fire?

24. What Hebrew king abolished sex-worship?

25. Who saw his neighbor's wife taking a bath and fell in love with her?

26. What man was seduced by his daughter-in-law in disguise?

27. What sisters were threatened with having their ears and noses cut off for permitting intimate attentions by foreign lovers?

28. What young man had sexual intercourse in public with ten women?

29. What prophet married a prostitute at the command of the Lord?

30. Who had three hundred concubines?

31. Where is described a man who died with "his breasts full of milk"?

32. What method was used to test a woman suspected of adultery?

33. What father offered his daughter to libertines, and why?

34. Who gave as a pledge to a harlot a ring, a cord, and a staff?

35. How many cases of incest are recorded in the Bible?

36. What is the Bible euphemism for a male prostitute?

37. What is the Bible euphemism for sexual intercourse?

38. How much was the slanderer of a virgin amerced?

39. Why did the Hebrews consider the sex act unclean?

40. What two Negro eunuchs are praised?

41. What four women of questionable sex-morality are listed in four consecutive verses in the New Testament?

42. What aphrodisiac is mentioned in the Bible?

ANSWERS TO QUESTIONS
RELATING TO SEX

1. By what man did 78 women have 88 children?

Rehoboam, Second Chronicles 11:21.—"And Rehoboam . . . took eighteen wives and threescore concubines; and begat twenty and eight sons, and threescore daughters."

2. Where is there a definite commandment against the wearing of men's clothes by women or the wearing of women's clothes by men?

Deuteronomy 22:5.—"The woman shall not wear that which pertaineth unto a man, neither shall a man put on a woman's garment: for all that do so are abomination unto the Lord thy God."

3. Who was killed for practising birth control?

Onan, Genesis 38:8–10.—"And Judah said unto Onan, Go in unto thy brother's wife, and marry her, and raise up seed to thy brother. And Onan knew that the seed should not be his; and it came to pass, when he went in unto his brother's wife, that he spilled it on the ground, lest that he should give seed to his brother. And the thing which he did displeased the Lord: wherefore he slew him also."

4. Under what kings did the Hebrews practise phallic worship?

Solomon and Rehoboam, Second Kings 23:13–14 and First Kings 14:21–24 (both in Moffatt's translation).—"The king [Josiah] desecrated the shrines east of Jerusalem, . . . which had been erected by Solomon king of Israel for Astarte the detestable idol of the Phoenicians and for Kemosh the detestable idol of the Moabites and for Milkom the detestable idol of the Ammonites. He smashed the obelisks, cut down the sacred poles, and filled up their site with dead men's bones."

"In Judah Rehoboam the son of Solomon reigned. . . . Judah did what was evil in the sight of the Eternal, . . . For they erected shrines, obelisks, and sacred poles, on every height and under every spreading tree; also there were temple-prostitutes in the land. . . ."

In these passages there are four words which indicate phallic worship to any student of the history of religion, namely, obelisks, sacred poles, temple-prostitutes, and Astarte.

5. What woman preacher taught fornication?

The prophetess Jezebel of Thyatira, Revelation 2:18–20. —"And unto the angel of the church in Thyatira write; . . . Notwithstanding I have a few things against thee, because thou sufferest that woman Jezebel, which calleth herself a prophetess, to teach and to seduce my servants to commit fornication, and to eat things sacrificed to idols." It is possible that the woman's real name was not Jezebel and that the writer called her that name because of the similarity of her character to that of the wife of Ahab. See First Kings 21:25 and Second Kings 9:22.

6. What woman made golden images of men and then made love to the images?

Jerusalem personified, Ezekiel 16:17.—"Thou hast also taken thy fair jewels of my gold and of my silver, which I had given thee, and madest to thyself images of men, and didst commit whoredom with them."

7. Who put on make-up to "vamp" a soldier?

Jezebel, Second Kings 9:30–33.—"And when Jehu was come to Jezreel, Jezebel heard of it; and she painted her face, and tired her head, and looked out at a window. . . . And he lifted up his face to the window, and said, Who is on my side? who? And there looked out to him two or three eunuchs. . . . And he said, Throw her down. So they threw her down: . . . and he trode her under foot."

8. Who warned his son to beware of a woman's eyelids?

Solomon, Proverbs 6:25.—"Lust not after her beauty in
thine heart; neither let her take thee with her eyelids."

9. What king's women were perfumed for a year before
   they came to him?

Ahasuerus', Esther 2:12.—"Now when every maid's turn
was come to go in to king Ahasuerus, after that she had
been twelve months, according to the manner of the women,
(for so were the days of their purifications accomplished,
to wit, six months with oil of myrrh, and six months with
sweet odours, and with other things for the purifying of the
women;) Then thus came every maiden unto the king; . . ."

10. What prophet said that the hire of a harlot would be
    "holiness to the Lord" and would be used to purchase
    food and clothing for the Lord's people?

Isaiah, Isaiah 23:17–18.—"And it shall come to pass . . .
that the Lord will visit Tyre, and she shall turn to her
hire, and shall commit fornication with all the kingdoms of
the world upon the face of the earth. And her merchandise
and her hire shall be holiness unto the Lord: it shall not
be treasured nor laid up; for her merchandise shall be for
them that dwell before the Lord, to eat sufficiently, and for
durable clothing."

11. Who kissed a beautiful young girl and then wept?

Jacob, Genesis 29:11, 17.—"And Jacob kissed Rachel, and
lifted up his voice, and wept. . . . Rachel was beautiful and
well favoured." Moffatt has, "Rachel was lovely and handsome." This weeping, however, was probably neither from
grief nor joy, but simply a form of salutation. See Genesis
45:2, 14, 15, and 46:29. Also First Samuel 20:41. For examples of the similar custom in other nations, see Frazer's
Folk-lore in the Old Testament, volume two, pages 82–93.

12. Who loved a girl much and hated her more as soon
    as he got her?

Amnon, Second Samuel 13:2, 14, 15.—"Amnon was so
upset by his passion for his sister Tamar, that it made him
ill—for she was a virgin, and it seemed to Amnon impossible
to get hold of her. . . . But . . . being stronger than she
was, he overpowered her and lay with her. Then Amnon

hated her fiercely; the hate he now felt for her was greater than the love he had felt for her." (This is Moffatt's rendering.)

13. Who advised a harlot to take a harp and sing around the city?

Isaiah, Isaiah 23:16.—"Take an harp, go about the city, thou harlot that hast been forgotten; make sweet melody, sing many songs, that thou mayest be remembered."

14. Who killed his brother for humbling his sister?

Absalom, Second Samuel 13:1, 22, 28, 29.—". . . Absalom the son of David had a fair sister, whose name was Tamar; and Amnon the son of David loved her . . . Absalom hated Amnon, because he had forced his sister Tamar. . . . Now Absalom had commanded his servants, saying, . . . when I say unto you, Smite Amnon; then kill him, fear not: . . . And the servants of Absalom did unto Amnon as Absalom had commanded. . . ."

15. The men of what city were struck blind because they tried to have sexual relations with celestial beings?

Sodom, Genesis 19:1–11.—Moffatt's translation, abridged, reads: "In the evening two of the angels reached Sodom. Lot was sitting at the gate-way of Sodom, and . . . as he pressed them, they turned with him and entered his house, . . . They had not lain down to rest before all the townsmen, the inhabitants of Sodom, beset the house, . . . shouting to Lot, 'Where are the men who came to visit you tonight? Bring them out to us that we may rape them.' . . . So they mobbed Lot and were on the point of breaking into the house, when the men put out their hands, pulled Lot inside, and closed the door. Then they plagued the townsfolk at the door with blindness, . . ."

16. What chapter describes the salesmanship of professional prostitutes?

Proverbs 7.

17. Where is a "single standard" of sexual immorality for men and women defended?

Hosea 4:14.—"But I will not punish your daughters for harlotry, nor your matrons for adultery, when the men themselves go off with harlots, and sacrifice with temple-prostitutes. . . ." (Moffatt.)

18. Who was struck barren for rebuking her husband for indecent exposure?

Michal, First Samuel 18:27 and Second Samuel 6:14, 20, 23.—". . . And Saul gave him [David] Michal his daughter to wife. . . ." "And David danced before the Lord with all his might; and David was girded with a linen ephod. . . . And Michal the daughter of Saul came out to meet David, and said, How glorious was the king of Israel to-day, who uncovered himself to-day in the eyes of the handmaids of his servants, as one of the vain fellows shamelessly uncovereth himself! . . . Therefore Michal the daughter of Saul had no child unto the day of her death."

19. Who "neighed after his neighbor's wife"?

Everyone in Israel, Jeremiah 5:8.—"They were as fed horses in the morning: every one neighed after his neighbour's wife."

20. What woman fell in love with young men from their portraits?

Aholibah, Ezekiel 23:11–17.—"And when . . . Aholibah saw this, . . . she doted upon the Assyrians her neighbours, captains and rulers clothed most gorgeously, horsemen riding upon horses, all of them desirable young men . . . for when she saw men pourtrayed upon the wall, the images of the Chaldeans pourtrayed with vermilion, . . . she doted upon them, and sent messengers unto them into Chaldea. And the Babylonians came to her into the bed of love, . . ."

Aholibah was Jerusalem personified, and the story was told by Ezekiel as a parable.

21. Who bought an adulteress for silver and grain?

Hosea, Hosea 3:1–2.—". . . an adulteress. . . . So I bought her to me for fifteen pieces of silver, and for an homer of barley, and an half homer of barley!" The piece of silver was a shekel, value probably about seventy-five cents. A homer's capacity we do not surely know, the estimates running from 8 to 11 bushels. A fair estimate of the value of a homer and a half of barley would be 15 shekels. He then paid for her thirty shekels (about $22.50), the price of a slave, see Exodus 21:32.

22. What woman tried to seduce a handsome young slave?

Potiphar's wife, Genesis 39:6–7.—". . . And Joseph was

a goodly person, and well favoured. And . . . his master's wife cast her eyes upon Joseph; and she said, Lie with me."

23. What two prophets committed adultery and were roasted in the fire?

Ahab and Zedekiah, Jeremiah 29:22–23.—". . . The Lord make thee like Zedekiah and like Ahab, whom the king of Babylon roasted in the fire; Because they have committed villany in Israel, and have committed adultery with their neighbours' wives, . . ."

24. What Hebrew king abolished sex-worship?

Josiah, Second Kings 23:4–7, Moffatt's translation.— "Then the king [Josiah] ordered Hilkiah the high-priest and the vice-priest and the warders to bring out of the temple of the Eternal all the vessels made for Baal and Astarte and the star-worship; these he burned outside Jerusalem. . . . He took the idol of Astarte out of the temple of the Eternal to the Kidron-ravine outside Jerusalem, where he burned it, grinding it to powder and flinging the powder on the graves of the common people. He demolished the houses of the sacred prostitutes who were in the temple of the Eternal, where the women wove tunics for Astarte." The worship of Astarte included sexual practices.

25. Who saw his neighbor's wife taking a bath and fell in love with her?

David, Second Samuel 11:2, 4.—"And it came to pass in an eveningtide, that David arose from off his bed, and walked upon the roof of the king's house: and from the roof he saw a woman washing herself; and the woman was very beautiful to look upon . . . And David sent messengers and took her; and she came in unto him, and he lay with her; . . ."

26. What man was seduced by his daughter-in-law in disguise?

Judah by Tamar, Genesis 38:13–18.—"And it was told Tamar, saying, Behold thy father in law goeth up to Timnath to shear his sheep. And she put her widow's garments off from her, and covered herself with a vail, and wrapped herself, and sat in an open place, which is by the way to Timnath; . . . When Judah saw her, he thought her to be an harlot; because she had covered her face. And he turned unto her by the way, and said, Go to, I pray thee, let me come in

unto thee; (for he knew not that she was his daughter in
law.) . . . And he . . . came in unto her, and she conceived
by him."

27. What sisters were threatened with having their ears
    and noses cut off for permitting intimate attentions
    by foreign lovers?

Aholah and Aholibah, Ezekiel 23:2–4, 25.—"Son of man,
there were two women, the daughters of one mother: And
they committed whoredoms in Egypt; they committed whoredoms in their youth: there were their breasts pressed, and
there they bruised the teats of their virginity. And the names
of them were Aholah the elder, and Aholibah her sister:
. . . Samaria is Aholah, and Jerusalem Aholibah. . . . And
I will set my jealousy against thee, and they shall deal
furiously with thee: they shall take away thy nose and thy
cars; . . ." (This fate was especially for Aholibah, but
throughout the chapter Ezekiel exhausts his vocabulary to
depict the punishments awaiting the sister nations.)

28. What young man had sexual intercourse in public with
    ten women?

Absalom, Second Samuel 15:16; 16:21–23.—"And the
king left ten women, which were concubines, to keep the
house. . . . And Ahithophel said unto Absalom, Go in unto
thy father's concubines, which he hath left to keep the
house; and all Israel shall hear that thou art abhorred of
thy father: then shall the hands of all that are with thee be
strong. So they spread Absalom a tent upon the top of the
house; and Absalom went in unto his father concubines in
the sight of all Israel. And the counsel of Ahithophel, which
he counselled in those days, was if a man had enquired at
the oracle of God: . . ."
This exhibition had a political significance, as the con-
text shows. The son or would-be successor of the king
strengthened his claim to succession if he was the first to
take over the king's harem, or the favorite wife or concubine.
Solomon put Adonijah to death simply because the latter
asked for Abishag, David's beautiful concubine, for Solomon
feared it was a trick to enable Adonijah to succeed the
recently deceased David. See First Kings 2:10–25.

29. What prophet married a prostitute at the command of
    the Lord?

Hosea, to illustrate a sermon, Hosea 1:2–3.—". . . And

the Lord said unto Hosea, Go, take unto thee a wife of whoredoms and children of whoredoms: for the land hath committed great whoredom, departing from the Lord. So he went and took Gomer the daughter of Diblaim; which conceived, and bare him a son."

30. Who had three hundred concubines?

Solomon, First Kings 11:1, 3.—"But king Solomon loved many strange women, . . . And he had . . . three hundred concubines: . . ."

31. Where is described a man who died with "his breasts full of milk"?

Job 21:23–24.—"One dieth in his full strength, . . . His breasts are full of milk, and his bones are moistened with marrow." RV has, "His pails are full of milk." Compare also Isaiah 60:16.—"Thou shalt also suck the milk of the Gentiles, and shalt suck the breast of kings: . . ."

32. What method was used to test a woman suspected of adultery?

She was made to drink holy water with holy dust in it. See Numbers 5:14–22.—". . . if the spirit of jealousy come upon him, and he be jealous of his wife, . . . Then shall the man bring his wife unto the priest, . . . And the priest shall take holy water in an earthen vessel; and of the dust that is on the floor of the tabernacle the priest shall take, and put it into the water: And the priest shall set the woman before the Lord, . . . And the priest shall charge her by an oath, and say unto the woman, If no man hath lain with thee, and if thou hast not gone aside to uncleanness with another instead of thy husband, be thou free from this bitter water that causeth the curse: But if thou hast gone aside to another instead of thy husband, . . . this water that causeth the curse shall go into thy bowels, to make thy belly to swell, and thy thigh to rot: And the woman shall say, Amen, amen."

33. What father offered his daughter to libertines, and why?

An old man of Gibeah, Judges 19:16–24.—"And, behold, there came an old man from his work out of the field at even, which was also of Mount Ephraim; and he sojourned in Gibeah: but the men of the place were Benjamites. And when he had lifted up his eyes, he saw a wayfaring man in the street of the city: . . . So he brought him into his house. . . . Now as they were making their hearts merry, behold, the men of the city, certain sons of Belial, beset the house round about, and beat at the door, and spake to the master of the house, the old man, saying, Bring forth the man that came into thine house, that we may know him. And the man, the master of the house, went out unto them, and said unto them, Nay, my brethren, nay, I pray you, do not so wickedly; seeing that this man is come into mine house, do not this folly. Behold, here is my daughter a maiden, and his concubine; them I will bring out now and humble ye them, and do with them what seemeth good unto you: but unto this man do not so vile a thing." See Genesis 19:1–11 for a similar story.

34. Who gave as a pledge to a harlot a ring, a cord, and a staff?

Judah, Genesis 38:18, RV.—"And he said, What pledge shall I give thee? And she said, Thy signet and thy cord, and thy staff that is in thy hand. And he gave them to her, and came in unto her,, and she conceived by him." Moffatt has, " 'Your signet-ring,' she said, 'your cord for it, and the stick in your hand'."

35. How many cases of incest are recorded in the Bible?

Nineteen, of eight kinds, as follows:
1. Lot with his elder daughter, Genesis 19:33.
2. Lot with his younger daughter, Genesis 19:35.
3. Abraham with his half-sister, Genesis 20:12.
4. Nahor with his niece, Genesis 11:27, 29.
5. Reuben with his father's concubine, Genesis 35:22; 49:4.
6. Amram with his aunt, Exodus 6:20.
7. Judah with his daughter-in-law, Genesis 38:16–18.
8. Amnon with his sister, Second Samuel 13:2, 14.
9–18. Absalom with his father's ten concubines, Second Samuel 15:16; 16:21–22.
19. Herod with his sister-in-law, Mark 6:17–18.
See also Amos 2:7 and First Corinthians 5:1.
And how about Cain (Genesis 4:17) and Seth (Genesis 4:26)?

36. What is the Bible euphemism for a male prostitute?

A dog, Deuteronomy 23:18.—"Thou shalt not bring the hire of a whore, or the price of a dog, into the house of the Lord thy God for any vow: for even both these are abomination unto the Lord thy God." Moffatt has, "catamite." Driver, in his commentary on Deuteronomy, says this word, "dog," is "an opprobrious designation of the male *kedeshim* referred to in verse 17," where the AV has "sodomite."

37. What is the Bible euphemism for sexual intercourse?

To commit adultery was to uncover or discover the skirt of the woman's husband. Compare the AV of Deuteronomy 22:30: "A man shall not take his father's wife, nor discover his father's skirt," with Moffatt's translation of the same: "No man shall marry a wife of his father or have intercourse with her." See also Ezekiel 16:8, and Ruth 3:9, where "spread the skirt over" seems to mean taking the woman to wife, or announcing that one intends to. The common phrases for sexual intercourse are, "go in unto," "lie with," or "know."

38. How much was the slanderer of a virgin amerced?

A hundred shekels (estimated at $65 by some and at $75 by others). Deuteronomy 22:16–19.—"And the damsel's father shall say unto the elders, I gave my daughter unto this man to wife, and he hateth her; And, lo, he hath given occasions of speech against her, saying, I found not thy daughter a maid; and yet these are the tokens of my daughter's virginity. And they shall spread the cloth before the elders of the city. And the elders of that city shall take that man and chastise him; And they shall amerce him in an hundred shekels of silver, and give them unto the father of the damsel, . . ." To amerce was to fine.

39. Why did the Hebrews consider the sex act unclean?

Because the Levitical law specifically stated that both parties to the act were ceremonially unclean until sundown, Leviticus 15:18.—"The woman also with whom man shall lie with seed of copulation, they shall both bathe themselves in water, and be unclean until the even."

40. What two Negro eunuchs are praised?

Ebed-melech and Candace's eunuch, Jeremiah 38:7, 39:15, 16, 18.—". . . Ebed-melech the Ethiopian, one of the eunuchs which was in the king's house, . . . Now the word of the Lord came unto Jeremiah, . . . saying, Go and speak to Ebed-melech the Ethiopian, saying, Thus saith the Lord

of hosts, the God of Israel; I will surely deliver thee, . . .
because thou hast put thy trust in me, saith the Lord."

Acts 8:27.—". . . a man of Ethiopia, an eunuch of great
authority under Candace queen of the Ethiopians, who had
the charge of all her treasure, and had come to Jerusalem for
to worship."

41. What four women of questionable sex-morality are listed in four consecutive verses in the New Testament?

Tamar, Rahab, Ruth, and Bathsheba, Matthew 1:3–6.—
"and Judah begat Perez and Zerah of Tamar, . . . and Salmon
begat Boaz of Rahab; and Boaz begat Obed of Ruth, . . .
And David begat Solomon of her that had been the wife of
Uriah;" These statements are in the RV account of the
genealogy of Jesus.

Tamar gave birth to Perez (through whom the line to
Jesus is traced) and to his twin brother Zerah as a direct
result of a very irregular sex-affair with Judah, her father-
in-law, described at length in the 38th chapter of Genesis.

Rahab was well known as Rahab the harlot, and is mentioned as a harlot in Joshua 2:1, 6:25, Hebrews 11:31, and
James 2:25.

Ruth's misconduct is not apparent to the casual reader
of the Authorized Version of the Bible, for it is well covered by euphemistic phrases. Moffatt is somewhat more
frank and translates Ruth 3:7 as follows: "When Boaz had
eaten and drunk, and had a merry time, he went to lie
down at the end of the grain heap. Then she [Ruth] crept
in noiselessly, uncovered his waist, and lay down there."
And if Ruth was entirely virtuous, why did the compiler of
the genealogy include her with Tamar, Rahab, and Bathsheba, and omit the virtuous wives of the thirty-three other
ancestors of Jesus?

Bathsheba's affair with David, Second Samuel 11:2–5, is
so well known as to require no emphasis here.

Allen, in his commentary on Matthew (International
Critical Commentary), gives an interesting pious explanation of the inclusion of these women in the genealogy of
Jesus, as follows: "These names are probably introduced
as those of women, in whose case circumstances were over-
ruled by the divine providence which, as it might have
seemed, should have excluded them from a place in the an-
cestral line of the Messiah."

42. What aphrodisiac is mentioned in the Bible?

The caper-berry, Ecclesiastes 12:5 RVm.—". . . and the almond-tree shall blossom, and the grasshopper shall be a burden, and desire shall fail: because man goeth to his everlasting home, . . ." The margin has "caper-berry" instead of "desire." Barton, in his commentary on Ecclesiastes, translates the phrase: "The caper-berry is made ineffectual," and states further, "The caper-berry was a plant used to excite sexual appetite. There can be little doubt that the Hebrew word here used refers to it, since it is the singular of the word which designates the same product in the Talmud."

The whole chapter is a graphic picture of the failing powers of old age.

The Septuagint version has "kapparis," and the plant has been identified botanically as *capparis spinosa*.

V

Wine and Strong Drink

1. Who gave royal wine in abundance to all comers for a week?

2. Where is a remarkably accurate "prophecy" of conditions similar to those obtaining under prohibition?

3. What woman said that poor men should drink and forget their poverty?

4. What young preacher was advised by an older one to drink wine instead of water?

5. What prophet tempted teetotalers with wine in the temple?

6. What father said to his son, "God give thee plenty of corn and wine"?

7. Who said new wine would make virgins flourish?

8. What woodchoppers were given 160,000 gallons of wine?

9. Who washed his garments in wine?

10. Where is an excellent word-picture of a drunken man?

11. Who was the first drunkard and how long did he live?

12. When were the apostles accused of being drunk?

13. How did Peter prove that they were sober?

14. What king was killed by his servant when drinking himself drunk?

15. Who recommended that old women should not drink too much wine?

16. When did thirty-three kings have a drinking-party?

17. Where does it say that both God and man like wine?

18. Who drank wine in bowls?

19. What king had a wine cellar?

20. Who had a "vineyard of red wine" which he watered every moment and watched over night and day?

21. When did Jesus make over a hundred gallons of wine?

22. Where are drunken priests described?

23. What ship-captain got drunk on home brew?

24. Where is wine compared to snakes?

25. When was a girl exchanged for a drink?

26. How many kinds of wine are mentioned in the Bible?

27. What king "dealt to every one of Israel, both man and woman, . . . a flagon of wine"?

ANSWERS TO QUESTIONS ON
WINE AND STRONG DRINK

1. Who gave royal wine in abundance to all comers for a week?

Ahasuerus (Xerxes), Esther 1:5–7.—". . . the king made a feast unto all the people . . . both unto great and small, seven days, . . . And they gave them drink in vessels of gold, . . . and royal wine in abundance, . . ."

2. Where is a remarkably accurate "prophecy" of conditions similar to those obtaining under prohibition?

Isaiah 24:5–11.—"The earth also is defiled under the inhabitants thereof; because they have transgressed the laws, changed the ordinance, broken the everlasting covenant. Therefore hath the curse devoured the earth, and they that dwell therein are desolate: . . . The new wine mourneth, the vine languisheth, all the merryhearted do sigh. The mirth of tabrets ceaseth, the noise of them that rejoice endeth, the joy of the harp ceaseth. They shall not drink wine with a song; strong drink shall be bitter to them that drink it. The city of confusion is broken down: every house is shut up, that no man may come in. There is crying for wine in the streets; all joy is darkened, the mirth of the land is gone."

.3. What woman said that poor men should drink and forget their poverty?

The mother of King Lemuel, Proverbs 31:1-7.—"The words of king Lemuel, the prophecy that his mother taught him. . . . Give strong drink unto him that is ready to perish, and wine unto those that be of heavy hearts. Let him drink, and forget his poverty, and remember his misery no more."

4. What young preacher was advised by an older one to drink wine instead of water?

Timothy, by Paul, First Timothy 5:23.—"Drink no longer water, but use a little wine for thy stomach's sake and thine often infirmities."

5. What prophet tempted teetotalers with wine in the temple?

Jeremiah, Jeremiah 35:4-6.—"And I brought them into the house of the Lord, . . . And I set before the sons of the house of the Rechabites pots full of wine, and cups, and I said unto them, Drink ye wine. But they said, We will drink no wine: for Jonadab the son of Rechab our father commanded us, saying, Ye shall drink no wine, neither ye, nor your sons for ever:" Jeremiah staged this affair as an advertisement and object lesson, asserting that the men of Judah should obey God as the Rechabites obeyed their father.

6. What father said to his son, "God give thee plenty of corn and wine"?

Isaac to Jacob, Genesis 27:28.—"Therefore God give thee of the dew of heaven, and the fatness of the earth, and plenty of corn and wine."

7. Who said new wine would make virgins flourish?

Zechariah, Zechariah 9:17 RV.—"For how great is his goodness, and how great is his beauty! grain shall make the young men flourish, and new wine the virgins."

8. What woodchoppers were given 160,000 gallons of wine?

Hiram's, preparing timbers for Solomon's temple, Second Chronicles 2:3, 10.—"And Solomon sent to Hiram the king of Tyre, saying, . . . behold, I will give to thy servants, the hewers that cut timber, . . . twenty thousand baths of wine, . . ." A bath was about eight gallons.

9. Who washed his garments in wine?

Judah, Genesis 49:10–12.—"The sceptre shall not depart from Judah, nor a lawgiver from between his feet, until Shiloh come; (RVm has "till he come to Shiloh") and unto him shall the gathering of the people be. Binding his foal unto the vine, and his ass's colt unto the choice vine; he washed his garments in wine, and his clothes in the blood of grapes: His eyes shall be red with wine, and his teeth white with milk." "Until Shiloh come" has been taken by some preachers to be a prophecy of the coming of Christ, although Shiloh is a place, not a person, and is not mentioned as a person elsewhere in the Bible. And if Shiloh be a person, and refers to Christ, it becomes embarrassing to account for the fact that his eyes are to be "red with wine."

10. Where is an excellent word-picture of a drunken man?

Proverbs 23:29–30, 33–35.—"Who hath woe? who hath sorrow? who hath contentions? who hath babbling? who hath wounds without cause? who hath redness of eyes? They that tarry long at the wine; they that go to seek mixed wine. . . . Thine eyes shall behold strange women, and thine heart shall utter perverse things. Yea, thou shalt be as he that lieth down in the midst of the sea, or as he that lieth upon the top of a mast. They have stricken me, thou shalt say, and I was not sick; they have beaten me, and I felt it not: when shall I awake? I will seek it yet again."

11. Who was the first drunkard and how long did he live?

Noah, 950 years, Genesis 9:20, 21, 29.—"And Noah . . . was drunken; . . . And all the days of Noah were nine hundred and fifty years: . . ."

12. When were the apostles accused of being drunk?

At Pentecost, Acts 2:13.—"Others mocking said, These men are full of new wine."

13. How did Peter prove that they were sober?

He said it was too early in the day for them to have become drunk, Acts 2:14–15.—"But Peter, standing up with the eleven, lifted up his voice, and said unto them, . . . these are not drunken, as ye suppose, seeing it is but the third hour of the day." (That is, nine o'clock in the morning.)

14. What king was killed by his servant when drinking himself drunk?

Elah, First Kings 16:9–10.—"And his [Elah's] servant Zimri, captain of half his chariots, conspired against him, as he was in Tirzah, drinking himself drunk in the house of Arza steward of his house in Tirzah. And Zimri went in and smote him, and killed him, . . ."

15. Who recommended that old women should not drink too much wine?

Paul, Titus 2:3.—"The aged women likewise, that they be . . . not given to much wine, . . ."

16. When did thirty-three kings have a drinking-party?

Ben-hadad and thirty-two other kings, First Kings 20:16. —". . . But Ben-hadad was drinking himself drunk in the pavilions, he and the kings, the thirty and two kings that helped him."

17. Where does it say that both God and man like wine?

Judges 9:13.—"And the vine said unto them, Should I leave my wine, which cheereth God and man, and go to be promoted over the trees?"

18. Who drank wine in bowls?

The Israelites, Amos 6:6.—"That drink wine in bowls, and anoint themselves with the chief ointments: . . ."

19. What king had a wine cellar?

David, First Chronicles 27:27.—". . . over the increase of the vineyards for the wine cellars was Zabdi the Shiphmite: . . ."

20. Who had a "vineyard of red wine" which he watered every moment and watched over night and day?

The Lord, Isaiah 27:2–3.—"In that day sing ye unto her, A vineyard of red wine. I the Lord do keep it; I will water it every moment: lest any hurt it, I will keep it night and day." Evidently the vineyard symbolizes the Lord's people.

21. When did Jesus make over a hundred gallons of wine?

At the Cana wedding, John 2:1–11.—"And the third day there was a marriage in Cana of Galilee; . . . And both Jesus

was called, and his disciples, to the marriage. . . . And there
were set there six waterpots of stone, . . . containing two or
three firkins apiece. Jesus saith unto them, Fill the waterpots with water. And they filled them up to the brim. And
he saith unto them, Draw out now, and bear unto the governor of the feast. And they bare it. When the ruler of the
feast had tasted the water that was made wine, . . . the governor of the feast called the bridegroom, And saith unto
him, Every man at the beginning doth set forth good wine;
and when men have well drunk, then that which is worse:
but thou hast kept the good wine until now."

A "firkin" contained a little over 8 gallons. The waterpots,
reckoning an average of 2½ firkins, would hold 20 gallons
each, making a total of 120 gallons, which was plenty for a
wedding party, especially as they had confessedly well drunk
already.

22. Where are drunken priests described?

Isaiah 28:7.—". . . the priest and the prophet have erred
through strong drink, they are swallowed up of wine, they
are out of the way through strong drink; they err in vision,
they stumble in judgment." They must have been really
quite drunk, for verse 8 continues, "For all tables are full of
vomit and filthiness, so that there is no place clean."

23. What ship-captain got drunk on home brew?

Noah, Genesis 9:20–21.—"And Noah began to be an
husbandman, and he planted a vineyard: And he drank of
the wine, and was drunken; and he was uncovered within
his tent."

24. Where is wine compared to snakes?

Proverbs 23:32.—"At the last it [wine] biteth like a serpent, and stingeth like an adder."

25. When was a girl exchanged for a drink?

Joel 3:3.—"And they have cast lots for my people; and
have given a boy for an harlot, and sold a girl for wine, that
they might drink."

26. How many kinds of wine are mentioned in the Bible?

There are eleven different Hebrew words translated "wine"
in the Old Testament, and two Greek words in the New.
The Hebrew words are, asis, chamar, chemer, enab, mimsak,
shekar, shemar, sobe, tirosh, yayin, and yeqeb. The Greek

words are *gleukos* and *oinos*. The commonest word for wine was *yayin*, which occurs 133 times.

27. What king "dealt to every one of Israel, both man and woman, . . . a flagon of wine"?

David, First Chronicles 16:2–3.—"And when David had made an end of offering the burnt offerings and the peace offerings, he blessed the people in the name of the Lord. And he dealt to every one of Israel, both man and woman, to every one a loaf of bread, and a good piece of flesh, and a flagon of wine."

VI

Work and Occupations

1. When did a ferry boat ply across the Jordan River?
2. What ten letter carriers are mentioned by name in the Bible?
3. What professional horse-traders are referred to four times?
4. What happened to the only "presidents" mentioned?
5. What was the penalty for working on the Sabbath?
6. Who had his wages changed ten times?
7. Who organized a walkout of bricklayers?
8. What were the qualifications of a bishop?
9. What agricultural implements were used as weapons?
10. Where are given directions for planting and threshing various kinds of grain?
11. Where is pride in good workmanship urged?
12. What preacher earned his living as a tent-maker?
13. What two lawyers are mentioned by name?
14. Who describes a baker preparing bread?
15. Where is an idol-factory described?
16. Who was the first blacksmith?
17. Who was a skilled worker in brass?
18. Who was the first professional lamplighter?
19. Who was the first shepherd?

20. Who was the first city-builder?

21. Where are apothecaries mentioned?

22. Where is the only place the word "leisure" is used?

23. What physician was an author?

24. What two prophets mention Greek slave-traders?

25. Who served in an emergency both as barber and tailor?

26. What workman using wheels was visited by Jeremiah?

27. Who was Jeremiah's secretary?

28. What prophet was a pomologist?

29. What merchants sold cedar chests of clothing?

30. What successful lawyer won a famous case?

31. What song-composer is credited with a thousand and five songs?

32. Where is mentioned the beating of swords into plow-shares and spears into pruning-hooks, and where the beating of plowshares into swords and pruning-hooks into spears?

ANSWERS TO QUESTIONS ON WORK AND OCCUPATIONS

1. When did a ferry boat ply across the Jordan River?

In the days of king David, Second Samuel 19:16-18.—"And Shimei came down with the men of Judah to meet king David . . . and they went over Jordan before the king. And there went over a ferry boat to carry over the king's household, and to do what he thought good. . . ."

2. What ten letter carriers are mentioned by name in the Bible?

The following persons are named in notes found in certain manuscripts at the end of the regular text of Romans, First and Second Corinthians, Ephesians, Philippians, Colossians, Philemon, and Hebrews. These are mostly ninth-century manuscripts, and the notes do not occur in the earlier

manuscripts, but the translators of the King James Authorized Version accepted them as true, and printed them at
the end of the various epistles: Phebe, Stephanus, Fortuna-
tus, Achaicus, Timotheus, Titus, Lucas, Tychicus, Epaphro-
ditus, and Onesimus.

3. What professional horse-traders are referred to four
times?

The house of Togarmah, Ezekiel 27:14.—"They of the
house of Togarmah traded in thy fairs with horses and horsemen and mules." They were Armenians. See also Genesis
10:3, First Chronicles 1:6, and Ezekiel 38:6.

4. What happened to the only "presidents" mentioned?

They were cast into a den of lions, Daniel 6:4, 24.—
"Then the presidents and princes sought to find occasion
against Daniel. . . . And the king commanded, and they
brought those men that had accused Daniel, and they cast
them into the den of lions, them, their children, and their
wives; and the lions had the mastery of them, and brake all
their bones in pieces or ever they came at the bottom of the
den."

5. What was the penalty for working on the Sabbath?

Death, Exodus 31:14.—"Ye shall keep the sabbath therefore; for it is holy unto you: every one that defileth it shall
surely be put to death: for whosoever doeth any work therein, that soul shall be cut off from among his people."

6. Who had his wages changed ten times?

Jacob, Genesis 31:4–7.—"And Jacob sent and called Rachel and Leah to the field unto his flock, And said unto
them, . . . your father hath deceived me, and changed my
wages ten times; . . ."

7. Who organized a walkout of bricklayers?

Moses and Aaron, Exodus 1:13–14; 4:29; 5:1; 12:51.—
"And the Egyptians made the children of Israel to serve
with rigour: And they made their lives bitter with hard
bondage, in morter, and in brick, . . . And Moses and Aaron
went and gathered together all the elders of the children of
Israel: . . . And afterward Moses and Aaron went in, and
told Pharaoh, Thus saith the Lord God of Israel, Let my
people go, . . . And it came to pass . . . that the Lord did
bring the children of Israel out of the land of Egypt. . . ."

8. What were the qualifications of a bishop?

Titus 1:7–9.—"For a bishop must be blameless, as the steward of God; not selfwilled, not soon angry, not given to wine, no striker, not given to filthy lucre; But a lover of hospitality, a lover of good men, sober, just, holy, temperate; Holding fast the faithful word as he hath been taught, . . ." See First Timothy 3:1–7 for an expanded list.

9. What agricultural implements were used as weapons?

Plowshares, coulters, axes, mattocks, forks, and goads. First Samuel 13:20–22.—"But all the Israelites went down to the Philistines, to sharpen every man his share, and his coulter, and his ax, and his mattock. Yet they had a file for the mattocks, and for the coulters, and for the forks, and for the axes, and to sharpen the goads."

10. Where are given directions for planting and threshing various kinds of grain?

Isaiah 28:24–28.—"Doth the plowman plow all day to sow? doth he open and break the clods of his ground? When he hath made plain the face thereof, doth he not cast abroad the fitches, and scatter the cummin, and cast in the principal wheat and the appointed barley and the rie in their place? . . . For the fitches are not threshed with a threshing instrument, neither is a cart wheel turned about upon the cummin; but the fitches are beaten out with a staff, and the cummin with a rod. Bread corn is bruised; because he will not ever be threshing it, nor break it with the wheel of his cart, nor bruise it with his horsemen."

11. Where is pride in good workmanship urged?

Second Timothy 2:15.—"Study to shew thyself approved unto God, a workman that needeth not to be ashamed, rightly dividing the word of truth." Also Exodus 31:3–5.—"And I have filled him [Bezaleel] with the spirit of God, in wisdom, and in understanding, and in knowledge, and in all manner of workmanship, To devise cunning works, to work in gold, and in silver, and in brass, And in cutting of stones, to set them, and in carving of timber, to work in all manner of workmanship."

12. What preacher earned his living as a tent-maker?

Paul, Acts 18:3.—"And because he [Paul] was of the same craft, he abode with them, and wrought; for by their occupation they were tentmakers."

13. What two lawyers are mentioned by name?

Gamaliel and Zenas, Acts 5:34.—". . . a Pharisee, named Gamaliel, a doctor of the law, . . ." Titus 3:13.—"Bring Zenas the lawyer and Apollos on their journey diligently, . . ."

14. Who describes a baker preparing bread?

Hosea, Hosea 7:4.—"They are all adulterers, as an oven heated by the baker, who ceaseth from raising after he hath kneaded the dough, until it be leavened."

15. Where is an idol-factory described?

Isaiah 44:9–17, Moffatt's translation.—"Makers of idols are all inane, and their adored images are futile: . . . The blacksmith works with the coals and hammers the idol into shape, plying his brawny arms, losing strength as he grows hungry and weary for a drink of water. The worker in wood draws lines on the block, marking them with a pencil; then he shapes the idol with his plane into a human figure, comely as a man, to occupy a shrine. In cutting timber for this purpose a man will fix upon some plane or oak, . . . Half of it he burns in the fire, roasting flesh upon the embers; he eats the roast meat and he is satisfied, warming himself and saying, 'Ha, I am warm now, I feel the glow!' The other half he turns into a god, into an idol, and bows down to it, worshipping it, praying to it, crying, 'Save me, for you are my god!' "

16. Who was the first blacksmith?

Tubal-cain, Genesis 4:22.—"And Zillah, she also bare Tubal-cain, an instructer of every artificer in brass and iron: . . ."

17. Who was a skilled worker in brass?

Hiram of Tyre (not king Hiram) First Kings 7:13–14.—"And king Solomon sent and fetched Hiram out of Tyre. He was a widow's son of the tribe of Naphtali, and his father was a man of Tyre, a worker in brass: and he was filled with wisdom, and understanding, and cunning to work all works in brass. And he came to king Solomon, and wrought all his work."

18. Who was the first professional lamplighter?

Aaron, Exodus 30:7–8.—"And Aaron shall burn thereon sweet incense every morning: when he dresseth the lamps, he shall burn incense upon it. And when Aaron lighteth the lamps at even, he shall burn incense upon it, . . ."

19. Who was the first shepherd?

Abel, Genesis 4:2.—"And Abel was a keeper of sheep, . . ." But compare Genesis 4:20: "And Adah bare Jabal: he was the father of such as dwell in tents, and of such as have cattle."

20. Who was the first city-builder?

Cain, Genesis 4:17.—"And Cain . . . builded a city, and called the name of the city, after the name of his son, Enoch."

21. Where are apothecaries mentioned?

Exodus 30:25.—". . . an ointment compound after the art of the apothecary: . . ." See also Exodus 30:35; 37:29; Second Chronicles 16:14; Nehemiah 3:8; Ecclesiastes 10:1.

22. Where is the only place the word "leisure" is used?

Mark 6:31.—"And he [Jesus] said unto them, Come ye yourselves apart into a desert place, and rest a while: for there were many coming and going, and they had no leisure so much as to eat."

23. What physician was an author?

Luke, Colossians 4:14.—"Luke, the beloved physician, . . ." He is credited with the authorship of the gospel of Luke and the book of the Acts of the Apostles, both of them dedicated to Theophilus.

24. What two prophets mention Greek slave-traders?

Ezekiel and Joel, Ezekiel 27:13.—"Javan, Tubal, and Meshech, they were thy merchants: they traded the persons of men and vessels of brass in thy market." Redpath, in his commentary on Ezekiel, says: "Javan is the same name as Ionia, and is generally looked upon as representing Greece." Joel 3:6.—"The children also of Judah and the children of Jerusalem have ye sold unto the Grecians, that ye might remove them far from their border."

25. Who served in an emergency both as barber and tailor?

Hanun, First Chronicles 19:4.—"Wherefore Hanun took David's servants, and shaved them, and cut off their garments in the midst. . . ."

26. What workman using wheels was visited by Jeremiah?

The potter, Jeremiah 18:3.—"Then I went down to the potter's house, and, behold, he wrought a work on the wheels."

27. Who was Jeremiah's secretary?

Baruch, Jeremiah 36:10, 17, 18.—"Then read Baruch in the book the words of Jeremiah. . . . And they asked Baruch, saying, Tell us now, How didst thou write all these words at his mouth? Then Baruch answered them, He pronounced all these words unto me with his mouth, and I wrote them with ink in the book."

28. What prophet was a pomologist?

Amos, Amos 7:14.—"Then answered Amos, and said to Amaziah, I was no prophet, neither was I a prophet's son; but I was an herdman, and a gatherer of sycomore fruit." The margin has "wild figs." But he became one of the greatest prophets of Israel.

29. What merchants sold cedar chests of clothing?

Ezekiel 27:23–24.—"Haran, and Canneh, and Eden, the merchants of Sheba, Asshur, and Chilmad, were thy merchants. These were thy merchants in all sorts of things, in blue clothes, and broidered work, and in chests of rich apparel, bound with cords, and made of cedar, among thy merchandise."

30. What successful lawyer won a famous case?

Gamaliel, Acts 5:34–40.—"Then stood there up one in the council, a Pharisee, named Gamaliel, a doctor of the law, had in reputation among all the people, and commanded to put the apostles forth a little space;" Then he addressed the council on behalf of the apostles, concluding cleverly with: "And now I say unto you, Refrain from these men, and let them alone: for if this counsel or this work be of men, it will come to nought: but if it be of God, ye cannot overthrow it; lest haply ye be found even to fight against God. And to him they agreed: . . ."

31. What song-composer is credited with a thousand and five songs?

Solomon, First Kings 4:32.—". . . and his [Solomon's] songs were a thousand and five."

32. Where is mentioned the beating of swords into plowshares and spears into pruning-hooks, and where the
beating of plowshares into swords and pruning-hooks
into spears?

Swords into plowshares, Isaiah 2:4 and Micah 4:3. Plowshares into swords, Joel 3:10.

VII

Death and Funerals

1. What woman gave a man butter and then killed him?
2. Who killed his seventy brothers on one stone?
3. What "very fat man" was stabbed to death?
4. What murdered girl was mourned by her girl chums four days a year?
5. What blind man's funeral is described in the Bible?
6. Who died the first natural death and what was his alleged age?
7. Who was the first person killed?
8. Where was the first cemetery?
9. What was the name of the cemetery for strangers and why was it so named?
10. What man lived in a cemetery?
11. When did one man execute 450?
12. Who was buried in a cave with his wife?
13. Who erected his own gravestone?
14. What brothers massacred all the men of a city to avenge their sister's honor?
15. Who was killed twice?
16. Who made lime from a king's skeleton?
17. Who put a wet blanket on a king and killed him?
18. What two Hebrews were embalmed by Egyptians?
19. Who accidentally hanged himself in a tree?

20. Who guarded seven corpses of hanged men from beasts and birds?

21. Who killed thieves who were robbing a garden?

22. Who was killed because he wanted to marry his late father's consort?

23. For what king was a "very great burning" made?

24. Who preached about a valley full of men's bones?

25. What dressmaker was raised from the dead?

26. Who was the first of the twelve disciples to be murdered?

27. At whose death did an earthquake occur?

28. Who was hanged on the gallows he had prepared for another?

29. Who fell off a seat and broke his neck?

30. Who hanged himself because his advice was not taken?

31. Who beheaded a man as he lay on his own bed?

32. What seven men were stoned to death?

33. Who were the six Bible suicides?

34. Who said, "The worm shall feed sweetly on him"?

35. What blind man killed 3,000 at a religious feast?

36. What attempt at a "furnace murder" failed?

37. Who cried, "Treason! Treason!" as she was condemned to die?

ANSWERS TO QUESTIONS ABOUT DEATH AND FUNERALS

1. What woman gave a man butter and then killed him?

Jael, Judges 5:25–26.—"He asked water, and she gave him milk; she brought forth butter in a lordly dish. She put her hand to the nail, and her right hand to the workmen's hammer; and with the hammer she smote Sisera, she smote off his head, when she had pierced and stricken through the temples."

2. Who killed his seventy brothers on one stone?

Abimelech, Judges 9:5.—"And he [Abimelech] went unto his father's house at Ophrah, and slew his brethren the sons of Jerubbaal, being threescore and ten persons, upon one stone: . . ."

3. What "very fat man" was stabbed to death?

Eglon, king of Moab, Judges 3:14–26.—"So the children of Israel served Eglon the king of Moab eighteen years. But . . . the Lord raised them up a deliverer, Ehud the son of Gera, . . . But Ehud made him a dagger which had two edges, of a cubit length; and he did gird it under his raiment upon his right thigh. And he brought the present unto Eglon king of Moab: and Eglon was a very fat man. . . . And Ehud said, I have a message from God unto thee. . . . And Ehud put forth his left hand, and took the dagger from his right thigh, and thrust it into his belly: And the haft also went in after the blade; . . . And Ehud escaped . . . unto Seirath."

4. What murdered girl was mourned by her girl chums four days a year?

Jephthah's daughter, Judges 11:39–40.—". . . And it was a custom in Israel, That the daughters of Israel went yearly to lament the daughter of Jephthah the Gileadite four days in a year."

5. What blind man's funeral is described in the Bible?

Samson's, Judges 16:31.—"Then his [Samson's] brethren and all the house of his father came down, and took him, and brought him up, and buried him between Zorah and Eshtaol in the burying place of Manoah his father. . . ."

6. Who died the first natural death and what was his alleged age?

Adam, Genesis 5:5.—"And all the days that Adam lived were nine hundred and thirty years: and he died."

7. Who was the first person killed?

Abel, Genesis 4:8.—"And Cain . . . rose up against Abel his brother, and slew him."

8. *Where was the first cemetery?*

At Mamre (Hebron) in Canaan, Genesis 23:17–20.—
"And the field of Ephron, which was in Machpelah, which
was before Mamre, the field, and the cave which was therein,
. . . were made sure unto Abraham for a possession of a bury-
ingplace by the sons of Heth." Verse 19: ". . . Mamre: the
same is Hebron in the land of Canaan."

9. *What was the name of the cemetery for strangers and
   why was it so named?*

It was called both "the potter's field" and "Aceldama,"
which means "the field of blood." The former name is used
in Matthew and the latter in Acts. In Matthew 27 it is stated
that Judas, repentant, returned to the priests the thirty pieces
of silver which they had paid him to betray Jesus. Verse 7
states: "And they took counsel, and bought with them the
potter's field, to bury strangers in." Evidently it was a plot
of ground near Jerusalem owned by a potter, but Matthew,
with his usual passion for connecting current events with
ancient prophecies, must needs bring in (verse 9) a quotation from "Jeremy the prophet," which really comes from
Zechariah 11:12–13, and obviously has no reference to the
case in hand.

The other name for the cemetery for strangers, "Aceldama," is stated in Acts 1:18–19 to have derived from the
fact that after Judas bought the field "with the reward of
iniquity," he fell headlong, "burst asunder in the midst, and
all his bowels gushed out." So it was called "the field of
blood." But there is good manuscript authority for "Acelda-
mach," which would mean, "the field of sleep," which was
probably the real name of the cemetery. It would therefore
be easy for anyone desiring to connect the cemetery with the
Judas story to drop the final "ch."

10. *What man lived in a cemetery?*

The man with the unclean spirit, Mark 5:2–3.—"And
when he [Jesus] was come out of the ship, immediately
there met him out of the tombs a man with an unclean
spirit, Who had his dwelling among the tombs; . . ."

11. *When did one man execute 450?*

Elijah, in his contest with the priests of Baal, First Kings
18:22, 40.—". . . but Baal's prophets are four hundred and
fifty men. . . . And Elijah said . . . Take the prophets of Baal;
let not one of them escape. And they took them: and Elijah

brought them down to the brook Kishon, and slew them there."

12. Who was buried in a cave with his wife?

Abraham, Genesis 25:9–10.—"And his sons Isaac and Ishmael buried him in the cave of Machpelah, in the field of Ephron. . . . The field which Abraham purchased of the sons of Heth: there was Abraham buried, and Sarah his wife."

13. Who erected his own gravestone?

Absalom, Second Samuel 18:18.—"Now Absalom in his lifetime had taken and reared up for himself a pillar, which is in the king's dale: for he said, I have no son to keep my name in remembrance: and he called the pillar after his own name: and it is called unto this day, Absalom's place." It is possible to harmonize this verse with 14:27: "And unto Absalom there were born three sons, . . ." by assuming that all three of the sons died very young.

14. What brothers massacred all the men of a city to avenge their sister's honor?

Simeon and Levi. Dinah, their sister, had been "defiled" by Shechem the son of Hamor the Hivite. Shechem wished to marry her and her brothers pretended to agree provided all the men of his city would be circumcised. Genesis 34:25: "And it came to pass on the third day, when they were sore, that two of the sons of Jacob, Simeon and Levi, Dinah's brethren, took each man his sword, and came upon the city boldly, and slew all the males." Incidentally, they confiscated the property and enslaved the wives and children of their victims. And when their father Jacob protested that their drastic measures had made him "to stink among the inhabitants of the land," their simple reply was, "Should he deal with our sister as with an harlot?" (34:26–31.) Evidently Simeon and Levi believed in lynching for rape, and did a thorough job of it.

15. Who was killed twice?

Goliath of Gath, First Samuel 17:4, 7, 50, 51 RV.—"And there went out a champion out of the camp of the Philistines, named Goliath, of Gath, whose height was six cubits and a span . . . [9 feet, 9 inches] And the staff of his spear was like a weaver's beam; . . . So David prevailed over the Philistine with a sling and a stone, and smote the Philistine, and slew him; but there was no sword in the hand of David. Then David ran, and stood over the Philistine, and took his sword, and drew it out of the sheath thereof, and slew him, and cut off his head therewith."

Note that, according to this record, David killed Goliath twice, once with the sling and stone and again with the sword. Here evidently two traditions have been blended, clumsily, by a later editor. But if this seems quibbling, turn to Second Samuel 21:19 RV.—"And there was again war with the Philistines at Gob; and Elhanan the son of Jaare-oregim the Bethlehemite slew Goliath the Gittite, the staff of whose spear was like a weaver's beam."

The discrepancy was noticed by the time First Chronicles was written, and an attempt to reconcile it was made in 20:5 by saying: ". . . Elhanan the son of Jair slew Lahmi the brother of Goliath the Gittite, . . ." and the translators of the King James Authorized Version, in Second Samuel 21:19, deliberately inserted the words, "the brother of," before "Goliath," as they confess by using italics.

It affords no way out of the dilemma to presume that Goliath of Gath and Goliath the Gittite were two different persons, for any person who came from Gath was a Gittite.

16. Who made lime from a king's skeleton?

Moab, Amos 2:1.—"Thus saith the Lord; for three transgressions of Moab, and for four, I will not turn away the punishment thereof; because he burned the bones of the king of Edom into lime:" That is, the Moabites did, for in chapters one and two Amos personifies the neighboring tribes in order to make vivid his condemnation of them.

17. Who put a wet blanket on a king and killed him?

Hazael killed king Ben-hadad, Second Kings 8:15 RV.— "And it came to pass on the morrow, that he [Hazael] took the coverlet, and dipped it in water, and spread it on his [Ben-hadad's] face, so that he died: and Hazael reigned in his stead."

18. What two Hebrews were embalmed by Egyptians?

Israel (Jacob) and Joseph, Genesis 50:2.—"And Joseph commanded his servants the physicians to embalm his father: and the physicians embalmed Israel." 50:26: "So Joseph died, being an hundred and ten years old: and they embalmed him, and he was put in a coffin in Egypt."

19. Who accidentally hanged himself in a tree?

Absalom, Second Samuel 18:9.—" . . . And Absalom rode upon a mule, and the mule went under the thick boughs of a great oak, and his head caught hold of the oak, and he was taken up between the heaven and the earth; and the mule that was under him went away." Joab later (verse 14) "took three darts in his hand, and thrust them through the heart of Absalom, while he was yet alive in the midst of the oak."

20. Who guarded seven corpses of hanged men from beasts and birds?

Rizpah, Second Samuel 21:8–10.—"But the king took the two sons of Rizpah . . . and the five sons of Michal . . . And he delivered them into the hands of the Gibeonites, and they hanged them in the hill before the Lord: and they fell all seven together, and were put to death in the days of harvest, . . . And Rizpah the daughter of Aiah took sackcloth, and spread it for her upon the rock, from the beginning of harvest until water dropped upon them out of heaven, and suffered neither the birds of the air to rest on them by day, nor the beasts of the field by night."

21. Who killed thieves who were robbing a garden?

Shammah, Second Samuel 23:11–12.—"And after him was Shammah the son of Agee the Hararite. And the Philistines were gathered together into a troop [margin, "for foraging"], where was a piece of ground full of lentiles: and the people fled from the Philistines. But he stood in the midst of the ground, and defended it, and slew the Philistines: and the Lord wrought a great victory."

22. Who was killed because he wanted to marry his late father's consort?

Adonijah, First Kings 2:22–25. Abishag the Shunammite was the fair damsel secured for king David in his old age because he "gat no heat." When he died Adonijah asked Bathsheba to ask David's successor, Solomon, that Abishag be given to him, Adonijah. "And king Solomon answered and said unto his mother, And why dost thou ask Abishag the Shunammite for Adonijah? ask for him the kingdom also; for he is mine elder brother; . . . Then king Solomon sware by the Lord, saying, God do so to me, and more also, if Adonijah have not spoken this word against his own life. . . . And king Solomon sent by the hand of Benaiah the son of Jehoiada; and he fell upon him that he died."

23. *For what king was a "very great burning" made?*

Asa, Second Chronicles 16:13–14.—"And Asa slept with his fathers, . . . And they buried him in his own sepulchres, which he had made for himself in the city of David, and laid him in the bed which was filled with sweet odours and divers kinds of spices prepared by the apothecaries' art: and they made a very great burning for him."

24. *Who preached about a valley full of men's bones?*

Ezekiel, Ezekiel 37:1–14.—"The hand of the Lord was upon me, . . . and set me down in the midst of the valley which was full of bones, . . . and, behold, there were very many in the open valley; and, lo, they were very dry. And he said unto me, Son of man, can these bones live? And I answered, O Lord God, thou knowest. Again he said unto me, Prophesy upon these bones, . . . So I prophesied as I was commanded: . . ."

25. *What dressmaker was raised from the dead?*

Dorcas, Acts 9:37–40.—"And it came to pass in those days, that she [Dorcas] was sick, and died: . . . and all the widows stood by . . . weeping, and shewing the coats and garments which Dorcas made while she was with them. But Peter put them all forth, and . . . said, Tabitha, arise. And she opened her eyes: and when she saw Peter, she sat up."

26. *Who was the first of the twelve disciples to be murdered?*

James, Acts 12:1–2.—"Now about that time Herod the king stretched forth his hands to vex certain of the church. And he killed James the brother of John with the sword."

27. *At whose death did an earthquake occur?*

Jesus', according to Matthew 27:50–53.—"Jesus, when he had cried again with a loud voice, yielded up the ghost. And, behold, the veil of the temple was rent in twain from the top to the bottom; and the earth did quake, and the rocks rent; And the graves were opened; and many bodies of the saints which slept arose, And came out of the graves after his resurrection, and went into the holy city, and appeared unto many." Buddhists likewise believe that there was a great earthquake at the death of Buddha.

28. Who was hanged on the gallows he had prepared for another?

Haman, Esther 7:10.—"So they hanged Haman on the gallows that he had prepared for Mordecai. . . ."

29. Who fell off a seat and broke his neck?

Eli, First Samuel 4:15, 18.—"Now Eli was ninety and eight years old; and his eyes were dim, that he could not see. . . . And it came to pass, . . . that he fell from off the seat backward by the side of the gate, and his neck brake, and he died: for he was an old man, and heavy. . . ."

30. Who hanged himself because his advice was not taken?

Ahithophel, Second Samuel 17:23.—"And when Ahithophel saw that his counsel was not followed, he saddled his ass, and arose, and gat him home to his house, to his city, and put his household in order, and hanged himself, and died, . . ."

31. Who beheaded a man as he lay on his own bed?

Rechab and Baanah killed Ishbosheth, Second Samuel 4:5–7.—"And . . . Rechab and Baanah went, and came about the heat of the day to the house of Ishbosheth, who lay on a bed at noon . . . and they smote him, and slew him, and beheaded him, and took his head, and gat them away through the plain all night."

32. What seven men were stoned to death?

1. The son of Shelemith, for cursing, Leviticus 24:11, 23.
2. A man who gathered sticks on the Sabbath, Numbers 15:32, 36.
3. Achan, for taking an accursed (tabu) thing, Joshua 6:18, 19; 7:1–26. Also his children and cattle.
4. Adoram, because he was a tax-gatherer of a hated king, First Kings 12:18.
5. Naboth, for alleged blasphemy, but really because king Ahab wanted his vineyard, First Kings 21:1–16.
6. Zechariah, because they disliked his preaching, Second Chronicles 24:20–21.
7. Stephen, for the same reason, Acts 7:54–60.

33. Who were the six Bible suicides?

1. Samson, by pulling down the house, Judges 16:30.
2. Saul, by falling on his sword, First Samuel 31:4.
3. Saul's armour-bearer, the same way, First Samuel 31:5.

4. Ahithophel, by hanging, Second Samuel 17:23.
5. Zimri, by burning the palace, First Kings 16:18.
6. Judas Iscariot, by hanging, Matthew 27:5. But Acts 1:18 states it was by falling headlong.

In the Apocrypha two suicides are recorded:

1. Ptolemy Macron, by poison, Second Maccabees 10:13.
2. Razis, by first falling on his sword, then leaping from a wall, and finally by plucking out his intestines through the wound made by the sword, Second Maccabees 14:41–46.

34. Who said, "The worm shall feed sweetly on him"?

Job, Job 24:20.

35. What blind man killed 3,000 at a religious feast?

Samson, Judges 16:23, 29, 30.—"Then the lords of the Philistines gathered them together for to offer a great sacrifice unto Dagon their god, and to rejoice: for they said, Our god hath delivered Samson our enemy into our hand. . . . And Samson took hold of the two middle pillars upon which the house stood, and on which it was borne up, of the one with his right hand, and of the other with his left. And Samson said, Let me die with the Philistines. And he bowed himself with all his might; and the house fell upon the lords, and upon all the people that were therein. So the dead which he slew at his death were more than they which he slew in his life." (Verse 27 states that there were about 3,000 on the roof alone.)

36. What attempt at a "furnace murder" failed?

Daniel 3:19–27.—"Then . . . Nebuchadnezzar . . . commanded that they should heat the furnace one seven times more than it was wont to be heated. And he commanded the most mighty men that were in his army to bind Shadrach, Meshach, and Abednego, and to cast them into the burning fiery furnace. Then these men . . . were cast into the midst of the burning fiery furnace. . . . Then Shadrach, Meshach, and Abednego came forth of the midst of the fire . . . upon whose bodies the fire had no power, nor was an hair of their head singed, neither were their coats changed, nor the smell of fire had passed on them."

37. Who cried, "Treason! Treason!" as she was condemned to die?

Athaliah, Second Kings 11:13–16.—"And when Athaliah heard the noise of the guard and of the people, she came to the people into the temple of the Lord. And when she looked, behold, the king stood by a pillar, as the manner was, and the princes and the trumpeters by the king, and all the people of the land rejoiced, and blew with trumpets: and Athaliah rent her clothes, and cried, Treason, Treason. But Jehoiada the priest commanded the captains of the hundreds, the officers of the host, and said unto them, Have her forth without the ranges: and him that followeth her kill with the sword. . . . And they laid hands on her; and she went by the way by the which the horses came into the king's house: and there was she slain."

VIII

About Children

1. What woman kidnaped a year-old boy and hid him for six years?
2. Who salted little babies?
3. Where is self-determination for children condemned?
4. What children were considered born in answer to prayer?
5. What king's seventy sons' heads were carried in baskets?
6. What boy died from sunstroke?
7. Who named his daughter after a kind of spice?
8. What captives desired to have their captor's little children dashed against the rocks?
9. When were children cast into a den of lions?
10. What prophet cursed little children for calling him names?
11. What blind man kissed his two grandsons?
12. Who burned his son alive as a sacrifice?
13. What four adopted children are mentioned in the Bible?
14. What two little children were taken into Egypt to escape massacre?
15. What woman's son died as she came to the doorstep of her home?
16. Whose child sneezed seven times?

17. Where is the death penalty commanded for disobedient children?

18. Where is vocational guidance for children advised?

19. Where is child beating commanded?

20. Whose little boy was named Mahershalalhashbaz, and why?

21. What proud father named a city for his boy?

22. What three boys had a father five hundred years old?

23. Did Adam and Eve have any daughters?

24. Who was the first child born after the flood?

25. Who sold their young brother into slavery?

26. Who told midwives to kill all boy babies when they were born?

27. What children's amusements and games are mentioned in the Bible?

28. Whose children were swallowed by an earthquake at the command of the Lord?

29. What five-year-old child was dropped by a careless nurse and lamed for life?

30. What eight-year-old boy was king of Jerusalem for one hundred days?

31. What slave boy became ruler of the land?

32. Is the birth of every child a sin on the part of the mother?

ANSWERS TO QUESTIONS
ABOUT CHILDREN

1. What woman kidnaped a year-old boy and hid him for six years?

Jehosheba, Second Kings 11:1–21.—"And when Athaliah the mother of Ahaziah saw that her son was dead, she arose and destroyed all the seed royal. But Jehosheba, the daughter of King Joram, sister of Ahaziah, took Joash [margin gives "Jehoash"] the son of Ahaziah, and stole him from among the king's sons which were slain; and they hid him, even him and his nurse, in the bedchamber from Athaliah, so that he was not slain. And he was with her hid in the house of the Lord six years. And Athaliah did reign over the land." The priest Jehoiada instigated a rebellion and put the boy on the throne, and (verse 21) "Seven years old was Jehoash when he began to reign."

2. Who salted little babies?

The Hebrews, Ezekiel 16:40, give a case of neglect when the usual procedure was not followed. "And as for thy nativity, in the day thou wast born thy navel was not cut, neither wast thou washed in water to supple thee; thou wast not salted at all, nor swaddled at all."

3. Where is self-determination for children condemned?

Proverbs 29:15.—"The rod and reproof give wisdom: but a child left to himself bringeth his mother to shame."

4. What children were considered born in answer to prayer?

Isaac, Genesis 15:2–5 and Genesis 21:1–3.
Esau and Jacob, Genesis 25:21–26.
Dan, Genesis 30:6.
Issachar, Zebulun, and Dinah, Genesis 30:17–21.
Joseph, Genesis 30:22–24.
Samuel, First Samuel 1:9–20.
John the Baptist, Luke 1:13.

5. What king's seventy sons' heads were carried in baskets?

Ahab's, Second Kings 10:1, 6, 7.—"And Ahab had seventy sons in Samaria. And Jehu wrote letters, and sent to Samaria, unto the rulers of Jezreel, to the elders, and to them that brought up Ahab's children, . . . Then he wrote a letter the second time to them, saying, If ye be mine, and if ye will hearken unto my voice, take ye the heads of the men your master's sons, and come to me to Jezreel by tomorrow this time. Now the king's sons, being seventy persons, were with the great men of the city, which brought them up. And it came to pass, when the letter came to them, that they took the king's sons, and slew seventy persons, and put their heads in baskets, and sent him [Jehu] them to Jezreel."

6. *What boy died from sunstroke?*

The son of the Shunammite woman, Second Kings 4:18–20.—"And when the child was grown, it fell on a day, that he went out to his father to the reapers. And he said unto his father, My head, my head. And he said to a lad, Carry him to his mother. And when he had taken him, and brought him to his mother, he sat on her knees till noon, and then died."

7. *Who named his daughter after a kind of spice?*

Job, Job 42:14.—"And he called the name of the first, Jemima; and the name of the second, Kezia; . . ." Kezia was the Hebrew for cassia, a coarse kind of cinnamon.

8. *What captives desired to have their captor's little children dashed against the rocks?*

The Hebrews in Babylon, Psalm 137:8–9.—"O daughter of Babylon, who art to be destroyed; happy shall he be, that rewardeth thee as thou hast served us. Happy shall he be, that taketh and dasheth thy little ones against the stones."

9. *When were children cast into a den of lions?*

Daniel 6:24.—"And the king commanded, and they brought those men which had accused Daniel, and they cast them into the den of lions, them, their children, and their wives; . . ."

10. *What prophet cursed little children for calling him names?*

Elisha, Second Kings 2:23–24.—"And he [Elisha] went up from thence unto Bethel: and as he was going up by the way, there came forth little children out of the city, and mocked him, and said unto him, Go up, thou bald head; go up, thou bald head. And he turned back, and looked on them, and cursed them in the name of the Lord. And there came forth two she bears out of the wood, and tare forty and two children of them."

11. *What blind man kissed his two grandsons?*

Jacob, Genesis 48:10.—"Now the eyes of Israel [Jacob] were dim for age, so that he could not see. And he brought them [Ephraim and Manasseh, his grandsons] near unto him; and he kissed them, and embraced them."

12. *Who burned his son alive as a sacrifice?*

Ahaz, Second Kings 16:2–3, Moffatt's translation.—"Ahaz was twenty years old when he began to reign, and he reigned in Jerusalem for sixteen years. He did not do what was right in the eyes of the Eternal his god, as his ancestor David had done; he lived on the lines of the kings of Israel, and he actually burned his son alive in sacrifice, following the abominable practice of the nations whom the Eternal had dispossessed to make room for Israel." AV has, "made his son to pass through the fire." For other instances, see Second Kings 17:17; 17:31; Jeremiah 32:35; Ezekiel 16:20–21.

13. What four adopted children are mentioned in the Bible?

Manasseh and Ephraim adopted by Jacob, Genesis 48:1–5.
Moses, by Pharaoh's daughter, Exodus 2:10.
Esther, by Mordecai, Esther 2:7.

14. What two little children were taken into Egypt to escape massacre?

Hadad and Jesus. First Kings 11:15–18.—"For it came to pass, when David was in Edom, and Joab the captain of the host was gone up to bury the slain, after he had smitten every male in Edom; . . . That Hadad fled, he and certain Edomites of his father's servants with him, to go into Egypt; Hadad being yet a little child. And they arose out of Midian, . . . and they came to Egypt, unto Pharaoh king of Egypt; which gave him an house, and appointed him victuals, and gave him land." Matthew 2:13–15: ". . . behold, the angel of the Lord appeareth to Joseph in a dream, saying, Arise, and take the young child and his mother, and flee into Egypt, and be thou there until I bring thee word: for Herod will seek the young child to destroy him. When he arose, he took the young child and his mother by night, and departed into Egypt: And was there until the death of Herod: . . ."

15. What woman's son died as she came to the doorstep of her home?

Jeroboam's wife's son, First Kings 14:17.—"And Jeroboam's wife arose, and departed, and came to Tirzah: and when she came to the threshold of the door, the child died;"

16. Whose child sneezed seven times?

The Shunammite woman's son, Second Kings 4:32–36.

—"And when Elisha was come into the house, behold, the child was dead, and laid upon his bed. He went in therefore, and shut the door upon them twain, and prayed unto the Lord. And he went up, and lay upon the child, and put his mouth upon his mouth, and his eyes upon his eyes, and his hands upon his hands: and he stretched himself upon the child; and the flesh of the child waxed warm. Then he returned, and walked in the house to and fro; and went up, and stretched himself upon him: and the child sneezed seven times, and the child opened his eyes. And he called Gehazi, and said, Call this Shunammite. So he called her. And when she was come in unto him, he said, Take up thy son."

17. Where is the death penalty commanded for disobedient children?

Deuteronomy 21:18–21.—"If a man have a stubborn and rebellious son, which will not obey the voice of his father, or the voice of his mother, and that, when they have chastened him, will not hearken unto them: Then shall his father and his mother lay hold on him, and bring him out unto the elders of his city, and unto the gate of his place; And they shall say unto the elders of his city, This our son is stubborn and rebellious, he will not obey our voice; he is a glutton, and a drunkard. And all the men of his city shall stone him with stones, that he die: so shalt thou put evil away from among you; and all Israel shall hear, and fear." See also Exodus 21:17, Leviticus 20:9.

18. Where is vocational guidance for children advised?

Proverbs 22:6, Moffatt's translation."—Train a child for his proper trade, and he will never leave it, even when he is old." The AV was ambiguous and was frequently misinterpreted. It ran,—"Train up a child in the way he should go: and when he is old, he will not depart from it." The marginal note admitted that the Hebrew really said, "Train up a child in his way" but many old-fashioned parents have used this verse as justification for severe training of the child in their way and contrary to his natural bent.

19. Where is child beating commanded?

Proverbs 23:13–14.—"Withhold not correction from the child: for if thou beatest him with the rod, he shall not die. Thou shalt beat him with the rod, and shalt deliver his soul from hell." See also 13:24; 19:18; 22:15; 29:15.

20. Whose little boy was named Mahershalalhashbaz, and why?

Isaiah's, Isaiah 8:3–4.—"And I [Isaiah] went unto the prophetess; and she conceived, and bare a son. Then said the Lord to me, Call his name Mahershalalhashbaz." This name means "a swift spoil and a speedy prey" and was given to the prophet's child to serve as a warning to the people of the approach of the Assyrians, as Isaiah points out in the next verse: "For before the child shall have knowledge to cry, My father, and my mother, the riches of Damascus and the spoil of Samaria shall be taken away before the king of Assyria."

21. What proud father named a city for his boy?

Cain, Genesis 4:17.—"And Cain knew his wife, and she conceived, and bare Enoch: and he builded a city, and called the name of the city, after the name of his son, Enoch."

22. What three boys had a father five hundred years old?

Shem, Ham, and Japheth, Genesis 5:32.—"And Noah was five hundred years old: and Noah begat Shem, Ham, and Japheth."

23. Did Adam and Eve have any daughters?

Yes. Cain, Abel, and Seth, the three sons of Adam and Eve, were born to them first, according to Genesis 4:1, 2, 25, and then Genesis 5:4 states: "And the days of Adam after he had begotten Seth were eight hundred years: and he begat sons and daughters:"

24. Who was the first child born after the flood?

Presumably Arphaxad, Genesis 11:10–11.—"These are the generations of Shem: Shem was an hundred years old, and begat Arphaxad two years after the flood: And Shem lived after he begat Arphaxad five hundred years, and begat sons and daughters." But Genesis 10:22 states: "The children of Shem; Elam, and Asshur, and Arphaxad, and Lud, and Aram." The question is whether or not Elam and Asshur are to be included among the sons mentioned in 11:11 as having been born after Arphaxad. Ham and Japheth, the other sons of Noah, also had children (see verses 2 and 6 of chapter 10) but Arphaxad is usually taken as the first child born after the flood, probably because of the definite statement, "two years after the flood."

25. Who sold their young brother into slavery?

Joseph's brothers, Genesis 37:26-28.—"And Judah said unto his brethren, What profit is it if we slay our brother, and conceal his blood? Come, and let us sell him to the Ishmeelites, and let not our hand be upon him; for he is our brother and our flesh. And his brethren were content. Then there passed by Midianites merchantmen; and they drew and lifted up Joseph out of the pit, and sold Joseph to the Ishmeelites for twenty pieces of silver: and they brought Joseph into Egypt."

26. Who told midwives to kill all boy babies when they were born?

The king of Egypt, Exodus 1:15-20.—"And the king of Egypt spake to the Hebrew midwives, of which the name of the one was Shiphrah, and the name of the other Puah: And he said, When ye do the office of a midwife to the Hebrew women, and see them upon the stools; if it be a son, then ye shall kill him: but if it be a daughter, then she shall live. But the midwives feared God, and did not as the king of Egypt commanded them, but saved the men children alive. And the king of Egypt called for the midwives, and said unto them, Why have ye done this thing, and have saved the men children alive? And the midwives said unto Pharaoh, Because the Hebrew women are not as the Egyptian women; for they are lively, and are delivered ere the midwives come in unto them. Therefore God dealt well with the midwives: and the people multiplied, and waxed very mighty."

27. What children's amusements and games are mentioned in the Bible?

Dancing, playing in the streets, and playing funeral. Job 21:11.—"They send forth their little ones like a flock, and their children dance." Zechariah 8:5: "And the streets of the city shall be full of boys and girls playing in the streets thereof." Matthew 11:16-17: "But whereunto shall I liken this generation? It is like unto children sitting in the markets, and calling unto their fellows, And saying, We have piped unto you, and ye have not danced; we have mourned unto you, and ye have not lamented." Perhaps mocking peculiar old men should be included (Second Kings 2:23-24), for it has always amused children.

28. Whose children were swallowed by an earthquake at the command of the Lord?

The children of Dathan and Abiram. The latter had rebelled at Moses' leadership. Numbers 16:27–34, Moffatt's translation.—". . . and when Dathan and Abiram, with their wives and little children, came out and stood at the entrance to their tents, Moses told the people to withdraw from the tents of these evil men and to touch nothing that belonged to them; 'lest,' he said, 'you are swept to ruin along with their sins.' Moses added, 'This will convince you that the Eternal has sent me to act, and that I am not acting on my own impulse: if these men die an ordinary death and suffer as all men suffer, then the Eternal has not sent me; but if the Eternal does something new, if the ground yawns and swallows up them and theirs, and they go down alive to the grave, then you may be sure that these men have despised the Eternal.' He had just finished speaking when the ground split under their feet; the earth did yawn and swallow up them and their households. So they and all theirs went down alive to the grave, the earth closed over them, and they vanished from the community. Then all the Israelites around fled at their shrieks, thinking the earth might swallow them also."

29. What five-year-old child was dropped by a careless nurse and lamed for life?

Mephibosheth, Second Samuel 4:4.—"And Jonathan, Saul's son, had a son that was lame of his feet. He was five years old when the tidings came of Saul and Jonathan out of Jezreel, and his nurse took him up, and fled: and it came to pass, as she made haste to flee, that he fell, and became lame. And his name was Mephibosheth."

30. What eight-year-old boy was king of Jerusalem for one hundred days?

Jehoiachin, Second Chronicles 36:9.—"Jehoiachin was eight years old when he began to reign, and he reigned three months and ten days in Jerusalem: and he did that which was evil in the sight of the Lord." One wonders what! In the Apocrypha, First Esdras 1:44 gives his age as 18 when he began to reign. His name is variously spelled Jeconiah, Coniah, Joakim, Jechonias, and Jechoniah, and he is frequently referred to in Jeremiah, and in Matthew 1:12 he is counted as one of the ancestors of Jesus.

31. What slave boy became ruler of the land?

Joseph, Genesis 39:1; 41:41.—"And Joseph was brought down to Egypt; and Potiphar . . . bought him. . . ." "And Pharaoh said unto Joseph, See, I have set thee over all the land of Egypt."

32. Is the birth of every child a sin on the part of the mother?

Yes, according to Leviticus 12:6–7.—"And when the days of her purifying are fulfilled, for a son, or for a daughter, she shall bring a lamb of the first year for a burnt offering, and a young pigeon, or a turtle-dove, for a sin offering, unto the door of the tabernacle of the congregation, unto the priest: Who shall offer it before the Lord, and make atonement for her; . . ."

The "churching of women" in some Christian churches is a survival of this ancient law.

It was rather inconsistent to look upon childbearing as a sin when the first command of God to man was said to have been (Genesis 1:28), "Be fruitful and multiply."

IX

Marriage Matters

1. Who was Cain's wife?
2. Where is a long description of a perfect wife?
3. What bridegroom gave a stag-party and schemed to get a linen-shower?
4. Where is a complete bridal toilet described?
5. What one cause for divorce did Jesus recognize?
6. Who tore his clothes and pulled out his hair because of racial intermarriage?
7. Who pulled out men's hair for marrying foreign wives?
8. Who advised Christians not to marry non-Christians?
9. Who deceived his son-in-law by substituting the bride's older sister on the wedding night?
10. What peculiar price did David pay for his first wife?
11. Who worked seven years to earn a wife?
12. How many wives had David?
13. How many wives and concubines had Solomon?
14. Who said, "Whoso findeth a wife findeth a good thing"?
15. Who was the first bigamist?
16. Where is it prophesied that seven women will offer to support themselves if one man will only marry them?
17. What bachelor of forty years married two women who were a grief to his parents?
18. Who said, "It is better to marry than to burn"?

19. What king gave his daughter a burned city for a bridal portion?

20. What Hebrew exile married the queen of Egypt's sister?

21. What Hebrew exile married the daughter of an Egyptian priest?

22. Who was commanded not to mourn for his wife?

23. What wife made a dummy of an idol and put it in bed to represent her husband?

24. Who advised young widows to marry?

25. What maidservant bore children to a man at his wife's request?

26. What judge of Israel was a great polygamist?

27. What father and son both passed off their wives as their sisters?

28. Who advised wives to be subject to their husbands in everything?

29. Who was the first husband to come home and brag about his day's work?

30. Who called his wife a heifer?

31. What famous Bible character had a Negro wife?

32. Who married the daughter of a god?

ANSWERS TO QUESTIONS ON MARRIAGE MATTERS

1. Who was Cain's wife?

This question has troubled every Bible reader, for the only woman previously mentioned was Cain's own mother, Eve, and Genesis 4:16–17 states only: "And Cain went out from the presence of the Lord, and dwelt in the land of Nod, on the east of Eden. And Cain knew his wife; and she conceived, and bare Enoch: and he builded a city, and called the name of the city, after the name of his son, Enoch."

There are other difficulties in these early stories, such as

where the people came from to inhabit the city which Cain
built, and what girl Cain's younger brother Seth married,
for Genesis 4:26 states: "And to Seth, to him also there was
born a son;" But the question of Cain's wife particularly has
always excited great interest in Christian Sunday schools.

The Hebrews, however, answered the question to their own
satisfaction long before there were any Christians. They took
their cue from Genesis 5:4, which states: "And the days of
Adam after he had begotten Seth were eight hundred years:
and he begat sons and daughters:"

There is a book, which should have been included in the
Apocrypha, called The Book of Jubilees. It is a midrash, or
commentary, on Genesis and the first 14 chapters of Exodus,
and was written by a Pharisee, probably between 109 and
106 B.C. It retells the early Bible story by arranging it in
"jubilees" of 49 years, each divided into seven weeks of
seven years, and fills in some of the gaps, including the
question about the wives of Cain and Seth—Book of Jubilees 4:1, 8-11: "And in the third week in the second
jubilee she [Eve] gave birth to Cain, and in the fourth
she gave birth to Abel, and in the fifth she gave birth to
her daughter Awan. . . . And in the sixth week he [Adam]
begat his daughter Azura. And Cain took Awan his sister
to be his wife and she bare him Enoch at the close of
the fourth jubilee. And in the first year of the first week of
the fifth jubilee, houses were built on the earth, and Cain
built a city, and called its name after the name of his son
Enoch. And Adam knew Eve his wife and she bare yet
nine sons. And in the fifth week of the fifth jubilee Seth
took Azura his sister to be his wife, and in the fourth
(year of the sixth week) she bare him Enos."

There really seems to be no other possible answer, if
the story is to be taken literally. The incest may shock our
modern morality-consciousness, but marriages between
brothers and sisters were common in Egyptian royal families
as late as the time of Akhenaten (1388-1358 B.C.)

2. Where is a long description of a perfect wife?

Proverbs 31:10-31, Moffatt's translation:

"A rare find is an able wife—
    she is worth far more than rubies!
Her husband may depend on her,
    and never lose by that;
she brings him profit and no loss,

from first to last.
She looks out wool and flax,
    and works it up with a will.
She is like merchant-ships,
    fetching foodstuffs from afar.
She rises before dawn,
    to feed her household,
    handing her maids their rations.
She buys land prudently;
    with her earnings she plants a vineyard.
She finds that industry is profitable;
    the lamp burns all night in her house.
She girds herself to work,
    and plies her arms with vigour;
she sets her hand to the distaff,
    her fingers hold the spindle.
She fears not snow for her household;
    for they all wear scarlet wool.
She has mantles made for herself,
    she is robed in linen and purple.
To poor folk she is generous,
    and lends a hand to the forlorn.
Her husband is a man of note,
    he sits with the sheikhs in council.
She makes linen yarn and sells it;
    she supplies girdles to the traders.
Strong and secure is her position;
    she can afford to laugh, looking ahead.
She talks shrewd sense,
    and offers kindly counsel.
She keeps an eye upon her household;
    she never eats the bread of idleness.
Her sons congratulate her,
    and thus her husband praises her:
'Many a woman does nobly,
    but you outdo them all!'
Charms may wane and beauty wither,
    keep your praise for a wife with brains;
give her due credit for her deeds,
    praise her in public for her services."

3. What bridegroom gave a stag-party and schemed to get
a linen-shower?

Samson, Judges 14:1, 2, 10–13, RV.—"And Samson . . .
told his father and mother, and said, I have seen a woman

in Timnah of the daughters of the Philistines: now therefore get her for me to wife. . . . And his father went down unto the woman: and Samson made there a feast; for so used the young men to do. And it came to pass, when they saw him, that they brought thirty companions to be with him. And Samson said unto them, Let me now put forth a riddle unto you: if ye can declare it unto me within the seven days of the feast, and find it out, then I will give you thirty linen garments and thirty changes of raiment; but if ye cannot declare it unto me, then shall ye give me thirty linen garments and thirty changes of raiment. . . ."

4. Where is a complete bridal toilet described?

Ezekiel 16:8–14, Moffatt's translation.—"Then, as I passed I saw you were ripe for love; so I spread my robe over you, to cover your nakedness, and pledged myself to you in marriage, making a compact with you—says the Lord the Eternal. Thus did you become my own. I bathed you in water, I washed all the blood off you, and anointed you with oil; I decked you with embroidered robes, I shod you with Egyptian leather, I swathed you in fine linen, I clothed you in silk; I adorned you with finery, bracelets on your arms, a necklace round your throat, a ring on your nose, ear-rings in your ears, and a lovely crown upon your head. You were adorned with silver and gold, robed in fine linen and silk and embroidered robes; your food was fine flour, honey, and oil. You blossomed into a great beauty, . . ."

The bride was Jerusalem personified.

5. What one cause for divorce did Jesus recognize?

Fornication by the wife, Matthew 19:9.—"And I say unto you, Whosoever shall put away his wife, except it be for fornication, and shall marry another, committeth adultery: and whoso marrieth her which is put away doth commit adultery." The same statement is attributed to Jesus in Matthew 5:32, but when Mark (10:11) and Luke (16:18) report this conversation, they say nothing about the exception for fornication. The phrase is considered by some critics to have been an interpolation by an editor.

6. Who tore his clothes and pulled out his hair because of racial intermarriage?

Ezra, Ezra 9:1–3.—". . . The people of Israel, and the priests, and the Levites, have not separated themselves from the people of the lands, doing according to their abominations, even of the Canaanites, the Hittites, . . . the Egyptians, and the Amorites. For they have taken of their daughters for themselves, and for their sons: so that the holy seed have mingled themselves with the people of those lands: . . . And when I heard this thing, I rent my garment and my mantle, and plucked off the hair of my head and of my beard, and sat down astonied."

7. Who pulled out men's hair for marrying foreign wives?

Nehemiah, Nehemiah 13:23–25.—"In those days also saw I Jews that had married wives of Ashdod, of Ammon, and of Moab: And their children spake half in the speech of Ashdod, and could not speak in the Jews' language, but according to the language of each people. And I contended with them, and cursed them, and plucked off their hair, . . ."

8. Who advised Christians not to marry non-Christians?

Paul, Second Corinthians 6:14–15.—"Be ye not unequally yoked together with unbelievers: for what fellowship hath righteousness with unrighteousness? and what communion hath light with darkness? And what concord hath Christ with Belial? or what part hath he that believeth with an infidel?"

9. Who deceived his son-in-law by substituting the bride's older sister on the wedding night?

Laban, Genesis 29:16–26.—"And Laban had two daughters: the name of the elder was Leah, and the name of the younger was Rachel. Leah was tender eyed; but Rachel was beautiful and well favoured. And Jacob loved Rachel; and said, I will serve thee seven years for Rachel thy younger daughter. And Jacob served seven years for Rachel; and they seemed unto him but a few days, for the love he had to her. And Jacob said unto Laban, Give me my wife, for my days are fulfilled, that I may go in unto her. And Laban gathered together all the men of the place, and made a feast. And it came to pass in the evening, that he took Leah his daughter, and brought her to him; and he went in unto her. And it came to pass, that in the morning, behold, it was Leah: and he said to Laban, What is this thou hast done unto me? did not I serve with thee for Rachel? wherefore then hast thou beguiled me? And Laban said, It must not be so done in our country, to give the younger before the firstborn."

The full force of this deception is not evident from the

AV, which calls Leah "tender eyed," whereas the correct translation pictures a much less attractive girl. Her eyes were "tender" in the sense of "weak." Moffatt has "dull eyes," and the Book of Jubilees (see answer to question one of this section) states, in chapter 28, verse 5: ". . . for Leah's eyes were weak, but her form was very handsome; but Rachel had beautiful eyes and a beautiful and very handsome form."

Jacob must have been very drunk, not to have known the difference, and one wonders where Rachel was while all this was going on!

10. What peculiar price did David pay for his first wife?

Two hundred Philistine prepuces, First Samuel 18:27.— "Wherefore David arose and went, he and his men, and slew of the Philistines two hundred men; and David brought their foreskins, and they gave them in full tale to the king, that he might be the king's son in law. And Saul gave him Michal his daughter to wife."

11. Who worked seven years to earn a wife?

Jacob, Genesis 29:20. "And Jacob served seven years for Rachel; and they seemed unto him but a few days, for the love he had to her."

12. How many wives had David?

No one knows, but plenty, for they included Michal, First Samuel 18:27, Abigail and Ahinoam, First Samuel 25:42–43, Bathsheba the wife of Uriah, Second Samuel 11:26–27, and an unknown number of others, Second Samuel 5:13.— "And David took him more concubines and wives out of Jerusalem, after he was come from Hebron: and there were yet sons and daughters born to David." Presumably these included the ten concubines mentioned in Second Samuel 15:16; 16:21–22; and 20:3. And finally there was Abishag, the beautiful virgin who lay in his bosom when he was "stricken in years; and they covered him with clothes, but he gat no heat," First Kings 1:1–4. It states that "the king knew her not," but she certainly should be counted among his wives or concubines.

13. How many wives and concubines had Solomon?

Seven hundred wives and three hundred concubines, First Kings 11:3.—"And he had seven hundred wives, princesses, and three hundred concubines: and his wives turned away his heart." Whether or not the queen of Sheba was one of his wives, perhaps a temporary one during her visit to him, First Kings 10:1–10, the Bible says nothing, but the Abyssinians maintain to this day that one of their kings, Ibn al Hakim, was the son of Solomon and the queen of Sheba, whose name they give as Makeda.

14. Who said, "Whoso findeth a wife findeth a good thing"?

Solomon, if he wrote Proverbs 18:22.—"Whoso findeth a wife findeth a good thing, and obtaineth favour of the Lord." And he must have obtained much favour.

15. Who was the first bigamist?

Lamech, Genesis 4:19.—"And Lamech took unto him two wives: the name of the one was Adah, and the name of the other was Zillah."

16. Where is it prophesied that seven women will offer to support themselves if one man will only marry them?

Isaiah 4:1.—"And in that day seven women shall take hold of one man, saying, We will eat our own bread, and wear our own apparel: only let us be called by thy name, to take away our reproach."

17. What bachelor of forty years married two women who were a grief to his parents?

Esau, Genesis 26:34–35.—"And Esau was forty years old when he took to wife Judith the daughter of Beeri the Hittite, and Bashemath the daughter of Elon the Hittite: Which were a grief of mind unto Isaac and to Rebekah."

18. Who said, "It is better to marry than to burn"?

Paul, First Corinthians 7:8–9.—"I say therefore to the unmarried and widows, It is good for them if they abide even as I. But if they cannot contain, let them marry: for it is better to marry than to burn." This does not refer to punishment in hell, but to what Moffatt calls being "aflame with passion."

19. What king gave his daughter a burned city for a bridal portion?

Pharaoh (probably of the 21st dynasty), First Kings 9:16. —"For Pharaoh king of Egypt had gone up, and taken Gezer, and burnt it with fire, and slain the Canaanites that dwelt in the city, and given it for a present unto his daughter, Solomon's wife."

20. What Hebrew exile married the queen of Egypt's sister?

Hadad, First Kings 11:19.—"And Hadad found great favour in the sight of Pharaoh, so that he gave him to wife the sister of his own wife, the sister of Tahpenes the queen."

21. What Hebrew exile married the daughter of an Egyptian priest?

Joseph, Genesis 41:45.—"And Pharaoh called Joseph's name Zaphnathpaaneah; and he gave him to wife Asenath the daughter of Potipherah priest of On."

22. Who was commanded not to mourn for his wife?

Ezekiel, Ezekiel 24:15-18.—"Also the word of the Lord came unto me, saying, Son of man, behold, I take away from thee the desire of thine eyes with a stroke: yet neither shalt thou mourn nor weep, neither shall thy tears run down. . . . So I spake unto the people in the morning: and at even my wife died; and I did in the morning as I was commanded."

23. What wife made a dummy of an idol and put it in bed to represent her husband?

Michal, First Samuel 19:13-16.—"And Michal took an image [margin, "teraphim"], and laid it in the bed, and put a pillow of goats' hair for his bolster, and covered it with a cloth. And when Saul sent messengers to take David, she said, He is sick. And Saul sent the messengers again to see David, saying, Bring him up to me in the bed, that I may slay him. And when the messengers were come in, behold, there was an image in the bed, with a pillow of goats' hair for his bolster."

24. Who advised young widows to marry?

Paul, First Timothy 5:14 RV.—"I desire therefore that the younger widows marry, bear children, rule the household, give no occasion to the adversary for reviling:"

25. What maidservant bore children to a man at his wife's request?

Bilhah, Genesis 30:3-7.—"And she [Rachel] said, Behold my maid Bilhah, go in unto her; and she shall bear upon my knees, that I may also have children by her. And she gave him Bilhah her handmaid to wife: and Jacob went in unto her. And Bilhah conceived, and bare Jacob a son. . . . And Bilhah Rachel's maid conceived again, and bare

Jacob a second son." The same story is told of Zilpah, the maid of Jacob's other wife Leah, Genesis 30:9–13. These four children, Dan, Naphtali, Gad, and Asher, together with Jacob's other children, became heads of the twelve tribes of Israel.

26. What judge of Israel was a great polygamist?

Gideon, Judges 8:30.—"And Gideon had threescore and ten sons of his body begotten: for he had many wives."

27. What father and son both passed off their wives as their sisters?

Abraham and Isaac. This story is told twice of Abraham (Genesis 12:10–20 and Genesis 20:1–18), and once of Isaac (Genesis 26:6–16). There are slight variations in the versions, but the general theme is the same—by calling his wife his sister the patriarch deceives the king of the country into which he ventures. The king takes the woman into his harem, and when he discovers she is a married woman, apologizes, protests at the deception, and indemnifies the husband. The patriarch and his wife leave the country with their possessions greatly increased.

28. Who advised wives to be subject to their husbands in everything?

Paul, Ephesians 5:22–24.—"Wives, submit yourselves unto your own husbands, as unto the Lord. For the husband is the head of the wife, even as Christ is the head of the church: and he is the saviour of the body. Therefore as the church is subject unto Christ, so let the wives be to their own husbands in every thing."

29. Who was the first husband to come home and brag about his day's work?

Lamech, Genesis 4:23–24 RV.—

> "And Lamech said unto his wives:
> Adah and Zillah, hear my voice;
> Ye wives of Lamech, hearken unto my speech:
> For I have slain a man for wounding me,
> And a young man for bruising me:
> If Cain shall be avenged sevenfold,
> Truly Lamech seventy and sevenfold."

30. Who called his wife a heifer?

Samson, Judges 14:18. Samson had told a riddle for the Philistines to guess. His wife wheedled the answer from him and then told it to the Philistines, who gave him the answer. "And he said unto them, if ye had not plowed with my heifer, ye had not found out my riddle."

31. *What famous Bible character had a Negro wife?*

Moses, Numbers 12:1.—"And Miriam and Aaron spake against Moses because of the Ethiopian woman whom he had married: for he had married an Ethiopian woman."

32. *Who married the daughter of a god?*

Judah, Malachi 2:11.—". . . Judah hath profaned the holiness of the Lord which he loved, and hath married the daughter of a strange god." This was Malachi's picturesque way of putting the fact that the people of Judah, by their intermarriage with nations which worshiped other gods than Jehovah, were profaning their religion.

X

Beasts, Birds, and Insects

1. Where in the Bible is portrayed the difficulty of domesticating a unicorn?

2. Where is described the sneezing of a crocodile?

3. What two kings fled from hornets?

4. Who prophesied that a pelican and a porcupine would sing together?

5. In what three places are peacocks mentioned?

6. Who made five golden mice?

7. Where are described sea-monsters suckling their young?

8. What animal had ten horns?

9. Where are four-footed fowls mentioned?

10. What beast had iron teeth and brass toe-nails?

11. What men had faces like lions?

12. How many horses did the Jews bring back from Babylon?

13. Of what land was it said that the owl, the raven, the pelican, and the porcupine would possess it?

14. Who prophesied that a meat-eating animal would eat straw?

15. What men blamed a beast for the evil they had done?

16. How much did Solomon pay for his horses?

17. Where is capital punishment for an animal prescribed?

18. What was the Hebrew penalty for eating the blood of beast or bird?

19. What was the Hebrew penalty for sculpturing any beast, bird, insect, or fish?

20. What chapter gives five methods of capturing birds?

21. What entire chapter is devoted to a description of the crocodile?

22. Who were told to be as wise as serpents and as harmless as doves?

23. What animal had seven horns and seven eyes?

24. Who had thirty sons who rode on thirty ass colts?

25. Who had seventy sons and grandsons who rode on seventy ass colts?

26. When did God make a promise to beasts and birds?

27. Where is the stork mentioned?

28. Where is there a vivid description of a war-horse?

29. When did camels wear necklaces?

30. How many golden calves were worshiped by the Hebrews?

31. Who mentioned a hen and chickens?

32. When did a he-goat butt a ram to death?

33. When was a donkey's head sold for eighty pieces of silver?

34. In what two places in the Bible is the bat classed as a bird?

35. Where is a prophecy that ostriches will appreciate irrigation?

36. From what animal's jaw-bone came a spring of water?

37. Where is a foster-mother partridge mentioned?

38. What whole book is largely occupied with a locust plague?

39. Where is a "nest among the stars" mentioned?

40. Whose horses were swifter than leopards?

41. Who changed dust into lice?

42. Where does it speak of the sole of a dove's foot?

43. Who said every kind of beast and bird had been tamed by man?

44. What mountain was so sacred that if an animal touched it, that animal was put to death?

45. How many animals of each kind did Noah take into the ark?

46. What sound was made by "the voice of the turtle"?

47. What horses had a queen's blood sprinkled on them?

48. What animal was reported to have drunk up a river?

49. To what animal are both Jesus and Satan compared?

50. In what verse is the chamois mentioned?

51. Where is the first mention of horses?

52. Who was companion to ostriches?

53. Who saw red, sorrel, and white horses at night?

54. Who found frogs on their beds and in their ovens?

55. Where are cockatrices mentioned?

56. What insects are described as having faces like men, hair like women, teeth like lions, and stings in their tails?

57. Who said "a living dog is better than a dead lion"?

58. Where is the chameleon mentioned?

59. When did God keep dogs from barking?

60. Where are apes mentioned?

61. Who set fire to three hundred foxes' tails?

62. What was the pygarg and where is it mentioned?

63. What bird is said to carry its young on its wings?

64. Who fed dragon meat to animals and birds?

ANSWERS TO QUESTIONS ABOUT
BEASTS, BIRDS, AND INSECTS

1. Where in the Bible is portrayed the difficulty of domesticating a unicorn?

Job 39:9-12.—"Will the unicorn be willing to serve thee, or abide by thy crib? Canst thou bind the unicorn with his band in the furrow? or will he harrow the valleys after thee? Wilt thou trust him, because his strength is great? or wilt thou leave thy labour to him? Wilt thou believe him, that he will bring home thy seed, and gather it into thy barn?" Instead of unicorn, the RV gives "wild ox." There is considerable uncertainty as to the animal meant by the Hebrew word "rem." Some take it to have been an antelope. It appears most likely to have been the now extinct aurochs (*Bos primigenius*) which was once plentiful in Europe and Asia. It was large, strong, and had long powerful horns. The AV translators used "unicorn" possibly because the Septuagint translation had "monokeros," the Greek equivalent. They should have known better, for Deuteronomy 33:17 mentions "the horns of a rem," and, of course, a unicorn can have but one horn. Consequently the AV translators solved the difficulty by translating it "the horns of unicorns." But they put in the margin, "an unicorn." Evidently belief in the fabulous unicorn persisted as late as the time of King James.

2. Where is described the sneezing of a crocodile?

Job 41:18.—"By his [the crocodile's] neesings a light doth shine, and his eyes are like the eyelids of the morning." The RV has, "His sneezings flash forth light, . . ." The word "neesing" is the original form of the word "sneezing," and is used to translate the very appropriate Hebrew word, "atishah."

3. What two kings fled from hornets?

The two kings of the Amorites, Joshua 24:12.—"And I sent the hornet before you, which drave them out from before you, even the two kings of the Amorites; . . ." These two kings were Sihon and Og, and their defeat is set forth in Numbers 21:21–35, but there is no mention of hornets in that passage. But the Lord had promised to send hornets to drive out their enemies, for which see Exodus 23:28 and Deuteronomy 7:20.

4. Who prophesied that a pelican and a porcupine would sing together?

Zephaniah, Zephaniah 2:14, RV.—". . . both the pelican and the porcupine shall lodge in the capitals thereof; their voice shall sing in the windows; . . ." AV has cormorant and bittern.

5. In what three places are peacocks mentioned?

First Kings 10:22.—"For the king [Solomon] had at sea a navy of Tharshish with the navy of Hiram: once in three years came the navy of Tharshish, bringing gold, and silver, ivory, and apes, and peacocks."

Second Chronicles 9:21 repeats First Kings 10:22.

Job 39:13.—"Gavest thou the goodly wings unto the peacocks? or wings and feathers unto the ostrich?" The RV differs greatly: "The wings of the ostrich wave proudly; but are they the pinions and plumage of love?"

6. Who made five golden mice?

The Philistines, First Samuel 6:1–18, especially verses 4–5.—"Then said they, What shall be the trespass offering which we shall return to him? They answered, Five golden emerods and five golden mice, according to the number of the lords of the Philistines: for one plague was on you all, and on your lords. Wherefore ye shall make images of your emerods, and images of your mice that mar the land; . . ."

7. Where are described sea-monsters suckling their young?

Lamentations 4:3.—"Even the sea-monsters draw out the breast, they give suck to their young ones: . . ." RV has jackals.

8. What animal had ten horns?

The apocalyptical beast of Revelation 13:1.—"And I stood upon the sand of the sea, and saw a beast rise up out of the sea, having seven heads and ten horns, . . ."

9. Where are four-footed fowls mentioned?

Leviticus 11:20.—"All fowls that creep, going upon all four, shall be an abomination unto you."

10. What beast had iron teeth and brass toe-nails?

The apocalyptical "fourth beast" of Daniel's dream, Daniel 7:7, 19.—"After this I saw in the night visions, and behold a fourth beast, . . . which was diverse from all the others, exceeding dreadful, whose teeth were of iron, and his nails of brass; which devoured, brake in pieces, and stamped the residue with his feet; . . ."

11. What men had faces like lions?

The mighty men of the Gadites, First Chronicles 12:8.— "And of the Gadites there separated themselves unto David into the hold to the wilderness men of might, and men of war fit for the battle, that could handle shield and buckler, whose faces were like the faces of lions, and were as swift as the roes upon the mountains;"

12. How many horses did the Jews bring back from Babylon?

736, Nehemiah 7:68.—"Their horses, seven hundred thirty and six:"

13. Of what land was it said that the owl, the raven, the pelican, and the porcupine would possess it?

Edom, Isaiah 34:11, RV.—"But the pelican and the porcupine shall possess it [Edom]; and the owl and the raven shall dwell therein: . . ." A similar prophecy about Assyria is found in Zephaniah 2:13–15.

14. Who prophesied that a meat-eating animal would eat straw?

Isaiah, Isaiah 65:25.—"The wolf and the lamb shall feed together, and the lion shall eat straw like the bullock: . . ."

15. What men blamed a beast for the evil they had done?

The brothers of Joseph, Genesis 37:12–36, especially verses 31–33.—"And they took Joseph's coat, and killed a kid of the goats, and dipped the coat in the blood; . . . and they brought it to their father; and said, This we have found: know now whether it be thy son's coat or no. And he knew it, and said, It is my son's coat; an evil beast hath devoured him; Joseph is without doubt rent in pieces."

16. *How much did Solomon pay for his horses?*

150 shekels of silver each, Second Chronicles 1:16–17.—
"And Solomon had horses brought out of Egypt, . . . And
they fetched up, and brought forth out of Egypt a chariot
for six hundred shekels of silver, and an horse for an hundred
and fifty: . . ." The silver shekel was worth about sixty-five
cents, as nearly as we can now determine, so Solomon paid a
little under a hundred dollars each for his horses.

17. *Where is capital punishment for an animal prescribed?*

Exodus 21:28.—"If an ox gore a man or a woman, that they
die: then the ox shall be surely stoned, and his flesh shall
not be eaten; but the owner of the ox shall be quit." See
also Exodus 19:12–13.

18. *What was the Hebrew penalty for eating the blood of
beast or bird?*

Banishment, Leviticus 7:26–27.—"Moreover ye shall eat
no manner of blood, whether it be of fowl or of beast,
in any of your dwellings. Whatsoever soul it be that eateth
any manner of blood, even that soul shall be cut off from
his people."

19. *What was the Hebrew penalty for sculpturing any
beast, bird, insect, or fish?*

Death to the nation, Deuteronomy 4:14–31, especially
verses 25–26.—"When thou shalt beget children, and children's children, and ye shall have remained long in the
land, and shall corrupt yourselves, and make a graven image,
or the likeness of any thing, and shall do evil in the sight
of the Lord thy God, to provoke him to anger: I call heaven
and earth to witness against you this day, that ye shall
soon utterly perish from off the land whereunto ye go over
Jordan to possess it; ye shall not prolong your days upon
it, but shall utterly be destroyed." The remainder of the section somewhat softens this extremely severe penalty.

20. *What chapter gives five methods of capturing birds?*

Job 18:8–10 RV.—"For he is cast into a net by his
own feet, and he walketh upon the toils. A gin shall take
him by the heel, And a snare shall lay hold on him. A
noose is hid for him in the ground, And a trap for him in
the way."

21. What entire chapter is devoted to a description of the crocodile?

Job 41. RV has leviathan, margin crocodile. AV has leviathan, margin, a whale or a whirlpool. But the description cannot possibly be mistaken for anything but a crocodile.

22. Who were told to be as wise as serpents and as harmless as doves?

The twelve apostles, Matthew 10:5, 16.—"These twelve Jesus sent forth, and commanded them, saying, . . . Behold, I send you forth as sheep in the midst of wolves: be ye therefore wise as serpents, and harmless as doves."

23. What animal had seven horns and seven eyes?

The apocalyptic "Lamb" of Revelation 5:6.—"And I beheld, and, lo, in the midst of the throne and of the four beasts, and in the midst of the elders, stood a Lamb as it had been slain, having seven horns and seven eyes, which are the seven Spirits of God sent forth into all the earth."

24. Who had thirty sons who rode on thirty ass colts?

Jair, Judges 10:3–4.—"And after him arose Jair, a Gileadite, and judged Israel twenty and two years. And he had thirty sons that rode on thirty ass colts, and they had thirty cities. . . ."

25. Who had seventy sons and grandsons who rode on seventy ass colts?

Abdon, Judges 12:13–14.—"And after him Abdon the son of Hillel, a Pirathonite, judged Israel. And he had forty sons and thirty nephews [margin and RV have "son's sons"], that rode on threescore and ten ass colts: and he judged Israel eight years."

26. When did God make a promise to beasts and birds?

After the flood, Genesis 9:8–11.—"And God spake unto Noah, and to his sons with him, saying, And I, behold, I establish my covenant with you, and with your seed after you; And with every living creature that is with you, of the fowl, of the cattle, and of every beast of the earth with you; from all that go out of the ark, to every beast of the earth. And I will establish my covenant with you; neither shall all flesh be cut off any more by the waters of a flood; neither shall there any more be a flood to destroy the earth."

27. *Where is the stork mentioned?*

Leviticus 11:19.—"And the stork, the heron after her kind, and the lapwing, . . ." These were some of the birds which might not be eaten. See also Deuteronomy 14:18, Job 39:13 (RV margin), Psalm 104:17, Jeremiah 8:7, Zechariah 5:9.

28. *Where is there a vivid description of a war-horse?*

Job 39:19–25.

29. *When did camels wear necklaces?*

In the days of Gideon, Judges 8:21, 26.—". . . And Gideon arose, and slew Zebah and Zalmunna, and took away the ornaments that were on their camels' necks. . . . the chains that were about their camels' necks."

30. *How many golden calves were worshiped by the Hebrews?*

Three, Exodus 32:1–8, especially verse 8.—". . . they have made them a molten calf, and have worshipped it, and have sacrificed thereunto, . . ." This was in the days of Moses. Again, in the time of king Jeroboam, First Kings 12:28–33, especially verse 28: ". . . the king took counsel, and made two calves of gold, and said unto them [his people], It is too much for you to go up to Jerusalem: behold thy gods, O Israel, which brought thee up out of the land of Egypt."

31. *Who mentioned a hen and chickens?*

Jesus, Matthew 23:37.—"O Jerusalem, Jerusalem, thou that killest the prophets, . . . how often would I have gathered thy children together, even as a hen gathereth her chickens under her wings, and ye would not!" See Luke 13:34.

32. *When did a he-goat butt a ram to death?*

In Daniel's apocalyptic dream, Daniel 8:1–12, especially verses 5 and 7.—"And as I was considering, behold, an he goat came from the west. . . . And I saw him come close unto the ram, and he was moved with choler against him, and smote the ram, and brake his two horns: and there was no power in the ram to stand before him, but he cast him down to the ground, and stamped upon him: and there was none that could deliver the ram out of his hand." The goat represented Alexander the Great; the ram, the Medo-Persian empire.

33. When was a donkey's head sold for eighty pieces of silver?

In the siege of Samaria, Second Kings 6:25.—"And there was a great famine in Samaria: and, behold, they besieged it, until an ass's head was sold for fourscore pieces of silver, . . ." 80 shekels of silver would amount to more than fifty dollars.

34. In what two places in the Bible is the bat classed as a bird?

Leviticus 11:13, 19.—"And these are they which ye shall have in abomination among the fowls; they shall not be eaten, . . . [then follows a long list, ending with] . . . the heron after her kind, and the lapwing, and the bat." The list is duplicated in Deuteronomy 14:11–18.

35. Where is a prophecy that ostriches will appreciate irrigation?

Isaiah 43:19–20, RV.—"Behold, I [Jehovah] will do a new thing; now shall it spring forth; shall ye not know it? I will even make a way in the wilderness, and rivers in the desert. The beasts of the field shall honor me, the jackals and the ostriches; because I give waters in the wilderness, and rivers in the desert, to give drink to my people, . . ."

36. From what animal's jaw-bone came a spring of water?

The ass's, Judges 15:15–19.—"And he [Samson] found a new jawbone of an ass, and put forth his hand, and took it, and slew a thousand men therewith. . . . And he was sore athirst, . . . But God clave a hollow place that was in the jaw, and there came water thereout; and when he had drunk, his spirit came again, and he revived: . . ."

37. Where is a foster-mother partridge mentioned?

Jeremiah 17:11 RV.—"As the partridge that sitteth on eggs which she hath not laid, so is he that getteth riches, and not by right; in the midst of his days they shall leave him, and at his end he shall be a fool."

38. What whole book is largely occupied with a locust plague?

Joel. Joel uses the locusts as a symbol of the hordes of his country's enemies.

39. Where is a "nest among the stars" mentioned?

Obadiah 1:4.—"Though thou exalt thyself as the eagle, and though thou set thy nest among the stars, thence will I bring thee down, saith the Lord."

40. Whose horses were swifter than leopards?

The Chaldeans, Habakkuk 1:6, 8.—"For, lo, I raise up the Chaldeans, that bitter and hasty nation, . . . Their horses also are swifter than the leopards, and are more fierce than the evening wolves: . . ."

41. Who changed dust into lice?

Aaron, according to Exodus 8:17.—". . . for Aaron stretched out his hand with his rod, and smote the dust of the earth, and it became lice in man, and in beast; all the dust of the land became lice throughout all the land of Egypt."

42. Where does it speak of the sole of a dove's foot?

In the Noah's Ark story, Genesis 8:9.—"But the dove found no rest for the sole of her foot, . . ."

43. Who said every kind of beast and bird had been tamed by man?

James, James 3:7.—"For every kind of beast, and of birds, and of serpents, and of things in the sea, is tamed, and hath been tamed of mankind: . . ."

44. What mountain was so sacred that if an animal touched it, that animal was put to death?

Sinai, Exodus 19:11–13.—". . . for the third day the Lord will come down in the sight of all the people upon mount Sinai. And thou shalt set bounds unto the people round about, saying, Take heed to yourselves, that ye go not up into the mount, or touch the border of it: whosoever toucheth the mount shall be surely put to death: There shall not an hand touch it, but he shall surely be stoned, or shot through; whether it be beast or man, it shall not live: . . ."

45. How many animals of each kind did Noah take into the ark?

Genesis 6:19, 7:8–9, and 7:15 all state two of each kind, but Genesis 7:2–5 says seven of each kind of the "clean" and two of each kind of the unclean.

Genesis 7:2, 5.—"Of every clean beast thou shalt take to thee by sevens, the male and his female: and of beasts that are not clean by two, the male and his female. . . . And Noah did according unto all that the Lord commanded him."

Genesis 7:8–9.—"Of clean beasts, and of beasts that are not clean, . . . There went in two and two unto Noah into the ark, the male and the female, as God had commanded Noah."

46. What sound was made by "the voice of the turtle"?

A cooing sound, for by "turtle" was meant "turtle-dove." The AV has "turtle" and the RV "turtle-dove."

Song of Solomon 2:12.—"The flowers appear upon the earth; the time of the singing of birds is come, and the voice of the turtle is heard in our land;"

47. What horses had a queen's blood sprinkled on them?

Jehu's horses, queen Jezebel's blood, Second Kings 9:30, 33.—"And when Jehu was come to Jezreel, Jezebel heard of it; and she painted her face, and tired her head, and looked out at a window . . . And he said, Throw her down. So they threw her down: and some of her blood was sprinkled on the wall, and on the horses: and he trode her under foot."

48. What animal was reported to have drunk up a river?

"Behemoth," which the AV margin interprets as "the elephant, as some think," but which the RV margin asserts was the hippopotamus. Job 40:15, 23: "Behold now behemoth, which I made with thee; he eateth grass as an ox. . . . Behold, he drinketh up a river, and hasteth not: he trusteth that he can draw up Jordan into his mouth."

49. To what animal are both Jesus and Satan compared?

The lion, Revelation 5:5.—"And one of the elders saith unto me, Weep not: behold, the Lion of the tribe of Juda, the Root of David, hath prevailed to open the book, and to loose the seven seals thereof." It is evident that here Jesus is meant, for Hebrews 7:14 asserts, ". . . our Lord sprang out of Juda;" and Revelation 22:16 reads: "I Jesus have sent mine angel to testify unto you these things in the churches.

I am the root and the offspring of David, and the bright and morning star." First Peter 5:8, however, compares the devil to a lion: "Be sober, be vigilant; because your adversary the devil, as a roaring lion, walketh about, seeking whom he may devour:"

50. *In what verse is the chamois mentioned?*

Deuteronomy 14:5 includes the chamois among the animals which might be eaten.—". . . and the wild ox, and the chamois."

51. *Where is the first mention of horses?*

Genesis 47:17.—"And they brought their cattle unto Joseph: and Joseph gave them bread in exchange for horses, . . ."

52. *Who was companion to ostriches?*

Job, Job 30:29, RV.—"I am a brother to jackals, And a companion to ostriches."

53. *Who saw red, sorrel, and white horses at night?*

Zechariah, Zechariah 1:8, RV.—"I saw in the night, and, behold, a man riding upon a red horse, and he stood among the myrtle-trees that were in the bottom; and behind him there were horses, red, sorrel, and white." In place of sorrel, the AV has "speckled," but the AV margin has "bay."

54. *Who found frogs on their beds and in their ovens?*

The Egyptians, according to Exodus 8:3, 6.—"And the river shall bring forth frogs abundantly, which shall go up and come into thine house, and into thy bedchamber, and upon thy bed, . . . and into thine ovens, and into thy kneadingtroughs: . . . And Aaron stretched out his hand over the waters of Egypt; and the frogs came up, and covered the land of Egypt."

55. *Where are cockatrices mentioned?*

Isaiah 11:8, 14:29, 59:5, Jeremiah 8:17, and in the margin of Proverbs 23:32, where the text has "adder." The most often quoted of these is Isaiah 11:8: ". . . and the weaned child shall put his hand on the cockatrice' den." The RV in these passages usually has "basilisk." Cockatrice and basilisk are both names for a fabulous serpent.

56. *What insects are described as having faces like men,*

hair like women, teeth like lions, and stings in their tails?

The apocalyptical locusts of Revelation 9:7–10.—"And the shapes of the locusts were like unto horses prepared unto battle; and on their heads were as it were crowns of gold, and their faces were as the faces of men. And they had hair as the hair of women, and their teeth were as the teeth of lions. . . . And they had tails like unto scorpions, and there were stings in their tails: . . ."

57. Who said "a living dog is better than a dead lion"?

The "preacher" author of Ecclesiastes, popularly interpreted as Solomon, because Ecclesiastes 1:1 reads: "The words of the Preacher, the son of David, king in Jerusalem." Ecclesiastes 9:4: "For to him that is joined to all the living there is hope: for a living dog is better than a dead lion."

58. Where is the chameleon mentioned?

Leviticus 11:30, among the "unclean creeping things" which might not be eaten: "And the ferret, and the chameleon, and the lizard, and the snail, and the mole."

59. When did God keep dogs from barking?

At the time of the last "plague" of the Egyptians, the plague of the death of the firstborn, Exodus 11:7.—"But against any of the children of Israel shall not a dog move his tongue, against man or beast: that ye may know how that the Lord doth put a difference between the Egyptians and Israel." Moffatt translates: "But not even a dog shall bark against any of the Israelites, against man or beast of them, . . ."

60. Where are apes mentioned?

First Kings 10:22, Second Chronicles 9:21.—". . . silver, ivory, and apes, and peacocks."

61. Who set fire to three hundred foxes' tails?

Samson, Judges 15:4–5.—"And Samson went and caught three hundred foxes, and took firebrands, and turned tail to tail, and put a firebrand in the midst between two tails. And when he had set the brands on fire, he let them go into the standing corn of the Philistines, and burnt up both the shocks, and also the standing corn, with the vineyards and olives."

62. What was the pygarg and where is it mentioned?

Probably a kind of antelope. It is listed among the edible animals in Deuteronomy 14:4–5.—"These are the beasts which ye shall eat: the ox, the sheep, and the goat, the hart, and the roebuck, and the fallow deer, and the wild goat, and the pygarg, and the wild ox, and the chamois." The margin of both the AV and the RV gives "bison" for pygarg, and notes that the Hebrew word is "dishon." The word pygarg was a transliteration of the Septuagint Greek word "pygargos," which means literally "white rump" and was the name of a Libyan antelope. The Hebrew word "dishon" is interpreted by scholars to mean a species of gazelle.

63. What bird is said to carry its young on its wings?

The eagle, Deuteronomy 32:11.—"As an eagle stirreth up her nest, fluttereth over her young, spreadeth abroad her wings, taketh them, beareth them on her wings:" See also Exodus 19:4.

64. Who fed dragon meat to animals and birds?

The Lord, Ezekiel 29:5.—". . . I have given thee [the great dragon that lieth in the midst of his rivers, verse 3] for meat to the beasts of the field and to the fowls of the heaven." The dragon was a metaphor for Pharaoh king of Egypt, see verses 2 and 3.

XI

Music

1. When and what did Jesus sing?

2. In what ancient orchestra was a bagpipe played?

3. What prophet condemned music-lovers?

4. In whose band did Jaaziel play?

5. What does "Selah" mean in the Psalms?

6. Who was the first musician and what instruments did he play?

7. Where is music compared to vinegar on soda?

8. Where is a "very lovely song" mentioned?

9. Who organized the first orchestra?

10. What cymbal player is credited with having written twelve of the psalms?

11. What musical instrument was played at a New Testament funeral?

12. Who advised Christians to sing?

13. What instruments did David's musicians play?

14. What choir-master is mentioned by name in the Bible?

15. Compare with reference to variety of instruments the two most famous orchestras in the Bible.

16. Where is described a singing school of 288 persons?

ANSWERS TO QUESTIONS
ABOUT MUSIC

1. When and what did Jesus sing?

At the Last Supper, Mark 14:26.—"And when they had sung an hymn, they went out into the mount of Olives." The margin has "psalm" in place of "hymn." This was the regular Passover supper which Jesus was keeping with his disciples. It was the Jewish custom at the Passover supper to sing "The Great Hallel," which consisted of Psalms 113 to 118 and 136. The part of this which was sung after the meal was Psalms 115 to 118, or, according to the school of Shammai, 114 to 118.

2. In what ancient orchestra was a bagpipe played?

Nebuchadnezzar's, Daniel 3:4–5 RV.—"Then the herald cried aloud, To you it is commanded, O peoples, nations, and languages, that at what time ye hear the sound of the cornet, flute, harp, sackbut, psaltery, dulcimer, and all kinds of music, ye fall down and worship the golden image that Nebuchadnezzar the king hath set up; . . ." In place of "dulcimer" the RV margin has "bagpipe." The bagpipe is a very ancient musical instrument. There is reason to suppose that it was known to the Egyptians, Chaldeans, Persians, Greeks, and Syrians. The Romans brought it to the British Isles.

3. What prophet condemned music-lovers?

Amos, Amos 6:1–5.—"Woe to them that are at ease in Zion, . . . that put far away the evil day, . . . that chant to the sound of the viol, and invent to themselves instruments of musick, . . ."

4. In whose band did Jaaziel play?

David's, First Chronicles 15:16–18.—"And David spake to the chief of the Levites to appoint their brethren to be the singers with instruments of musick, psalteries, and harps, and cymbals, sounding, by lifting up the voice with joy. So the Levites appointed Heman . . . and Jaaziel, and . . ."

Jaaziel's instrument was (see verse 20, margin) the psaltery, a primitive form of the modern zither.

5. What does "Selah" mean in the Psalms?

Probably a musical notation meaning, "Lift up" (your voices), or "Loud," like the modern, "Forte." It is found 71 times in the Psalms and twice in Habakkuk 3.

6. Who was the first musician and what instruments did he play?

Jubal, Genesis 4:21.—"And his brother's name was Jubal: he was the father of all such as handle the harp and organ." Moffatt has "lyre and pipe." The Hebrew words, kinnor and ugab, are difficult to translate, as about all we know about them is that the former was a stringed instrument and the latter a wind.

7. Where is music compared to vinegar on soda?

Proverbs 25:20 RV.—"As one that taketh off a garment in cold weather, and as vinegar upon soda, so is he that singeth songs to a heavy heart." AV has "vinegar upon nitre."

8. Where is a "very lovely song" mentioned?

Ezekiel 33:32.—"And, lo, thou art unto them as a very lovely song of one that hath a pleasant voice, and can play well on an instrument: for they hear thy words, but they do them not."

9. Who organized the first orchestra?

David, Second Samuel 6:5.—"And David and all the house of Israel played before the Lord on all manner of instruments made of fir wood, even on harps, and on psalteries, and on timbrels, and on cornets, and on cymbals." Moffatt gives lutes, lyres, drums, rattles, and cymbals. But the fact that these instruments were said to have been made of wood does not mean that cornets could not have been included, for wooden cornets were used in Germany as late as the eighteenth century and are called for in Bach's cantatas. For more about David's orchestra, see First Chronicles, chapters 15 and 25, also the great orchestra of 4,000 in 23:5.

10. What cymbal player is credited with having written twelve of the psalms?

Asaph, First Chronicles 15:19.—"So the singers, Heman,

Asaph, and Ethan, were appointed to sound with cymbals of brass." The psalms credited to him are Psalms 50 and 73 to 83.

11. What musical instrument was played at a New Testament funeral?

The flute, Matthew 9:23-24 RV.—"And when Jesus came into the ruler's house, and saw the flute-players, and the crowd making a tumult, he said, Give place: for the damsel is not dead, but sleepeth. . . ."

12. Who advised Christians to sing?

Paul, Colossians 3:16.—"Let the word of Christ dwell in you richly in all wisdom; teaching and admonishing one another in psalms and hymns and spiritual songs, singing with grace in your hearts to the Lord."

13. What instruments did David's musicians play?

Cornets, trumpets, cymbals, psalteries, and harps, First Chronicles 15:28.—"Thus all Israel brought up the ark of the covenant of the Lord with shouting, and with sound of the cornet, and with trumpets, and with cymbals, making a noise with psalteries and harps." Also timbrels, see Second Samuel 6:5. The timbrel was a hand drum.

14. What choir-master is mentioned by name in the Bible?

Chenaniah, First Chronicles 15:22, 27.—"And Chenaniah, chief of the Levites, was for song: he instructed about the song, because he was skilful." "And David was clothed with a robe of fine linen, and all the Levites that bare the ark, and the singers, and Chenaniah the master of the song with the singers: . . ."

15. Compare with reference to variety of instruments the two most famous orchestras in the Bible.

David's and Nebuchadnezzar's both had psalteries, harps, and cornets, but David's had cymbals, timbrels, and trumpets, which are not mentioned in Nebuchadnezzar's. The latter, however, had flutes, sackbuts, and dulcimers (bagpipes), which David's did not have. But Nebuchadnezzar's is credited with having had "also all kinds of music." See Second Samuel 6:5; First Chronicles 15:16-28; and Daniel 3:5. The word translated "sackbut" is in Hebrew *sabbekha*, probably like the Greek *sambuke*, a stringed instrument, perhaps a large harp. It was an easy mistake to identify the sabbekha with the sackbut, or trombone (from the French saquebute, literally pull, push).

16. Where is described a singing school of 288 persons?

First Chronicles 25:7.—"So the number of them, with their brethren that were instructed in the songs of the Lord, even all that were cunning, was two hundred four-score and eight."

XII

Books, Writing, and Education

1. Who was the first book censor and what happened to him?

2. Where was located the only library building mentioned in the Bible?

3. Where is it stated that teachers and scholars gambled?

4. Where is a diamond-pointed pen mentioned?

5. What author gave a copy of his book to an officer and told him to tie a stone to it and throw it into a river?

6. Who wrote on the plaster on the wall?

7. Where is a legal transfer of real estate described in detail?

8. Where is recorded the first intelligence test?

9. Where are paper and ink mentioned?

10. Who taught the only "school" mentioned in the Bible?

11. Who first used a pen?

12. What students built their own dormitory?

13. In what three languages was the Bible written?

14. What book of the Bible closes with a threat against anyone editing it?

15. Who was proud of his large handwriting?

16. What ancient books, now lost, are mentioned in the Bible?

17. Of what tribe were 42,000 men killed because of their incorrect pronunciation of one word?

18. What is the shortest time on record for acquiring a foreign language?

19. What town clerk quieted a riot?

20. Where are tutors of an heir mentioned?

21. Where is a schoolmaster referred to?

22. Who warned Christians against philosophy?

23. What apostle had a library?

24. When did foreigners rank higher than natives in an intelligence test?

25. What is the Bible origin of the phrase, "D.V." (God willing)?

26. How many proverbs did Solomon speak?

27. When did the devil quote scripture to his purpose, and did he quote it correctly?

28. Who considered "much study" to be "a weariness of the flesh"?

29. Was the conclusion, "For thine is the kingdom, and the power, and the glory, for ever. Amen" a part of the Lord's Prayer originally?

30. With what part of the body did the people of Bible times think they thought?

ANSWERS TO QUESTIONS ABOUT BOOKS, WRITING, AND EDUCATION

1. Who was the first book censor and what happened to him?

Jehoiakim, king of Judah, Jeremiah 36:1–32, summarized here in verses 4, 21–23, 27–28, and 30.—"Then Jeremiah called Baruch the son of Neriah; and Baruch wrote from the mouth of Jeremiah all the words of the Lord, which he had spoken unto him, upon a roll of a book. . . . So the king sent Jehudi to fetch the roll: . . . And Jehudi read it in the ears of the king, and in the ears of all the princes which stood beside the king. Now the king sat in the winterhouse in the ninth month: and there was a fire on the hearth burning before him. And it came to pass, that when [as often as] Jehudi had read three or four leaves, [RV margin "columns"] he [the king] cut it with the penknife, and cast it into the fire that was on the hearth, until all the roll was consumed. . . . Then the word of the Lord came to Jeremiah, after that the king had burned the roll, . . . saying, Take thee again another roll, and write in it all the former words that were in the first roll, which Jehoiakim the king of Judah hath burned. . . . Therefore thus saith the Lord of Jehoiakim king of Judah; He shall have none to sit upon the throne of David: and his dead body shall be cast out in the day to the heat, and in the night to the frost."

Was this prophecy fulfilled? Second Kings 24.6 states: "So Jehoiakim slept with his fathers: and Jehoiachin his son reigned in his stead." But Dr. A. S. Peake, in his commentary on Jeremiah, says: ". . . the prediction was probably fulfilled. Had it not been, it would have been suppressed . . . and against this consideration the conventional formula in 2 Kings xxiv.6 weighs scarcely at all, especially since the fact of burial and the situation of the grave are so significantly omitted."

2. Where was located the only library building mentioned in the Bible?

In Ecbatana, Ezra 6:1-2.—"Then Darius the king made a decree, and search was made in the house of the rolls, where the treasures were laid up in Babylon. And there was found at Achmetha, in the palace that is in the province of the Medes, a roll, and therein was a record. . . ." Marginal references give "books" in place of "rolls," and "Ecbatana" in place of "Achmetha." Evidently the writer was hazy on his geography and thought that Babylon included Media. Ecbatana was the capital of Media. Probably the house of the books was one building in the group known collectively as the palace. And the books were very likely not "rolls" but clay tablets.

3. Where is it stated that teachers and scholars gambled?

First Chronicles 25:8.—"And they cast lots, ward against ward, as well the small as the great, the teacher as the scholar." Casting lots was evidently throwing some form of dice, or marked tablets, and was believed to be governed by the will of the Lord. Proverbs 16:33 states, "The lot is cast into the lap; but the whole disposing thereof is of the Lord." Other occasions when lots were used are recorded in Leviticus 16:8, Isaiah 34:17, Jonah 1:7, and even in Acts

1:26, when lots were cast to determine the successor of Judas for the twelfth disciple.

4. Where is a diamond-pointed pen mentioned?

Jeremiah 17:1.—"The sin of Judah is written with a pen of iron, and with the point of a diamond: . . ." Probably the idea was not that the iron pen had a diamond point, but that two instruments of writing were employed. There is however no word "and" in the Hebrew of this passage after the word "iron."

5. What author gave a copy of his book to an officer and told him to tie a stone to it and throw it into a river?

Jeremiah, Jeremiah 51:59–64 RV.—". . . Now Seraiah was chief chamberlain. And Jeremiah wrote in a book all the evil that should come upon Babylon. . . . And Jeremiah said to Seraiah, When thou comest to Babylon, then see that thou read all these words, . . . And it shall be, when thou hast made an end of reading this book, that thou shalt bind a stone to it, and cast it into the midst of the Euphrates: and thou shalt say, Thus shall Babylon sink, and shall not rise again . . ."

6. Who wrote on the plaster on the wall?

Presumably God, Daniel 5:5.—"In the same hour came forth fingers of a man's hand, and wrote over against the candlestick upon the plaister of the wall of the king's palace: and the king saw the part of the hand that wrote."

7. Where is a legal transfer of real estate described in detail?

Jeremiah 32:9–14.—"And I bought the field of Hanameel my uncle's son, that was in Anathoth, and weighed him the money, even seventeen shekels of silver. And I subscribed the evidence, and sealed it, and took witnesses, and weighed him the money in the balances. So I took the evidence of the purchase, both that which was sealed according to the law and custom, and that which was open: And I gave the evidence of the purchase unto Baruch the son of Neriah, the son of Maaseiah, in the sight of Hanameel mine uncle's son, and in the presence of the witnesses that subscribed the book of the purchase, before all the Jews that sat in the court of the prison. And I charged Baruch before them, saying, Thus saith the Lord of hosts, the God of Israel; Take these evidences, this evidence of the purchase, both which is sealed, and this evidence which is open; and put them in an earthen vessel, that they may continue many days."

8. *Where is recorded the first intelligence test?*

First Kings 10:1-3.—"And when the queen of Sheba heard of the fame of Solomon concerning the name of the Lord, she came to prove him with hard questions. And she came to Jerusalem with a very great train, . . . and when she was come to Solomon, she communed with him of all that was in her heart. And Solomon told her all her questions: there was not anything hid from the king, which he told her not."

9. *Where are paper and ink mentioned?*

Second John 1:12.—"Having many things to write unto you, I would not write with paper and ink: but I trust to come unto you, and speak face to face, that our joy may be full." See also Jeremiah 36:18; Third John 1:13.

10. *Who taught the only "school" mentioned in the Bible?*

Tyrannus, Acts 19:9.—". . . disputing daily in the school of one Tyrannus."

11. *Who first used a pen?*

The Zebulunites are the first ones mentioned in the Bible, Judges 5:14.—". . . and out of Zebulun they that handle the pen of the writer."

12. *What students built their own dormitory?*

The sons of the prophets, Second Kings 6:1-2.—"And the sons of the prophets said unto Elisha, Behold now, the place where we dwell with thee is too strait for us. Let us go, we pray thee, unto Jordan, and take thence every man a beam, and let us make place there, where we may dwell. And he answered, Go ye." There were several bands of these "sons of the prophets," one at Bethel (2:3), one at Jericho (2:5), and one at Gilgal (4:38). They may have been guilds or brotherhoods, banded together for religious and economic reasons largely, but it is likely that there was an educational aspect as well, for 4:38 says: ". . . the sons of the prophets were sitting before him: . . ." that is, before Elisha, and that phrase would indicate a class before a teacher.

13. *In what three languages was the Bible written?*

The Old Testament was written mostly in Hebrew, but ten chapters or parts were in Aramaic (Ezra 4:8 to 6:18, and 7:12–26. Daniel, chapters 2 to 7 inclusive). The Old Testament and the Apocrypha were translated into Greek in the third century b.c. (parts perhaps as late as the first century b.c.) and that translation is known as the Septuagint or Alexandrian version. In the first century b.c. the Old Testament, most of it, at least, was translated into Aramaic, known as the Targums. The New Testament was written in Greek, although scholars believe that there was probably an Aramaic original source for some of the gospel material.

14. What book of the Bible closes with a threat against anyone editing it?

Revelation, Revelation 22:18–19.—"For I testify unto every man that heareth the words of the prophecy of this book, If any man shall add unto these things, God shall add unto him the plagues that are written in this book: And if any man shall take away from the words of the book of this prophecy, God shall take away his part out of the book of life, and out of the holy city, and from the things which are written in this book."

15. Who was proud of his large handwriting?

Paul, Galatians 6:11 RV.—"See with how large letters I write unto you with mine own hand."

16. What ancient books, now lost, are mentioned in the Bible?

The Book of the Wars of the Lord (which is a collection of victory songs), mentioned and quoted from in Numbers 21:14–15, and The Book of Jasher (or Jashar) (which is a collection of poems on great events), mentioned and quoted from in Joshua 10:12–13 and Second Samuel 1:17–27.

There are many "books" mentioned by the writer of Chronicles, attributed to Samuel the Seer, Nathan the Prophet, Gad the Seer, Abijah the Shilonite, Iddo the Seer, Shemaiah the Prophet, Jehu son of Hanini, besides The Book of the Kings of Israel, The Book of the Kings of Judah and Israel, and The Book of the Acts of Uzziah, all mentioned in First Chronicles 29:29, Second Chronicles 9:29; 12:15; 13:22; 20:34; 26:22; and 32:32. These are all, however, references to parts of books now in the Bible, or to documents used as sources by Bible writers.

Jude 1:14–15 mentions and quotes from The Book of

Enoch—Enoch 1:9 and 5:4—but the Book of Enoch cannot be reckoned a lost book, as an Ethiopic version of it was discovered in Abyssinia in 1773, and in 1952 fragments of no less than eight different Enochan manuscripts in the original Aramaic, some of them containing sections not found in the Ethiopic manuscript, were discovered in a Qumran cave near Jerusalem. It had a great influence upon Christian thought, and many quotations from it and parallels to it have been identified in the letters of Paul and even in the sayings of Jesus.

17. Of what tribe were 42,000 men killed because of their incorrect pronunciation of one word?

The tribe of Ephraim, Judges 12:5–6.—"And the Gilead-ites took the passages of Jordan before the Ephraimites: and it was so, that when those Ephraimites which were escaped said, Let me go over; that the men of Gilead said unto him, Art thou an Ephraimite? If he said, Nay; Then said they unto him, Say now Shibboleth: and he said Sibboleth: for he could not frame to pronounce it right. Then they took him, and slew him at the passages of the Jordan: and there fell at that time of the Ephraimites forty and two thousand."

18. What is the shortest time on record for acquiring a foreign language?

"Suddenly," Acts 2:1–4.—"And when the day of Pente-cost was fully come, they were all with one accord in one place. And suddenly there came a sound from heaven as of a rushing mighty wind, . . . And they were all filled with the Holy Ghost, and began to speak with other tongues, as the Spirit gave them utterance." Verses 9 to 11 name the coun-tries, the languages of which were thus acquired.

19. What town clerk quieted a riot?

The town clerk of Ephesus, Acts 19:35–41.—"And when the town clerk had appeased the people, he said, Ye men of Ephesus, . . . ye ought to be quiet, and to do nothing rashly . . . For we are in danger to be called in question for this day's uproar, there being no cause whereby we may give an account of this concourse. And when he had thus spoken, he dismissed the assembly." The town clerk, or grammateus, was a very important public official of the towns and cities of the Greek provinces of the Roman Empire.

20. Where are tutors of an heir mentioned?

Galatians 4·1–2.—"Now I say, That the heir, as long as he is a child, . . is under tutors and governors until the time appointed of the father."

21. Where is a schoolmaster referred to?

Galatians 3 24–25.—"Wherefore the law was our schoolmaster to bring us unto Christ, that we might be justified by faith. But after that faith is come, we are no longer under a schoolmaster."

22. Who warned Christians against philosophy?

Paul, Colossians 2:8.—"Beware lest any man spoil you through philosophy and vain deceit, after the tradition of men, after the rudiments of the world, and not after Christ." Paul was too much of a student and philosopher himself to condemn all philosophy, and was warning the Christians of Colossae against a particular philosophy which was greatly influencing them, a sort of theosophic belief in intermediate spirits, angelic or demonic, between man and God. These spirits were in charge of various elements, such as earth, water, air, etc., and were therefore called elemental spirits or elementals. The phrase in verse 8 translated "rudiments of the world" refers to them. Moffatt recognizes the real meaning of the verse by translating it as follows,—"Beware of anyone getting hold of you by means of a theosophy which is specious make-believe, on the lines of human tradition, corresponding to the Elemental spirits of the world and not to Christ." The principalities and powers mentioned in verses 10 and 15 were some of these elemental spirits.

23. What apostle had a library?

Paul, Second Timothy 4:13.—"The cloke that I left at Troas with Carpus, when thou comest, bring with thee, and the books, but especially the parchments." These *biblia* and *membranas* would be priceless now, had they been preserved, for our oldest manuscripts of the New Testament were written three centuries later, and these books and parchments of Paul's were probably early compilations of the acts and words of Jesus, with perhaps copies of Paul's own letters. The *membranas*, however, may have been blank parchment sheets prepared for writing.

24. When did foreigners rank higher than natives in an intelligence test?

Daniel 1:19–20.—". . . among them all was found none like Daniel, Hananiah, Mishael, and Azariah: therefore stood they before the king. And in all matters of wisdom and understanding, that the king enquired of them, he found them ten times better than all the magicians and astrologers that were in all his realm."

25. What is the Bible origin of the phrase, "D.V." (God willing)?

James 4:15.—"For that ye ought to say, If the Lord will, we shall live, and do this, or that." The Latin Vulgate version of "If the Lord will" is "Si Dominus voluerit," which became shortened in common usage to "Deo volente."

26. How many proverbs did Solomon speak?

3000, First Kings 4:32.—"And he spake three thousand proverbs: . . ."

27. When did the devil quote scripture to his purpose, and did he quote it correctly?

At the temptation of Jesus, Matthew 4:5–6.—"Then the devil taketh him up into the holy city, And setteth him on a pinnacle of the temple, And saith unto him, If thou be the Son of God, cast thyself down: for it is written, He shall give his angels charge concerning thee: and in their hands they shall bear thee up, lest at any time thou dash thy foot against a stone." The devil was quoting, correctly, from Psalm 91:11–12. Jesus, answering him (verses 7 and 10), quoted Deuteronomy 6:16; 6:13; and 10:20, but inserted the word "only," ("him only shalt thou serve"). The honors for accuracy were slightly with the devil. It is interesting to note that both the devil and Jesus quoted from the Septuagint (Greek) version, which differs slightly from the Hebrew. Or perhaps it is the writer of Matthew who is responsible for the quotations, if not for the whole conversation, for Mark (1:13) has only "tempted of Satan." But see also Luke 4:1–13.

28. Who considered "much study" to be "a weariness of the flesh"?

The Preacher, Ecclesiastes 1:1; 12:12.—"The words of the Preacher, the son of David, king in Jerusalem." (Solomon.) "And further, by these, my son, be admonished: of making many books there is no end; and much study is a weariness of the flesh." This is usually misquoted, "to the flesh."

29. Was the conclusion, "For thine is the kingdom, and the power, and the glory, for ever. Amen" a part of the Lord's Prayer originally?

Not according to Luke 11:2–4 nor the Revised Version of Matthew 6:9–13. It was probably a doxology response used in the early church after the recitation of the prayer, which crept into the text. It is not found in the oldest manuscripts.

30. With what part of the body did the people of Bible times think they thought?

With the heart, Proverbs 23:7.—"For as he thinketh in his heart, so is he: . . ." See also Esther 6:6; Isaiah 10:7; Matthew 9:4. The Hebrews, in common with their contemporaries, were ignorant of the function of the brain. The words "brain" or "brains" do not occur in the Bible. Moffatt on Proverbs 31:30 speaks of a "wife with brains," but he is translating very freely a Greek text which refers to a "woman with understanding." The Babylonians thought the mind was located in the liver. Even Aristotle, who dissected bodies, thought that, because the brain was so cold, it must be used for refrigerating the blood!

XIII

Oddities

1. What verse has been held to be a prophecy about radio?

2. What five automobile parts are named in one Bible chapter?

3. Who had a car of state with a purple seat "inlaid with love"?

4. Whose hair stood up when he saw a ghost?

5. Who was So?

6. Where are immortal worms mentioned?

7. Whose "bowels boiled"?

8. When did a noise make no sound?

9. What boy's hand was older than his elder brother?

10. Who said he would chastise his people with scorpions for whips?

11. When did ears swallow ears?

12. Who prophesied that the moon would be as bright as the sun?

13. Where are near-sighted Christians mentioned?

14. Who had holy oil on his beard?

15. Were fishes taken into the ark?

16. Where is a hammock mentioned?

17. Who burned a snake alive?

18. Who expected to meet whom in the air?

19. What did Ahijah say about Abijah?

20. Who were Uz and Buz?

21. Who were Bedad and Hadad?

22. Who were Oholah and Oholibah?

23. Who were Gog and Magog?

24. Who were Tryphena and Tryphosa?

25. Who told a riddle about two eagles?

26. Who told a riddle about a lion?

27. Who walked forty days without eating?

28. How many decks were there on Noah's Ark?

29. Who made an iron axe-head swim?

30. What Hebrew named one of his sons "Ham"?

31. When was heaven bent?

32. What ass-herd discovered hot springs?

33. What two children's father was their grandfather also?

34. Whose nose smelt like apples?

35. What is the only Biblical reference to dwarfs?

36. Where is the only place Easter is mentioned in the Bible?

37. What is the middle chapter of the Bible?

38. What is the middle verse of the Bible?

39. How many words in the Bible?

40. What is the shortest verse in the Old Testament?

41. What is the shortest verse in the New Testament?

42. What psalm has four verses alike?

43. Where else in the Bible does the eighteenth psalm appear?

44. What is the longest psalm?

45. What is the shortest psalm?

46. What is the longest word in the Bible?

47. What psalm is a mosaic of two other psalms?

48. What psalm is an acrostic?

49. What book in the Bible does not contain the name of God?

50. How many groups of the magic number seven are there in the Book of Revelation?

51. What two chapters are almost identical?

52. What verse has all the letters of the English alphabet except "j", and another except "q"?

53. What was "The To Remain Bible"?

54. What was "The Wicked Bible"?

55. What was "The Breeches Bible"?

56. What was "The Vinegar Bible"?

57. What was "The Treacle Bible"?

58. What was "The Printers Bible"?

59. What was "The Ears to Ear Bible"?

60. What was "The Bug Bible"?

61. What was "The Standing Fishes Bible"?

62. What was "The Wife-Hater Bible"?

63. What was "The Murderers Bible"?

ANSWERS TO QUESTIONS
ABOUT ODDITIES

1. What verse has been held to be a prophecy about radio?

Zephaniah 1:10.—"And it shall come to pass in that day, saith the Lord, that there shall be the noise of a cry from the fish gate, and an howling from the second, and a great crashing from the hills."

2. What five automobile parts are named in one Bible chapter?

"Hoods," "rings," "mufflers," "chains," "round tires like the moon." It is, of course, a mere coincidence that these words so familiar in this automobile age were used by the

English translators to denote various parts of the costume of fashionable women in Isaiah's day. See Isaiah 3:18–23.— "In that day the Lord will take away the bravery of their tinkling ornaments about their feet, and their cauls, and their round tires like the moon, The chains, and the bracelets, and the mufflers, . . . The rings, and nose jewels, . . . The glasses, and the fine linen, and the hoods, and the vails."

3. Who had a car of state with a purple seat "inlaid with love"?

Solomon, Song of Solomon 3:9–10 RV.—"King Solomon made himself a palanquin [margin, "car of state"] of the wood of Lebanon. He made the pillars thereof of silver, the bottom thereof of gold, the seat of it of purple, the midst thereof being paved [margin, "inlaid"] with love, from the daughters of Jerusalem." Instead of palanquin the AV has "chariot" and Moffatt has "sedan." Just how it could be inlaid with love is not apparent. Moffatt has "inlaid with ebony," but the Hebrew and Greek texts both have plainly "love." It does not seem to have occurred to any of the reverend scholars to make the only translation consistent with both the Hebrew text and the well known amorous propensities of King Solomon, namely, "the seat of it of purple, the midst thereof being pressed down by the love of the daughters of Jerusalem." Sedan petting-parties are evidently not so "modern" after all.

4. Whose hair stood up when he saw a ghost?

The hair of Eliphaz, one of Job's friends, Job 4:15–16.— "Then a spirit passed before my face; the hair of my flesh stood up: It stood still, but I could not discern the form thereof: . . ."

5. Who was So?

King of Egypt, according to Second Kings 17:4.— ". . . Hoshea . . . had sent messengers to So king of Egypt, . . ." This could not have been so, for no king of that name or of similar name ruled in Egypt at that time. Possibly the individual referred to was Sibi, commander-in-chief of a North Arabian tribe, the Musri, confused with Mizraim (Egypt).

6. Where are immortal worms mentioned?

Isaiah 66:24.—"And they shall go forth, and look upon

the carcases of the men that have transgressed against me: for their worm shall not die, neither shall their fire be quenched; and they shall be an abhorring unto all flesh."

See also Mark 9:44, 46, 48.

7. Whose "bowels boiled"?

Job's, Job 30:27.—"My bowels boiled, and rested not: the days of affliction prevented me." RV has: "My heart is troubled, . . ."

8. When did a noise make no sound?

When Elijah was on Mount Horeb and Jehovah spoke to him in "a still small voice," First Kings 19:12. The RV margin points out that the Hebrew says, "a sound of gentle stillness."

9. What boy's hand was older than his elder brother?

Zerah's, Genesis 38:27–30 RV.—"And it came to pass in the time of her [Tamar's] travail, that, behold, twins were in her womb. And it came to pass, when she travailed, that one put out a hand: and the midwife took and bound upon his hand a scarlet thread, saying, This came out first. And it came to pass, as he drew back his hand, that, behold, his brother came out: and she said, Wherefore hast thou made a breach for thyself? therefore his name was called Perez. And afterward came out his brother, that had the scarlet thread upon his hand: and his name was called Zerah."

10. Who said he would chastise his people with scorpions for whips?

Rehoboam, First Kings 12:13–14.—"And the king [Rehoboam] answered the people roughly, saying . . . My father made your yoke heavy, and I will add to your yoke: my father also chastised you with whips, but I will chastise you with scorpions."

11. When did ears swallow ears?

In Pharaoh's dream, Genesis 41:5–7.—"And he slept and dreamed the second time: and, behold, seven ears of corn came up upon one stalk, rank and good. And, behold, seven thin ears and blasted with the east wind sprung up after them. And the seven thin ears devoured the seven rank and full ears. And Pharaoh awoke, and, behold, it was a dream."

12. Who prophesied that the moon would be as bright as the sun?

Isaiah 30:26.—"Moreover the light of the moon shall be as the light of the sun, . . ."

13. Where are near-sighted Christians mentioned?

Second Peter 1:9 RV.—"For he that lacketh these things is blind, seeing only what is near, . . ."

14. Who had holy oil on his beard?

Aaron, Psalms 133:2.—"It is like the precious ointment upon the head, that ran down upon the beard, even Aaron's beard: . . ." For the recipe for this "oil of holy ointment" and its use, see Exodus 30:22–33.

15. Were fishes taken into the ark?

Yes, according to Genesis 7:15.—"And they went in unto Noah into the ark, two and two of all flesh, wherein is the breath of life." But a flood certainly would not exterminate the fishes, and verse 22 is careful to say: "All in whose nostrils was the breath of life, of all that was in the dry land, died." Verse 15 should have had an exception for the fishes. And it certainly would have been difficult to take into the ark even a fraction of the species of fish. The flood story is full of impossibilities and inconsistencies, if one takes it literally.

16. Where is a hammock mentioned?

Isaiah 24:20 RV.—"The earth shall stagger like a drunken man, and shall sway to and fro like a hammock; . . ." AV has "cottage."

17. Who burned a snake alive?

Paul, Acts 28:3, 5.—"And when Paul had gathered a bundle of sticks, and laid them on the fire, there came a viper out of the heat, and fastened on his hand. . . . And he shook off the beast into the fire, and felt no harm."

18. Who expected to meet whom in the air?

Paul expected to meet Jesus in the air, First Thessalonians 4:16–17.—"For the Lord himself will descend from heaven with a shout, with the voice of the archangel, and with the trump of God: and the dead in Christ shall rise first: Then we which are alive and remain shall be caught up together

with them in the clouds, to meet the Lord in the air: and
so shall we ever be with the Lord."

19. What did Ahijah say about Abijah?

That he would die, First Kings 14:1–12.—"At that time
Abijah the son of Jeroboam fell sick. . . . And Jeroboam's
wife . . . arose, and went to Shiloh, and came to the house
of Ahijah. . . . And it was so, when Ahijah heard the sound
of her feet, as she came in at the door, that he said, Come
in, thou wife of Jeroboam; . . . for I am sent to thee
with heavy tidings. . . . Arise thou therefore, get thee to thine
own house: and when thy feet enter into the city, the
child shall die."

20. Who were Uz and Buz?

The first two sons of Nahor and Milcah, Genesis 22:20–
21 RV.—". . . it was told Abraham, saying, Behold, Milcah,
she also hath borne children unto thy brother Nahor: Uz his
firstborn, and Buz his brother, . . ." AV has "Huz" and
"Buz."

21. Who were Bedad and Hadad?

Father and son, Edomites, Genesis 36:35.—". . . and
Hadad the son of Bedad, . . ."

22. Who were Oholah and Oholibah?

Sister cities, Samaria and Jerusalem, personified, Ezekiel
23:4 RV.—"And the names of them were Oholah the elder,
and Oholibah her sister: and they became mine, and they
bare sons and daughters. And as for their names, Samaria is
Oholah, and Jerusalem Oholibah." AV has "Aholah" and
"Aholibah."

23. Who were Gog and Magog?

In Genesis 10:2 Magog is the son of Japheth, but in
Ezekiel 38:2 Magog is the land from which Gog came. See
also the rest of the chapter and chapter 39. In Revelation
20:8 Gog and Magog are the heathen nations to be led by
Satan against the faithful at the millennium.

24. Who were Tryphena and Tryphosa?

Roman Christians, Romans 16:12.—"Salute Tryphena and
Tryphosa, who labour in the Lord . . ."

25. Who told a riddle about two eagles?

Ezekiel, Ezekiel 17. This is termed a riddle, but is a long and rather complicated parable.

26. Who told a riddle about a lion?

Samson, Judges 14:12–20. The riddle was: "Out of the eater came forth meat, and out of the strong came forth sweetness." And the answer was: "What is sweeter than honey? and what is stronger than a lion?" Samson was referring to "a swarm of bees and honey in the carcase of the lion," verse 8.

27. Who walked forty days without eating?

Elijah, First Kings 19:8.—"And he [Elijah] arose, and did eat and drink, and went in the strength of that meat forty days and forty nights unto Horeb the mount of God."

28. How many decks were there on Noah's Ark?

Three, Genesis 6:16.—"A window shalt thou make to the ark, and in a cubit shalt thou finish it above; and the door of the ark shalt thou set in the side thereof; with lower, second, and third stories shalt thou make it." Moffatt has, "also put three decks in it," in place of the last phrase.

29. Who made an iron axe-head swim?

Elisha, Second Kings 6:5–7.—"But as one was felling a beam, the ax head fell into the water: and he cried, and said, Alas, master! for it was borrowed. And the man of God [Elisha] said, Where fell it? And he shewed him the place. And he cut a stick, and cast it in thither; and the iron did swim. Therefore said he, Take it up to thee. And he put out his hand, and took it."

30. What Hebrew named one of his sons "Ham"?

Noah, Genesis 6:10.—"And Noah begat three sons, Shem, Ham, and Japheth."

31. When was heaven bent?

When God came down, Psalm 18:9.—"He bowed the heavens also, and came down: and darkness was under his feet." Moffatt has, "as down he came on the bending sky, the storm-cloud at his feet."

32. What ass-herd discovered hot springs?

Anah, Genesis 36:24, RV.—". . . this is Anah who found

the hot springs in the wilderness, as he fed the asses of Zibeon his father."

33. What two children's father was their grandfather also?

Lot was father and grandfather of Moab and Benammi, Genesis 19:36–38.—"Thus were both the daughters of Lot with child by their father. And the firstborn bare a son, and called his name Moab: the same is the father of the Moabites unto this day. And the younger, she also bare a son, and called his name Benammi: the same is the father of the children of Ammon unto this day." This story (verses 30–38) of the double incest has been assumed by many scholars to be a Hebrew method of expressing contempt for their neighbors, the Moabites and the Ammonites.

34. Whose nose smelt like apples?

The prince's daughter of the Song of Solomon 7:1, 8.—"How beautiful are thy feet with shoes, O prince's daughter! the joints of thy thighs are like jewels, . . . now also thy breasts shall be as clusters of the vine, and the smell of thy nose like apples;" RV has "the smell of thy breath," but the Hebrew says "nose." The meaning, evidently, is "the smell of the breath of thy nostrils."

35. What is the only Biblical reference to dwarfs?

Among those prohibited from officiating at offerings, Leviticus 21:20.—"Or crookbackt, or a dwarf, or that hath a blemish. . . ."

36. Where is the only place Easter is mentioned in the Bible?

Acts 12:4.—"And when he [Herod] had apprehended him [Peter], he put him in prison, . . . intending after Easter to bring him forth to the people." RV has "after the Passover," for, of course, the word Easter had not then been associated with the resurrection of Christ.

37. What is the middle chapter of the Bible?

Psalm 117.

38. What is the middle verse of the Bible?

Psalm 118:8 (AV).

39. How many words in the Bible?

773,746 (AV).

40. What is the shortest verse in the Old Testament?

First Chronicles 1:25.—"Eber, Peleg, Reu."

41. What is the shortest verse in the New Testament?

John 11:35.—"Jesus wept."

42. What psalm has four verses alike?

Psalm 107, verses 8, 15, 21, and 31.

43. Where else in the Bible does the eighteenth psalm appear?

Second Samuel 22.

44. What is the longest psalm?

Psalm 119.

45. What is the shortest psalm?

Psalm 117.

46. What is the longest word in the Bible?

Mahershalalhashbaz, Isaiah 8:1, 3.

47. What psalm is a mosaic of two other psalms?

Psalm 108 is composed of Psalm 57:8–12 and Psalm 60:7–14.

48. What psalm is an acrostic?

Psalm 119. The 176 verses are divided into 22 sections of eight verses each, one section for each letter of the Hebrew alphabet. Each verse in each section begins, in the Hebrew, with the letter of the alphabet heading that section, that is, for instance, each of the first eight verses begins with a Hebrew word beginning with aleph. This acrostic form is not preserved in the English translation.

49. What book in the Bible does not contain the name of God?

The Book of Esther.

50. How many groups of the magic number seven are there in the Book of Revelation?

Eighteen, including the seven churches of Asia (Revelation 1:4), spirits (1:4), candlesticks (1:12), stars (1:16), angels (1:20), lamps (4:5), seals (5:1), horns (5:6), eyes (5:6), trumpets (8:2), thunders (10:3), thousand persons

(11:13), heads (12:3), diadems (12:3), plagues (15:1), bowls (16:1), mountains (17:9), and kings (17:10).

51. What two chapters are almost identical?

Second Kings 19 and Isaiah 37.

52. What verse has all the letters of the English alphabet except "j", and another except "q"?

(a) except "j", Ezra 7:21, both AV and RV; (b) except "q," I Chronicles 12:40.

53. What was "The To Remain Bible"?

In 1805, in proof-reading a Bible, a man questioned whether or not a certain comma should be removed. His editor answered the question by writing on the margin, "to remain." The two words were included in the type of the body of the text, so that Galatians 4:29 read in two subsequent editions: "But as then he that was born after the flesh persecuted him that was born after the spirit to remain, even so it is now."

54. What was "The Wicked Bible"?

A printer of a 1631 edition was fined three hundred pounds for leaving the "not" out of one of the Ten Commandments so that Exodus 20:14 read: "Thou shalt commit adultery."

55. What was "The Breeches Bible"?

The Geneva version of 1560 translated Genesis 3:7: "making themselves breeches out of fig-leaves," which the AV renders, "aprons." The Hebrew word "chagorah" means "anything girded on."

56. What was "The Vinegar Bible"?

An edition of 1717 headed the 20th chapter of Luke, "The parable of the vinegar" instead of "vineyard."

57. What was "The Treacle Bible"?

An edition of 1568 rendered Jeremiah 8:22: "Is there no treacle [AV "balm"] in Gilead?" The "Rosin Bible" is another name for the Douai Bible of 1609 (preferred by Roman Catholics) which uses "rosin" for "balm." The Hebrew word "tsori" means "balsam," and is so translated by Moffatt.

58. What was "The Printers Bible"?

Psalm 119:161 reads: "Princes have persecuted me without a cause:" The first word was printed "Printers" by a careless printer in an edition printed sometime before 1702.

59. What was "The Ears to Ear Bible"?

Matthew 13:43 reads: ". . . Who hath ears to hear, let him hear," but in an 1810 edition it appeared as "ears to ear."

60. What was "The Bug Bible"?

An edition of 1551 translated Psalm 91:5: "Thou shalt not be afraid of bugs by night;" which the AV has, "the terror by night;"

61. What was "The Standing Fishes Bible"?

An 1806 Bible left the "r" out of "fishers" in Ezekiel 47:10: "And it shall come to pass that the fishers will stand upon it."

62. What was "The Wife-Hater Bible"?

An 1810 Bible made an odd mistake on Luke 14:26: "If any man come to me and hate not his father, and mother, and wife, and children, and brethren, and sisters, yea, and his own life also, he cannot be my disciple." The word "life" was printed "wife."

63. What was "The Murderers Bible"?

The word "murmurers" was misprinted "murderers" in the 16th verse of the one-chapter book of Jude in an edition of 1801.

XIV

Somewhat Amusing

1. When did Hebrews wear kilts?
2. What man wore a hat trimmed with blue lace?
3. Who gave soup to an angel?
4. Who went fishing naked?
5. Who ate a mouse behind a tree?
6. Where does it speak of a king hunting a flea?
7. What man wore iron horns?
8. What prophet said he would go naked and make a noise like an ostrich?
9. Who prayed inside a fish?
10. Who asked God to put his tears in a bottle?
11. Who named his son "Hen"?
12. What mob shouted one sentence two hours?
13. What man wore a veil?
14. Who was called an ass as a compliment?
15. Who collected men's earrings to his sorrow?
16. What priests wore linen shorts?
17. Who threatened to make a sea-serpent bite the Israelites?
18. What two disciples did Jesus nickname "Sons of Thunder"?
19. What disciples were mistaken for Jupiter and Mercury?
20. What soldiers imitated dogs?

21. What men were ashamed to have been shaved?

22. Who asked God to let him alone so that he could take a little comfort before he died?

23. Who cut his hair once a year?

24. Who "embraced dunghills"?

25. Who had "collops of fat on his flanks"?

26. Who were called "slow bellies"?

27. What man was shaved when he was asleep?

28. Who named his walking-sticks "Beauty" and "Bands"?

29. Whose chariot was washed in a women's bathing pool?

30. Who thought his conscience was in his kidneys?

ANSWERS TO QUESTIONS
SOMEWHAT AMUSING

1. When did Hebrews wear kilts?

When Hanun forced them to, First Chronicles 19:4.— "Wherefore Hanun took David's servants, and shaved them, and cut off their garments in the midst hard by their buttocks, and sent them away."

2. What man wore a hat trimmed with blue lace?

Aaron, Exodus 28:37–38, and see Exodus 39:31.—"And thou shalt put it on a blue lace, that it may be upon the mitre; . . . And it shall be upon Aaron's forehead, . . ." RVm has "turban" for "mitre."

3. Who gave soup to an angel?

Gideon, Judges 6:11, 19.—"And there came an angel of the Lord, and sat under an oak. . . . And Gideon went in, and made ready a kid, . . . and he put the broth in a pot, and brought it out to him under the oak, and presented it."

4. Who went fishing naked?

Peter, John 21:7.—"Now when Simon Peter heard that it was the Lord, he girt his fisher's coat unto him, (for he was naked,) and did cast himself into the sea."

5. *Who ate a mouse behind a tree?*

Evidently celebrants of "heathen" mysteries, Isaiah 66:17.
—"They that sanctify themselves, and purify themselves in
the gardens behind one tree in the midst, eating swine's
flesh, and the abomination, and the mouse, shall be consumed together, saith the Lord."

The tree was probably an "asherah" or sacred tree, and
the custom a survival of tree-worship, or possibly phallic
worship. See Deuteronomy 16:21, 22.

For an interesting account of sacred mice, read First Samuel, chapter 6.

6. *Where does it speak of a king hunting a flea?*

First Samuel 26:20.—". . . for the king of Israel is come
out to seek a flea, as when one doth hunt a partridge in
the mountains."

7. *What man wore iron horns?*

Zedekiah, First Kings 22:11.—"And Zedekiah the son of
Chenaanah made him horns of iron. . . ."

8. *What prophet said he would go naked and make a
noise like an ostrich?*

Micah, Micah 1:8 (RV).—"I will go stripped and naked;
I will make a wailing like the jackals, and a lamentation
like the ostriches." AV has "dragons" and "owls."

9. *Who prayed inside a fish?*

Jonah, Jonah 2:1.—"Then Jonah prayed unto the Lord
his God out of the fish's belly."

10. *Who asked God to put his tears in a bottle?*

David, Psalms 56:8.—". . . put thou my tears into thy
bottle: . . ."

11. *Who named his son "Hen"?*

Zephaniah, Zechariah 6:14.—". . . Hen the son of Zephaniah, . . ."

12. *What mob shouted one sentence two hours?*

The Ephesian populace, Acts 19:34.—". . . all with one
voice about the space of two hours cried out, Great is Diana
of the Ephesians."

13. What man wore a veil?

Moses, Exodus 34:33.—"And till Moses had done speaking with them, he put a vail on his face."

14. Who was called an ass as a compliment?

Issachar, Genesis 49:14.—"Issachar is a strong ass couching down between two burdens."

15. Who collected men's earrings to his sorrow?

Gideon, Judges 8:24–27.—"And Gideon said . . . give me every man the earrings of his prey . . . And Gideon made an ephod thereof and put it in his city, even in Ophrah: and all Israel went thither a whoring after it: which thing became a snare unto Gideon, and to his house."

The "ephod" was evidently an idol, or some article used in divination or worship, for see Judges 17:5 and First Samuel 21:9.

16. What priests wore linen shorts?

Aaron and his sons, Exodus 28:42–43.—"And thou shalt make them linen breeches to cover their nakedness; from the loins even unto the thighs they shall reach: And they shall be upon Aaron, and upon his sons, . . ."

17. Who threatened to make a sea-serpent bite the Israelites?

The Lord, Amos 9:3.—". . . and though they be hid from my sight in the bottom of the sea, thence will I command the serpent and he shall bite them:"

For further evidence of belief in sea-serpents and sea-dragons, see Isaiah 27:1.

18. What two disciples did Jesus nickname "Sons of Thunder"?

James and John, Mark 3:17.—"And James the son of Zebedee, and John the brother of James; and he surnamed them Boanerges, which is, The sons of thunder:"

19. What disciples were mistaken for Jupiter and Mercury?

Barnabas and Paul, Acts 14:12.—"And they called Barnabas, Jupiter; and Paul, Mercurius, because he was the chief speaker."

20. What soldiers imitated dogs?

Gideon's, Judges 7:5.—". . . and the Lord said unto Gideon, Every one that lappeth of the water with his tongue, as a dog lappeth, him shalt thou set by himself; . . ."

21. What men were ashamed to have been shaved?

David's servants, First Chronicles 19:4, 5.—". . . shaved them, . . . for the men were greatly ashamed."

22. Who asked God to let him alone so that he could take a little comfort before he died?

Job, Job 10:20–21.—". . . let me alone, that I may take comfort a little, Before I go whence I shall not return, even to the land of darkness and the shadow of death;"

23. Who cut his hair once a year?

Absalom, Second Samuel 14:26.—"And when he polled his head, (for it was at every year's end that he polled it: because the hair was heavy on him, therefore he polled it:) he weighed the hair of his head at two hundred shekels after the king's weight." (Six pounds and four ounces.)

24. Who "embraced dunghills"?

They that were brought up in scarlet, Lamentations 4:5. —". . . they that were brought up in scarlet embrace dunghills."

25. Who had "collops of fat on his flanks"?

The "wicked man" mentioned in Job 15:20, 27.—"The wicked man . . . Because he covereth his face with his fatness, and maketh collops of fat on his flanks."

26. Who were called "slow bellies"?

The Cretians, Titus 1:12.—"One of themselves, even a prophet of their own, said, The Cretians are always liars, evil beasts, slow bellies." The prophet is identified by some scholars as Epimenides.

27. What man was shaved when he was asleep?

Samson, Judges 16:19.—"And she made him sleep upon her knees; and she called for a man, and she caused him to shave off the seven locks of his head; . . ."

28. Who named his walking-sticks "Beauty" and "Bands"?

Zechariah, Zechariah 11:7.—". . . And I took unto me two staves; the one I called Beauty, and the other I called Bands; . . ."

29. Whose chariot was washed in a women's bathing pool?

Ahab's, First Kings 22:38.—"And they washed the chariot by the pool of Samaria: and the dogs licked up his blood (now the harlots washed themselves there); . . ." So in the RV. The AV has in place of the last phrase the following, "and they washed his armour;"

30. Who thought his conscience was in his kidneys?

The Psalmist, Psalms 73:21.—"Thus my heart was grieved, and I was pricked in my reins." Also Psalms 16:7.—". . . my reins also instruct me in the night seasons."

Such was evidently the common belief of Bible times. See Proverbs 23:16, Revelation 2:23. The word "reins" comes from the Latin, renes, kidneys. The Talmud (Berakhoth 61a) says that one kidney prompts man to do good, the other to do evil. The kidneys, then, as the seat of morality, were the most important organs of the body, and were especially reserved for Jehovah and sacrificed to him as a burnt offering. See Leviticus 3:4–5.

XV

Contradictions

1. Who was Jesus' grandfather on his father's side?

2. Who moved David to take a census?

3. How many times did the cock crow when Peter denied Jesus?

4. Who killed the giant Goliath?

5. Who killed Saul?

6. Does God tempt men?

7. How many horses had Solomon?

8. How many beatitudes did Jesus give in the Sermon on the Mount?

9. What was the exact inscription on the cross of Jesus?

10. Does every man sin?

11. Who bought the potter's field?

12. Who prophesied the potter's field?

13. In what chapter did Paul contradict himself?

14. Where is absolutely contradictory advice given in adjacent verses?

15. What important verse in the Authorized Version (King James) is omitted in the Revised Version?

16. What childless woman had five sons?

17. What king was eight when he was eighteen?

18. Who advised marriage and who advised against it?

19. Did those with Saul (Paul) at his conversion hear a voice?

20. Where was Jesus three days after his baptism?

21. How many apostles were in office between the resurrection and the ascension of Jesus?

22. From which one of David's sons was Jesus descended?

ANSWERS TO QUESTIONS
ABOUT CONTRADICTIONS

1. Who was Jesus' grandfather on his father's side?

Matthew says "Jacob," but Luke says "Heli." Matthew 1:16.—"And Jacob begat Joseph the husband of Mary, of whom was born Jesus, who is called Christ." Luke 3:23.—"And Jesus himself began to be about thirty years of age, being (as was supposed) the son of Joseph, which was the son of Heli." This contradiction has troubled Christians much, and is only one of many in these two genealogies.

2. Who moved David to take a census?

Second Samuel says "the Lord," but First Chronicles says "Satan." Second Samuel 24:1–2.—"And again the anger of the Lord was kindled against Israel, and he moved David against them to say, Go, number Israel and Judah. For the king said to Joab. . . . Go now . . . and number ye the people." First Chronicles 21:1–2.—"And Satan stood up against Israel, and provoked David to number Israel. And David said to Joab . . . Go, number Israel . . ."

3. How many times did the cock crow when Peter denied Jesus?

Mark says twice, but Matthew, Luke, and John say once. Mark 14:72.—"And the second time the cock crew. And Peter called to mind the word that Jesus said unto him, Before the cock crow twice, thou shalt deny me thrice. And when he thought thereon, he wept." Matthew 26:74–75.— ". . . And immediately the cock crew. And Peter remembered the word of Jesus, which said unto him, Before the cock crow, thou shalt deny me thrice. And he went out, and wept bitterly." See also Luke 22:60–61 and John 13:38; 18:27.

4. Who killed the giant Goliath?

Both David and Elhanan, First Samuel 17:23, 50.—". . . there came up the champion, the Philistine of Gath, Goliath by name, out of the armies of the Philistines, . . . So David prevailed over the Philistine with a sling and with a stone, and smote the Philistine, and slew him; . . ." Second Samuel 21:19 RV.—". . . and Elhanan the son of Jaareoregim the Bethlehemite slew Goliath the Gittite, the staff of whose spear was like a weaver's beam." First Chronicles 20:5 tries to reconcile the contradiction by saying that Elhanan slew the brother of Goliath. The Authorized Version deliberately inserts "the brother of" in the text of Second Samuel 21:19, as is shown by the italics used.

5. Who killed Saul?

First Samuel says that Saul killed himself, but Second Samuel that an Amalekite slew him. First Samuel 31:4–6.— ". . . Therefore Saul took a sword, and fell upon it . . . So Saul died, . . ." Second Samuel 1 tells how an Amalekite reported to David how he had killed Saul at the latter's request, and (verse 15) ". . . David called one of the young men, and said, Go near, and fall upon him [the Amalekite] . . ." thus punishing him for having killed "the Lord's anointed." Was this story told in Second Samuel to remove from Saul the stigma of the self-destruction reported in First Samuel?

6. Does God tempt men?

Genesis says yes, but James says no. Genesis 22:1.—"And it came to pass after these things, that God did tempt Abraham, . . ." Then follows the story of how God did it. James 1:13.—"Let no man say when he is tempted, I am tempted of God: for God cannot be tempted with evil, neither tempteth he any man:"

7. How many horses had Solomon?

First Kings says 40,000; Second Chronicles 4,000. First Kings 4:26.—"And Solomon had forty thousand stalls of horses for his chariots, . . ." Second Chronicles 9:25.—"And Solomon had four thousand stalls for horses and chariots, . . ."

8. How many beatitudes did Jesus give in the Sermon on the Mount?

Matthew 5:3–11 gives nine beatitudes, but Luke 6:20–23 has only four.

9. *What was the exact inscription on the cross of Jesus?*

Matthew 27:37.—"THIS IS JESUS THE KING OF THE JEWS."
Mark 15:26.—"THE KING OF THE JEWS."
Luke 23:38.—"THIS IS THE KING OF THE JEWS."
John 19:19.—"JESUS OF NAZARETH THE KING OF THE JEWS."

10. *Does every man sin?*

First Kings 8:46.—". . . for there is no man that sinneth not, . . ." So also Second Chronicles 6:36; Proverbs 20:9; Ecclesiastes 7:20; and First John 1:8–10. But First John 3:9 says that some men do not and cannot.—"Whosoever is born of God doth not commit sin; for his seed remaineth in him: and he cannot sin, because he is born of God."

11. *Who bought the potter's field?*

Acts says that Judas bought it, but Matthew says that the chief priests did. Acts 1:18–19.—"Now this man purchased a field with the reward of iniquity; and falling headlong, he burst asunder in the midst, and all his bowels gushed out. And it was known to all the dwellers at Jerusalem; insomuch as that field is called, Aceldama, that is to say, The field of blood." Matthew 27:6–8.—"And the chief priests took the silver pieces, and said, It is not lawful for to put them into the treasury, because it is the price of blood. And they took counsel, and bought with them the potter's field, to bury strangers in. Wherefore that field was called, The field of blood, unto this day." Note also that there is another contradiction in the fact that Acts states that it was called the field of blood because of Judas' blood; but Matthew, because of Jesus' blood.

12. *Who prophesied the potter's field?*

Matthew 27:9–10 states: "Then was fulfilled that which was spoken by Jeremy the prophet, saying, And they took the thirty pieces of silver, the price of him that was valued, whom they of the children of Israel did value; And gave them for the potter's field, as the Lord appointed me." But there is no such passage in Jeremiah. What the writer of Matthew had in mind was probably Zechariah 11:12–13: "And I said unto them, If ye think good, give me my price; and if not, forbear. So they weighed for my price thirty pieces of silver. And the Lord said unto me, Cast it unto the potter: a goodly price that I was prised at of them. And I took the thirty pieces of silver, and cast them to the potter in the house of the Lord." It is evident that neither Jeremiah nor Zechariah had any foreknowledge of the potter's field, and that the connection between the incidents is only a matter of coincidence of words and phrases.

13. In what chapter did Paul contradict himself?

Galatians 6. In verse 2 Paul says: "Bear ye one another's burdens, and so fulfil the law of Christ." In verse 5 he says: "For every man shall bear his own burden."

14. Where is absolutely contradictory advice given in adjacent verses?

Proverbs 26. Verse 4 advises: "Answer not a fool according to his folly, lest thou also be like unto him." Verse 5 says: "Answer a fool according to his folly, lest he be wise in his own conceit."

15. What important verse in the Authorized Version (King James) is omitted in the Revised Version?

First John 5:7—"For there are three that bear record in heaven, the Father, the Word, and the Holy Ghost: and these three are one." This verse in the Authorized Version is not included in the Revised Version because it is not in the earliest Greek manuscripts, and is evidently a gloss introduced by some pious but unethical soul who desired to have the doctrine of the Trinity included in the Bible. The RV splits the 6th verse and takes the latter part of the 6th to make the 7th.

16. What childless woman had five sons?

Michal. Second Samuel 6:23.—"Therefore Michal the daughter of Saul had no child unto the day of her death." This was her punishment for reproving her husband, David, for indecent exposure, which was evidently considered perfectly all right for him to do inasmuch as he was dancing before the Lord in a religious procession. But Second Samuel 21:8 speaks of "the five sons of Michal the daughter of Saul, whom she brought up for Adriel the son of Barzillai the Meholathite:" But the AV admits in the margin that what the Hebrew really says is:—"bare to Adriel." It is evident from First Samuel 18:19, where it is stated that Merab, another daughter of Saul, was the wife of Adriel, that "Michal" must have been written for "Merab" in Second Samuel 21:8 by a copyist's mistake.

17. What king was eight when he was eighteen?

Jehoiachin. Second Kings 24:8.—"Jehoiachin was eighteen years old when he began to reign, and he reigned in Jerusalem three months . . ." Second Chronicles 36:9.— "Jehoiachin was eight years old when he began to reign, and he reigned three months and ten days in Jerusalem: . . ."

18. Who advised marriage and who advised against it?

Solomon was for marriage and Paul was against it. Proverbs 18:22.—"Whoso findeth a wife findeth a good thing, and obtaineth favour of the Lord." As for Paul, see First Corinthians 7, the whole chapter. He says in verse 1: "It is good for a man not to touch a woman," but in verse 2 he admits that men and women had better marry in order to avoid fornication. In verse 27 he says: "Art thou bound unto a wife? Seek not to be loosed. Art thou loosed from a wife? seek not a wife." In verses 39 and 40 he says: "The wife is bound by the law as long as her husband liveth; but if her husband be dead, she is at liberty to be married to whom she will; only in the Lord. But she is happier if she so abide, after my judgment: and I think also that I have the spirit of God." So Paul was not so enthusiastic about marriage as Solomon was.

19. Did those with Saul (Paul) at his conversion hear a voice?

Acts 9:7 states: "And the men which journeyed with him stood speechless, hearing a voice, but seeing no man." But in reporting the same event Paul himself (Acts 22:9) said: "And they that were with me saw indeed the light, and were afraid; but they heard not the voice of him that spake to me."

20. Where was Jesus three days after his baptism?

Mark 1:12–13 states that "immediately" after the baptism, "the spirit driveth him into the wilderness. And he was there in the wilderness forty days, tempted of Satan; . . ." But the writer of the Fourth Gospel distinctly states (John 1:35) that the next day after the baptism Jesus called Andrew and Simon Peter to be his disciples, that on the second day (1:43) Jesus went into Galilee and called Philip and Nathanael as disciples, and that on the third day (2:1–11) he was at the wedding in Cana of Galilee.

21. How many apostles were in office between the resurrection and the ascension of Jesus?

Twelve, according to First Corinthians 15:5.—"And that he was seen of Cephas, then of the twelve:" But Judas hanged himself (Matthew 27:3–5) before the resurrection, and Matthias was not elected (Acts 1:9–26) until after the ascension.

22. From which one of David's sons was Jesus descended?

The genealogy in Matthew traces Jesus' ancestry through Solomon (Matthew 1:6–7) while the genealogy in Luke traces it through Nathan, another son of David (Luke 3:31).

XVI

Miracles and Wonders

1. Where are hailstones described weighing over one hundred pounds each?

2. Where did a phantom hand appear?

3. When did two sticks become one?

4. Who changed the specific gravity of a metal?

5. When did fire consume stones?

6. What historical person, mentioned eleven times in the Bible, had neither father, mother, nor other ancestors, was not born and did not die?

7. In what city did a wall fall on 27,000 men?

8. What prophet was gifted with clairaudience?

9. When were sick people cured by a man's shadow falling on them?

10. When did an iron gate open of its own accord?

11. Who died at the age of 120 without senility?

12. What king made a speech and was immediately "eaten of worms"?

13. What sorcerer was struck with blindness?

14. What man's hair became feathers?

15. Who saw a flying roll?

16. What two men walked on the water?

17. How many Bible characters are said to have risen or to have been raised from the dead?

18. Who believed there are "fiery flying serpents"?

19. Where is a sea-serpent mentioned?

20. Who held a conversation with an ass?

ANSWERS TO QUESTIONS ON
MIRACLES AND WONDERS

1. Where are hailstones described weighing over one hundred pounds each?

Revelation 16:21.—"And there fell upon men a great hail out of heaven, every stone about the weight of a talent: . . ." A talent weighed between 108 and 130 pounds. For other great hailstones in the Bible, see Joshua 10:11; Exodus 9:22–35; and Revelation 11:19. Hail is always viewed in the Bible as a punishment from God, and is so mentioned over thirty times. Macalister, in Hastings' Dictionary of the Bible, vol. 2, p. 282, lists other hailstones on record as larger even than the ones of Revelation 16:21.

2. Where did a phantom hand appear?

At Belshazzar's feast, writing on the wall, Daniel 5:5.— "In the same hour came forth fingers of a man's hand, and wrote over against the candlestick upon the plaister of the wall of the king's palace: and the king saw the part of the hand that wrote."

3. When did two sticks become one?

Ezekiel 37:15–17.—"The word of the Lord came again unto me, saying, Moreover, thou son of man, take thee one stick, and write upon it, for Judah, and for the children of Israel his companions: then take another stick, and write upon it, For Joseph, the stick of Ephraim, and for all the house of Israel his companions: And join them one to another into one stick; and they shall become one in thine hand."

4. Who changed the specific gravity of a metal?

Elisha, Second Kings 6:5–6.—"But as one was felling a beam, the axe head fell into the water: . . . And the man of God . . . cut down a stick, and cast it in thither; and the iron did swim."

5. When did fire consume stones?

First Kings 18:38.—"Then the fire of the Lord fell, and consumed the burnt sacrifice, and the wood, and the stones, and the dust, and licked up the water that was in the trench."

6. What historical person, mentioned eleven times in the Bible, had neither father, mother, nor other ancestors, was not born and did not die?

Melchisedec (sometimes spelled Melchizedek), Hebrews 7:1-3.—"For this Melchisedec, king of Salem, priest of the most high God, who met Abraham returning from the slaughter of the kings, and blessed him; To whom also Abraham gave a tenth part of all; first being by interpretation King of righteousness, and after that also King of Salem, which is, King of peace; Without father, without mother, without descent, having neither beginning of days, nor end of life; but made like unto the Son of God; abideth a priest continually."

For "without descent" the margin has "without pedigree," and the RV "without genealogy."

For other mention of this strange person, see Genesis 14:18; Psalm 110:4; Hebrews 5:6, 10; 6:20; 7:10, 11, 15, 17, 21. It is evident that the author of Hebrews is interested in making out that Melchisedec was a prototype of Christ, and that to secure his end and make the parallel complete, he changed and expanded the passage in Genesis 14, where it was the king of Sodom who met Abraham returning from the slaughter of the kings. Why the author of Hebrews did not adduce the "bread and wine" of Genesis 14:18 as a prototype of the Lord's Supper is hard to understand, unless the eucharist was of later origin than the date of the composition of Hebrews.

Needless to say, Melchisedec has been very popular as a sermon subject, as there is just enough of the miraculous, the mysterious, and the symbolic to intrigue interpreters.

7. In what city did a wall fall on 27,000 men?

Aphek, First Kings 20:30.—"But the rest fled to Aphek, into the city; and there a wall fell upon twenty and seven thousand of the men that were left. . . ."

8. What prophet was gifted with clairaudience?

Elisha, Second Kings 6:12.— '. . . but Elisha, the prophet

that is in Israel, telleth the king of Israel the words that thou speakest in thy bedchamber."

9. When were sick people cured by a man's shadow falling on them?

Acts 5:15-16.—"Insomuch that they brought forth the sick into the streets, and laid them on beds and couches, that at the least the shadow of Peter passing by might overshadow some of them. There came also a multitude out of the cities round about unto Jerusalem, bringing sick folks, and them which were vexed with unclean spirits: and they were healed every one."

For many instances of superstitions about the magical effects of shadows, see Frazer's Golden Bough, volume 3, pp. 77-83.

10. When did an iron gate open of its own accord?

Acts 12:10.—"When they were past the first and the second ward, they came unto the iron gate that leadeth unto the city; which opened to them of his own accord: and they went out, . . ."

11. Who died at the age of 120 without senility?

Moses, Deuteronomy 34:7.—"And Moses was an hundred and twenty years old when he died: his eye was not dim, nor his natural force abated." For the last phrase, the Hebrew has, as the margin indicates, "nor his moisture fled."

12. What king made a speech and was immediately "eaten of worms"?

Herod, Acts 12:21-23.—"And upon a set day Herod, arrayed in royal apparel, sat upon his throne, and made an oration unto them. And the people gave a shout, saying, It is the voice of a god, and not of a man. And immediately the angel of the Lord smote him, because he gave not God the glory: and he was eaten of worms, and gave up the ghost."

13. What sorcerer was struck with blindness?

Elymas, Acts 13:8-11.—"But Elymas the sorcerer . . . withstood them, . . . And immediately there fell on him a mist and a darkness; and he went about seeking some to lead him by the hand."

14. What man's hair became feathers?

Nebuchadnezzar's, Daniel 4:33.—"The same hour was the

thing fulfilled upon Nebuchadnezzar: and he was driven from men, and did eat grass as oxen, and his body was wet with the dew of heaven, till his hairs were grown like eagles' feathers, and his nails like birds' claws."

15. Who saw a flying roll?

Zechariah, Zechariah 5:1–2.—"Then I turned, and lifted up mine eyes, and looked, and behold a flying roll. And he said unto me, What seest thou? And I answered, I see a flying roll; the length thereof is twenty cubits, and the breadth thereof ten cubits." The roll was, properly, a "scroll" (as Moffatt translates) and was inscribed with a curse for thieves and false swearers. See verses 3 and 4.

16. What two men walked on the water?

Jesus and Peter, Matthew 14:25–33, especially 25 and 29. —"And in the fourth watch of the night Jesus went unto them, walking on the sea. . . . And when Peter was come down out of the ship, he walked on the water, to go to Jesus."

17. How many Bible characters are said to have risen or to have been raised from the dead?

Twelve, (1) The son of the Widow of Zarephath, First Kings 17:22. (2) The son of the Shunammite woman, Second Kings 4:32–35. (3) The man whose body touched the bones of Elisha, Second Kings 13:21. (4) Jesus Christ, Matthew 28:5–7; Mark 16:6; Luke 24:6. (5) The son of the Widow of Nain, Luke 7:12–15. (6) The daughter of Jairus, Luke 8:53–55. (7) Lazarus, John 11:43–44. (8) Tabitha (Dorcas), Acts 9:40. (9) Eutychus, Acts 20:9–12. (10) Samuel, First Samuel 28:14. (11 and 12) Moses and Elijah, Luke 9:30. The last three instances (10, 11, and 12) are of a different sort from the first nine, and seem more like spiritistic materializations.

In Matthew 27:52–53 there is a strange account, not given by the other gospel writers, of a wholesale resurrection of the dead: "And the graves were opened; and many bodies of the saints which slept arose, And came out of the graves after his resurrection, and went into the holy city, and appeared unto many."

18. Who believed there are "fiery flying serpents"?

Isaiah, Isaiah 30:6.—"The burden of the beasts of the south: into the land of trouble and anguish, from which

come the young and old lion, the viper and fiery flying serpent, . . ." See also Isaiah 14:29.

19. Where is a sea-serpent mentioned?

Amos 9:3.—". . . and though they be hid from my sight
in the bottom of the sea, thence will I command the serpent, and he shall bite them:" See also Isaiah 27:1. There
was also in Hebrew mythology a fabled sea-monster called
Rahab, mentioned in Psalm 87:4; Psalm 89:10; and Isaiah
51:9, also in the RV of Job 9:13; Job 26:12; and Isaiah
30:7. The Babylonians believed in a similar sea-monster,
Tiamat, supposed to have eleven helpers. Inasmuch as the
helpers of Rahab are mentioned in Job 9:13 RV, it is likely
that Rahab was the Hebrew version of Tiamat.

20. Who held a conversation with an ass?

Balaam, Numbers 22:28–30.—"And the Lord opened the
mouth of the ass, and she said unto Balaam, What have I
done unto thee, that thou hast smitten me these three times?
And Balaam said unto the ass, Because thou hast mocked
me: I would there were a sword in mine hand, for now
would I kill thee. And the ass said unto Balaam, Am not I
thine ass, upon which thou hast ridden ever since I was
thine unto this day? was I ever wont to do so unto thee?
And he said, Nay."

For interesting parallels of the supposed intelligence of
animals and their understanding of human speech, see Frazer's Golden Bough, volume 3, pages 398–400.

XVII

Kings

1. What king had his thumbs and great toes cut off for having thus treated seventy captive kings?

2. What king reigned seven days and then cremated himself?

3. What king sulked in bed because he failed to make a real estate deal?

4. What king fell out of his bedroom window?

5. What dead king was laid on a perfumed bed?

6. What king stopped a Hebrew invasion by sacrificing his oldest son?

7. What king installed a city waterworks system?

8. What king was killed by a chance arrow?

9. What king lived in quarantine?

10. What king's knees knocked together for fright?

11. What king saw his sons killed and then was blinded?

12. What harlot's son ruled Israel six years?

13. What king sentenced his ten concubines to life imprisonment?

14. What king was displeased with a gift of twenty cities?

15. What king imported apes and peacocks?

16. What king inherited a sun-clock from his father?

17. What king suffered two years from a foot-disease and consulted physicians instead of the Lord?

18. What king's hand dried up?

19. What king committed suicide by falling on his sword?

20. What king began to reign at seven years of age?

21. What king began to reign at eight years of age?

22. What present did King Tou bring to King David?

23. What Hebrew king cut his conquered enemies with saws, harrows, and axes?

24. What king cut up a book with a penknife and burned it?

25. What king's household crossed the Jordan River in a ferry-boat?

26. What five kings hid in a cave?

27. What king caused 10,000 prisoners to be killed by precipitation?

28. What king lay all night on the ground when his son was sick?

29. Who advised Christians to be in subjection to kings, governors, and masters?

30. What king had a throne of ivory overlaid with gold?

31. What prophet predicted that kings would act as nursemaids?

32. What king was killed when he was drunk?

33. What fat king was stabbed to death by a left-handed man?

34. What king had 900 chariots of iron?

35. What king had a house made of ivory?

36. What king was given a daily allowance by another king?

37. What king of Egypt killed a king of Judah in battle?

38. What king gave a prophet 40 camel-loads of presents?

39. What king attended a religious service and then killed all the worshipers?

40. What king consulted a spiritistic medium and was punished by death?

ANSWERS TO QUESTIONS
ABOUT KINGS

1. *What king had his thumbs and great toes cut off for having thus treated seventy captive kings?*

Adoni-bezek, Judges 1:6–7.—"But Adoni-bezek fled; and they pursued after him, and caught him, and cut off his thumbs and his great toes. And Adoni-bezek said, Three-score and ten kings, having their thumbs and their great toes cut off, gathered their meat under my table: as I have done, so God hath requited me. And they brought him to Jerusalem, and there he died."

2. *What king reigned seven days and then cremated himself?*

Zimri, First Kings 16:15–18.—"In the twenty and seventh year of Asa king of Judah did Zimri reign seven days in Tirzah. . . . And Omri went up from Gibbethon, and all Israel with him, and they besieged Tirzah. And it came to pass, when Zimri saw that the city was taken, that he went into the palace of the king's house, and burnt the king's house over him with fire, and died."

3. *What king sulked in bed because he failed to make a real estate deal?*

Ahab, First Kings 21:2–4.—"And Ahab spake unto Naboth, saying, Give me thy vineyard, that I may have it for a garden of herbs, because it is near unto my house: and I will give thee for it a better vineyard than it; or, if it seem good to thee, I will give thee the worth of it in money. And Naboth said unto Ahab, The Lord forbid it me, that I should give the inheritance of my fathers unto thee. And Ahab came into his house heavy and displeased. . . . And he laid him down upon his bed, and turned away his face, and would eat no bread."

4. *What king fell out of his bedroom window?*

Ahaziah, Second Kings 1:2.—"And Ahaziah fell down through a lattice in his upper chamber that was in Samaria, and was sick: . . ."

5. What dead king was laid on a perfumed bed?

Asa, Second Chronicles 16:13–14.—"And Asa slept with his fathers, . . . And they buried him in his own sepulchre, which he had made for himself in the city of David, and laid him in the bed which was filled with sweet odours and divers kinds of spices prepared by the apothecaries' art: . . ."

6. What king stopped a Hebrew invasion by sacrificing his oldest son?

The King of Moab, Second Kings 3:26–27. (The meaning is much clearer in Moffatt's translation.)—"The king of Moab, when he saw that the battle was too hot for him, took seven hundred swordsmen to cut his way through to the king of Edom. This failed. So he took his eldest son, the heir to the throne, and sacrificed him on the wall. It brought such a storm of indignation against Israel, that the Israelites had to leave him alone and return home."

7. What king installed a city waterworks system?

Hezekiah, Second Kings 20:20.—"And the rest of the acts of Hezekiah, and all his might, and how he made a pool, and a conduit, and brought water into the city, are they not written in the book of the chronicles of the kings of Judah?"

8. What king was killed by a chance arrow?

Ahab, First Kings 22:34.—"And a certain man drew a bow at a venture, and smote the king of Israel between the joints of the harness: . . ." Verse 37 tells of his death.

9. What king lived in quarantine?

Azariah (Uzziah), Second Kings 15:5.—"And the Lord smote the king, so that he was a leper unto the day of his death, and dwelt in a several house. . . ." RV has "separate house" and RV margin has "infirmary."

10. What king's knees knocked together for fright?

Belshazzar, when the hand wrote his doom on the wall, Daniel 5:6.—"Then the king's countenance was changed, and his thoughts troubled him, so that the joints of his loins were loosed, and his knees smote one against another."

11. What king saw his sons killed and then was blinded?

Zedekiah, Second Kings 25:7.—"And they slew the sons of Zedekiah before his eyes, and put out the eyes of Zedekiah, and bound him with fetters of brass, and carried him to Babylon."

12. What harlot's son ruled Israel six years?

Jephthah, Judges 11:1; 12:7.—"Now Jephthah the Gileadite was a mighty man of valour, and he was the son of an harlot: . . . And Jephthah judged Israel six years. Then died Jephthah the Gileadite, and was buried in one of the cities of Gilead."

13. What king sentenced his ten concubines to life imprisonment?

David, Second Samuel 20:3.—"And David came to his house at Jerusalem; and the king took the ten women his concubines, whom he had left to keep the house, and put them in ward, and fed them, but went not in unto them. So they were shut up unto the day of their death, living in widowhood."

14. What king was displeased with a gift of twenty cities?

Hiram, king of Tyre, First Kings 9:11–13.—". . . then king Solomon gave Hiram twenty cities in the land of Galilee. And Hiram came out from Tyre to see the cities which Solomon had given him; and they pleased him not. And he said, What cities are these which thou hast given me, my brother? And he called them the land of Cabul unto this day." The margin gives Cabul as meaning displeasing or dirty, but the word seems to mean sandy.

15. What king imported apes and peacocks?

Solomon, First Kings 10:22.—"For the king had at sea a navy of Tharshish with the navy of Hiram: once in three years came the navy of Tharshish, bringing gold, and silver, ivory, and apes, and peacocks."

16. What king inherited a sun-clock from his father?

Hezekiah, from his father, Ahaz, Second Kings 20:10–11. —"And Hezekiah answered, . . . let the shadow return backward ten degrees. And Isaiah the prophet cried unto the Lord: and he brought the shadow ten degrees backward, by which it had gone down in the dial of Ahaz." In the parallel account in Isaiah 38:8 it is called "the sun dial of Ahaz."

17. What king suffered two years from a foot-disease and consulted physicians instead of the Lord?

Asa, Second Chronicles 16:12–13.—"And Asa in the thirty and ninth year of his reign was diseased in his feet, until his disease was exceeding great: yet in his disease he sought not to the Lord, but to the physicians. And Asa slept with his fathers, and died in the one and fortieth year of his reign."

18. What king's hand dried up?

Jeroboam's, First Kings 13:4.—"And it came to pass, when king Jeroboam heard the saying of the man of God, which had cried against the altar in Bethel, that he put forth his hand from the altar, saying, Lay hold on him. And his hand, which he put forth against him, dried up, so that he could not pull it in again to him."

19. What king committed suicide by falling on his sword?

Saul, First Chronicles 10:4.—". . . So Saul took a sword, and fell upon it."

20. What king began to reign at seven years of age?

Jehoash (sometimes called Joash) of Judah, Second Kings 11:21.—"Seven years old was Jehoash when he began to reign."

21. What king began to reign at eight years of age?

Josiah of Judah, Second Kings 22:1.—"Josiah was eight years old when he began to reign, . . ."

22. What present did King Tou bring to King David?

Vessels of gold, silver, and brass, First Chronicles 18:9–10.—"Now when Tou king of Hamath heard how David had smitten all the host of Hadarezer king of Zobah; He sent Hadoram his son to king David, . . . and with him all manner of vessels of gold and silver and brass."

23. What Hebrew king cut his conquered enemies with saws, harrows, and axes?

David, First Chronicles 20:1–3.—". . . And Joab smote Rabbah, and destroyed it. And David took the crown of their king from off his head, . . . and he brought also exceeding much spoil out of the city. And he brought out the people that were in it, and cut them with saws, and with harrows of iron, and with axes. Even so dealt David with all the cities of the children of Ammon. . . ."

24. What king cut up a book with a penknife and burned it?

Jehoiakim, Jeremiah 36:22–23 (Moffatt's translation).—
"The king was in his winter apartments, with a brazier burning in front of him. Whenever Jehudi read three or four leaves, the king would slash them off with a pen-knife and fling them into the fire burning upon the brazier, till the whole of the roll was consumed in the fire burning upon the brazier."

25. What king's household crossed the Jordan River in a ferry-boat?

David's, Second Samuel 19:18.—"And there went over a ferry boat to carry over the king's household, . . ."

26. What five kings hid in a cave?

Joshua 10:3, 16.—". . . Adoni-zedec king of Jerusalem . . . Hoham king of Hebron . . . Piram king of Jarmuth . . . Japhia king of Lachish, and Debir king of Eglon . . . these five kings fled, and hid themselves in a cave at Makkedah."

27. What king caused 10,000 prisoners to be killed by precipitation?

Amaziah, Second Chronicles 25:11, 12.—"And Amaziah strengthened himself, and led forth his people, and went to the valley of salt, and smote of the children of Seir ten thousand. And other ten thousand left alive did the children of Judah carry away captive, and brought them unto the top of the rock, and cast them down from the top of the rock, that they all were broken in pieces."

28. What king lay all night on the ground when his son was sick?

David, Second Samuel 12:15–16.—". . . And the Lord struck the child that Uriah's wife bare unto David, and it was very sick. David therefore besought God for the child; and David fasted, and went in, and lay all night upon the earth."

29. Who advised Christians to be in subjection to kings, governors, and masters?

The author of First Peter 2:13, 14, 18.—"Submit yourselves to every ordinance of man for the Lord's sake: whether it be to the king, as supreme; or unto governors, . . . Servants, be subject to your masters with all fear; not only to the good and gentle, but also to the froward."

30. What king had a throne of ivory overlaid with gold?

Solomon, First Kings 10:18.—"Moreover the king made a great throne of ivory, and overlaid it with the best gold."

31. What prophet predicted that kings would act as nurse-maids?

Isaiah, Isaiah 49:23.—"And kings shall be thy nursing fathers, . . ."

32. What king was killed when he was drunk?

Elah, by Zimri, First Kings 16:9–10.—"And his [Elah's] servant Zimri, captain of half his chariots, conspired against him, as he was in Tirzah, drinking himself drunk in the house of Arza steward of his house in Tirzah. And Zimri went in and smote him, and killed him, . . ."

33. What fat king was stabbed to death by a left-handed man?

Eglon, king of Moab, was stabbed by Ehud, Judges 3:17, 21, 22.—". . . and Eglon was a very fat man. . . . And Ehud put forth his left hand, and took the dagger from his right thigh, and thrust it into his belly: And the haft also went in after the blade; and the fat closed upon the blade, so that he could not draw the dagger out of his belly; . . ."

34. What king had 900 chariots of iron?

Jabin, king of Canaan, Judges 4:2–3.—"And the Lord sold them into the hand of Jabin king of Canaan, that reigned in Hazor; . . . And the children of Israel cried unto the Lord: for he had nine hundred chariots of iron; and twenty years he mightily oppressed the children of Israel."

35. What king had a house made of ivory?

Ahab, First Kings 22:39.—"Now the rest of the acts of Ahab and all that he did, and the ivory house which he made, . . ."

36. What king was given a daily allowance by another king?

Jehoiachin, by Evil-merodach, Second Kings 25:27, 30.— "Evil-merodach king of Babylon . . . did lift up the head of Jehoiachin king of Judah out of prison; . . . And his allowance was a continual allowance given him of the king, a daily rate for every day, all the days of his life."

37. What king of Egypt killed a king of Judah in battle?

Pharaoh-nechoh killed Josiah, Second Kings 23:29.—"In

his days Pharaoh-nechoh king of Egypt went up against the king of Assyria to the river Euphrates: and king Josiah went against him; and he slew him at Megiddo, when he had seen him."

38. What king gave a prophet 40 camel-loads of presents?

Ben-hadad, Second Kings 8:7–9.—"And Elisha came to Damascus; and Ben-hadad the king of Syria was sick; . . . And the king said unto Hazael, Take a present in thine hand, and go, meet the man of God, and enquire of the Lord by him, saying, Shall I recover of this disease? So Hazael went to meet him, and took a present with him, even of every good thing of Damascus, forty camels' burden, . . ."

39. What king attended a religious service and then killed all the worshipers?

Jehu, Second Kings 10:18, 19, 25.—"And Jehu gathered all the people together, and said unto them, Ahab served Baal a little; but Jehu shall serve him much. Now therefore call unto me all the prophets of Baal, all his servants, and all his priests; let none be wanting: for I have a great sacrifice to do to Baal; whosoever shall be wanting, he shall not live. But Jehu did it in subtilty, to the intent that he might destroy the worshippers of Baal. . . . And it came to pass, as soon as he had made an end of offering the burnt offering, that Jehu said to the guard and to the captains, Go in, and slay them; let none come forth. And they smote them with the edge of the sword; and the guard and the captains cast them out, . . ."

40. What king consulted a spiritistic medium and was punished by death?

Saul, First Samuel 28:7; First Chronicles 10:13–14.—"Then said Saul unto his servants, Seek me a woman that hath a familiar spirit, that I may go to her, and enquire of her. . . ." "So Saul died for his transgression which he committed against the Lord, even against the word of the Lord, which he kept not, and also for asking counsel of one that had a familiar spirit, to enquire of it; And enquired not of the Lord: therefore he slew him, and turned the kingdom unto David the son of Jesse."

XVIII

Queens

1. What queen's son burnt a phallic image she had made?

2. What queen forged her husband's signature to important letters?

3. Where are sixty queens mentioned?

4. What queen weaned her nephew?

5. What wicked queen had a daughter who was a wicked queen?

6. What queen was devoured by dogs?

7. What queen was killed in a driveway?

8. What queen was deposed for refusing to obey her drunken husband?

9. Who prophesied that queens should lick the dust?

10. Who said, "I sit a queen and am no widow"?

11. What queen's disguise was penetrated by a blind man?

12. What queen gave what king an intelligence test of many questions in which he ranked 100%?

ANSWERS TO QUESTIONS ABOUT QUEENS

1. What queen's son burnt a phallic image she had made?

Maachah's son Asa, Second Chronicles 15:16.—"And also

concerning Maachah the mother of Asa the king, he removed her from being queen, because she had made an idol in a grove: and Asa cut down her idol, and stamped it, and burnt it at the brook Kidron." For "idol" the margin has "horror." RV has "an abominable image for an Asherah." Moffatt has "an obscene object for Astarte." The Vulgate (old Latin) version has "*similacrum Priapi*."

2. What queen forged her husband's signature to important letters?

Jezebel, First Kings 21:8.—"So she [Jezebel] wrote letters in Ahab's name, and sealed them with his seal, and sent the letters to the elders and to the nobles that were in his city, . . ."

3. Where are sixty queens mentioned?

Song of Solomon 6:8.—"There are threescore queens, . . ."

4. What queen weaned her nephew?

Tahpenes, First Kings 11:20.—"And the sister of Tahpenes bare him Genubath his son, whom Tahpenes weaned in Pharaoh's house: . . ."

5. What wicked queen had a daughter who was a wicked queen?

Jezebel, whose daughter was Athaliah, First Kings 21:25; Second Kings 8:16, 18; Second Chronicles 24:7.—"But there was none like unto Ahab, which did sell himself to work wickedness in the sight of the Lord, whom Jezebel his wife stirred up." ". . . Jehoram the son of Jehoshaphat king of Judah began to reign. . . . And he walked in the ways of the kings of Israel, as did the house of Ahab: for the daughter of Ahab was his wife: and he did evil in the sight of the Lord." ". . . Athaliah, that wicked woman, . . ."

6. What queen was devoured by dogs?

Jezebel, Second Kings 9:35–36.—"And they went to bury her: but they found no more of her than the skull, and the feet, and the palms of her hands. Wherefore they came again, and told him. And he said, This is the word of the Lord, which he spake by his servant Elijah the Tishbite, saying, In the portion of Jezreel shall dogs eat the flesh of Jezebel:"

7. What queen was killed in a driveway?

Athaliah, Second Kings 11:16.—"And they laid hands on her [Athaliah]; and she went by the way by the which the horses came into the king's house: and there was she slain."

8. What queen was deposed for refusing to obey her drunken husband?

Vashti, Esther 1:10–21 (abridged).—"On the seventh day, when the heart of the king was merry with wine, he commanded . . . To bring Vashti the queen before the king with the crown royal, to shew the people and the princes her beauty: for she was fair to look on. But the queen Vashti refused to come . . . therefore was the king very wroth, and his anger burned in him . . . And Memucan answered before the king and the princes, . . . If it please the king, let there go a royal commandment . . . That Vashti come no more before king Ahasuerus; and let the king give her royal estate unto another that is better than she. . . . And the saying pleased the king and the princes; and the king did according to the word of Memucan:"

9. Who prophesied that queens should lick the dust?

Isaiah, Isaiah 49:23.—". . . and their queens thy nursing mothers: they shall bow down to thee with their face toward the earth, and lick up the dust of thy feet; . . ."

10. Who said, "I sit a queen and am no widow"?

Babylon (Rome personified), Revelation 18:2, 7.—"And he cried mightily with a strong voice, saying, Babylon the great is fallen, is fallen, . . . How much she hath glorified herself, and lived deliciously, so much torment and sorrow give her: for she saith in her heart, I sit a queen, and am no widow, and shall see no sorrow."

11. What queen's disguise was penetrated by a blind man?

The wife of Jeroboam, First Kings 14:2, 4, 6.—"And Jeroboam said to his wife, Arise, I pray thee, and disguise thyself, . . . And Jeroboam's wife did so, and arose, and went to Shiloh, and came to the house of Ahijah. But Ahijah could not see; for his eyes were set by reason of his age. . . . And it was so, when Ahijah heard the sound of her feet, as she came in at the door, that he said, Come in, thou wife of Jeroboam; why feigneth thou thyself to be another? . . ."

12. What queen gave what king an intelligence test of many questions in which he ranked 100%?

The Queen of Sheba tested Solomon, First Kings 10:1–3.
—"And when the queen of Sheba heard of the fame of Solomon concerning the name of the Lord, she came to prove him with hard questions . . . and when she was come to Solomon, she communed with him of all that was in her heart. And Solomon told her all her questions: there was not any thing hid from the king, which he told her not."

XIX

About Women

1. What woman swore because she lost some money?

2. What woman lived in the only "college" mentioned in the Bible?

3. What New Testament book is a letter written to a lady?

4. Who were the first women to demand their property rights?

5. What woman judge held court under a palm-tree?

6. What woman was the first person to be buried in a cemetery?

7. What captain's mother hoped her son's soldiers would each get two girls as part of the spoil?

8. What prophet set a woman up in the oil business?

9. What woman said, "A worthy woman who can find?"

10. Where is a nagging woman compared to a rainy day?

11. Who was the Scarlet Woman?

12. What woman was carried through the air in a bushel measure?

13. How old was the first woman whose age is recorded?

14. What woman protested at her brother's marrying a Negro woman?

15. What woman lied to her father to save her husband?

16. Where did women knead dough in the streets?

17. What woman cried seven days with company in the house?

18. Who said that if women wanted to learn anything they should ask their husbands at home?

19. In what early Christian church was a notorious woman member so bad that she was called Jezebel?

20. What business woman was Paul's first convert?

21. Who said it was better to live on the roof than with a quarrelsome woman?

22. Who lost his wife to his best man?

23. Who had seven daughters who were shepherdesses?

24. What woman in silent prayer was thought by a priest to be intoxicated?

25. What noted Hebrew had many wives but loved a man more?

26. What beautiful girl was named for a vanity-case?

27. Whose daughter was Noah?

28. What woman became a mineral?

29. Whose daughter stole her father's idols and sat on them?

30. What woman perfumed her bed with cinnamon?

31. What widow was intimate with her brother-in-law and had twins by her father-in-law?

32. What woman had five husbands?

33. Whose skull was broken by a stone cast by a woman?

34. What woman used a hammer effectively?

35. Was Delilah Samson's wife?

36. What servant-girl, with child by the 86-year-old man of the house, was driven out by his wife?

37. What was Eve's other name?

38. What woman's advice was sought by five men?

39. What two women were the mothers of their half-brothers?

40. Who named his daughter after his beautiful sister?

41. What man who had just killed 450 men fled from an angry woman?

42. To what did Solomon liken a woman of the sort now termed, "beautiful but dumb"?

43. What women became masons?

44. What girl dancer caused a murder?

45. What did Salome do?

46. Who said that if a girl's father had spit in her face, she should be ashamed seven days?

ANSWERS TO QUESTIONS
ABOUT WOMEN

1. What woman swore because she lost some money?

Micah's mother, Judges 17:1–2.—"And there was a man of mount Ephraim, whose name was Micah. And he said unto his mother, The eleven hundred shekels of silver that were taken from thee, about which thou cursedst, and spakest of also in mine ears, behold, the silver is with me; I took it. . . ."

2. What woman lived in the only "college" mentioned in the Bible?

Huldah the prophetess, Second Kings 22:14.—". . . Huldah the prophetess, . . . (now she dwelt in Jerusalem in the college;) . . ." Second Chronicles 34:22 is a parallel account. This "college" may have referred only to a district or ward of the city. RV translates it "in the second quarter." But some scholars think that it was a place of instruction. The confusion is due to the fact that the Hebrew idea of a school or college was a place of repetition, and the word for "second" is easily confused with the word for "repetition," since both are from the same root.

3. What New Testament book is a letter written to a lady?

Second John, as is shown by verse 1.—"The elder unto the elect lady and her children, whom I love in the truth; . . ."

4. Who were the first women to demand their property rights?

The five daughters of Zelophehad, Numbers 27:1–7.—
"Then came the daughters of Zelophehad. . . . And they
stood before Moses . . . and all the congregation, . . . saying
. . . Why should the name of our father be done away from
among his family, because he hath no son? Give unto us
therefore a possession among the brethren of our father. . . .
And the Lord spake unto Moses, saying, The Daughters of
Zelophehad speak right: thou shalt surely give them a possession. . . ."

5. What woman judge held court under a palm-tree?

Deborah, Judges 4:4–5.—"And Deborah, a prophetess, the
wife of Lapidoth, she judged Israel at that time. And she
dwelt under the palm tree of Deborah between Ramah and
Bethel in mount Ephraim: and the children of Israel came
up to her for judgment."

6. What woman was the first person to be buried in a
cemetery?

Sarah, Genesis 23:19–20.—". . . Abraham buried Sarah his
wife in the cave of the field of Machpelah . . . And the
field, and the cave that is therein, were made sure unto Abraham for a possession of a burying-place by the sons of Heth."

7. What captain's mother hoped her son's soldiers would
each get two girls as part of the spoil?

Sisera's, Judges 5:28, 30.—"The mother of Sisera looked
out at a window, and cried through the lattice, . . . have
they not divided the prey; to every man a damsel or
two; . . . ?"

8. What prophet set a woman up in the oil business?

Elisha, Second Kings 4:2–7.—"And Elisha said unto her,
. . . Go, borrow thee vessels abroad of all thy neighbors,
. . . And it came to pass, when the vessels were full, . . .
Then she came and told the man of God. And he said, Go,
sell the oil, and pay thy debt, and live thou and thy chil-
dren of the rest."

9. What woman said, "A worthy woman who can find?"

The mother of King Lemuel, Proverbs 31:1, 10 RV.—
"The words of king Lemuel; the oracle which his mother
taught him. . . . A worthy woman who can find? . . ."

10. Where is a nagging woman compared to a rainy day?

Proverbs 27:15.—"A continual dropping in a very rainy day and a contentious woman are alike."

11. Who was the Scarlet Woman?

Probably the City of Rome personified, Revelation 17, especially 4–6 and 18.—"And the woman was arrayed in purple and scarlet colour, and decked with gold and precious stones and pearls, having a golden cup in her hand full of abominations and filthiness of her fornication: And upon her forehead was a name written, MYSTERY, BABYLON THE GREAT, THE MOTHER OF HARLOTS AND ABOMINATIONS OF THE EARTH. And I saw the woman drunken with the blood of the saints, and with the blood of the martyrs of Jesus: . . . And the woman which thou sawest is that great city, whi_h reigneth over the kings of the earth."

At one time Protestants used to refer to the Church of Rome as the Scarlet Woman.

12. What woman was carried through the air in a bushel measure?

The woman named "Wickedness" or "Sin" in Zechariah's vision, Zechariah 5:5–11 (Moffatt's translation).—"Then the angel who talked to me came forward and said to me, 'Raise your eyes and look at this barrel which is emerging.' I said, 'What is it?' He answered, 'This barrel which you see emerging is their iniquity all over the land.' Then a disc of lead was lifted, and there sat a woman inside the barrel! 'This,' he said, 'is Sin'; and he pushed her down inside the barrel and flung the leaden cover over the opening. Then, raising my eyes, I looked and saw two women coming out, with the wind in their wings—they had wings like the wings of a stork—and they lifted the barrel high between earth and heaven. I said to the angel who talked to me, 'Where are they carrying the barrel?' He replied, 'To the land of Shinar, to build a shed for it; and whenever the shed is ready, the barrel shall be placed there on its own base.' "

The word which Moffatt translates "barrel" is really "ephah," as the AV has it. The ephah was a common measure among the Hebrews and contained slightly more than our bushel. Our barrel contains two and one half bushels, and could hold a small woman, but by using the word "barrel" Moffatt reduces the effect of extreme compression and discomfort, which Zechariah evidently intended to convey, as well as the element of the miraculous.

13. How old was the first woman whose age is recorded?

127 years, Sarah, Genesis 23:1.—"And Sarah was an hundred and seven and twenty years old: these were the years of the life of Sarah."

14. What woman protested at her brother's marrying a Negro woman?

Miriam, Numbers 12:1.—"And Miriam and Aaron spake against Moses because of the Ethiopian woman whom he had married: . . ."

15. What woman lied to her father to save her husband?

Michal, First Samuel 19:12, 14, 17.—"So Michal let David down through a window: and he went, and fled, and escaped. . . . And when Saul sent messengers to take David, she said, He is sick. . . . And Saul said unto Michal, Why hast thou deceived me so, and sent away mine enemy, that he is escaped? . . ."

16. Where did women knead dough in the streets?

In Jerusalem, Jeremiah 7:17–18.—"Seest thou not what they do in the cities of Judah and in the streets of Jerusalem? The children gather wood, and the fathers kindle the fire, and the women knead their dough, to make cakes to the queen of heaven, . . ." The queen of heaven was Ishtar, a Babylonian goddess, and the cakes were shaped like the images of the goddess or were stamped with her likeness. The modern parallel would be hot cross buns.

17. What woman cried seven days with company in the house?

The woman of Timnath, Samson's wife, Judges 14:17.—"And she wept before him the seven days, while their feast lasted: . . ."

18. Who said that if women wanted to learn anything they should ask their husbands at home?

Paul, First Corinthians 14:34–35.—"Let your women keep silence in the churches: for it is not permitted unto them to speak; but they are commanded to be under obedience, as also saith the law. And if they will learn anything, let them ask their husbands at home: . . ." This passage is responsible for much of the difficulty experienced by women preachers seeking positions, no matter how well qualified they may be.

19. In what early Christian church was a notorious woman
    member so bad that she was called Jezebel?

Thyatira, Revelation 2:18, 20.—"And unto the angel of
the church in Thyatira write; . . . Notwithstanding I have a
few things against thee, because thou sufferest that woman
Jezebel, which calleth herself a prophetess, to teach and to
seduce my servants to commit fornication, and to eat things
sacrificed to idols."

20. What business woman was Paul's first convert?

Lydia, seller of purple, Acts 16:14-15.—"And a certain
woman named Lydia, a seller of purple, of the city of Thyatira, which worshipped God, heard us: whose heart the Lord
opened, that she attended unto the things which were spoken of Paul. And when she was baptized, and her household, she besought us, saying, If ye have judged me to be
faithful to the Lord, come into my house, and abide there.
And she constrained us." This purple was a dye extracted
from a shell-fish.

21. Who said it was better to live on the roof than with a
    quarrelsome woman?

Solomon, if he was the author of Proverbs 21:9 RV.—"It
is better to dwell in the corner of the housetop, than with
a contentious woman in a wide house." AV has "brawling
woman." Proverbs 21:19 has the same idea, but substitutes
"wilderness" for "housetop." Probably, by the time he had
written ten more proverbs, something had occurred which
led Solomon to desire to be even farther away.

22. Who lost his wife to his best man?

Samson, Judges 14:20 (Moffatt's translation).—"And
Samson's wife was given to one of his companions, who had
been his best man." AV has "his companion, whom he had
used as his friend," a phrase which means best man. See John
3:29, where "the friend of the bridegroom" is very evidently
the best man at the wedding ceremony.

23. Who had seven daughters who were shepherdesses?

Reuel, the priest of Midian, Exodus 2:16.—"Now the
priest of Midian [Reuel, see verse 18] had seven daughters: and they came and drew water, and filled the troughs
to water their father's flock."

24. What woman in silent prayer was thought by a priest to be intoxicated?

Hannah, First Samuel 1:12–15.—"And it came to pass, as she continued praying before the Lord, that Eli marked her mouth. Now Hannah, she spake in her heart; only her lips moved, but her voice was not heard: therefore Eli thought she had been drunken. And Eli said unto her, How long wilt thou be drunken? put away thy wine from thee. And Hannah answered and said, No, my lord, I am a woman of a sorrowful spirit: I have drunk neither wine nor strong drink, but have poured out my soul before the Lord."

25. What noted Hebrew had many wives but loved a man more?

David, who, after he had married Michal, Abigail, and Ahinoam, "took him more wives and concubines out of Jerusalem," Second Samuel 5:13. Yet, at the death of his friend Jonathan, he lamented, Second Samuel 1:26: "I am distressed for thee, my brother Jonathan: very pleasant hast thou been unto me: thy love to me was wonderful, passing the love of women."

26. What beautiful girl was named for a vanity-case?

The third daughter of Job, Job 42:14–15.—"And he called the name of the first, Jemima; and the name of the second, Kezia; and the name of the third, Keren-happuch. And in all the land were no women found so fair as the daughters of Job: . . ." Keren-happuch is Hebrew for "horn of antimony." It was the custom to tinge the eyelashes with a dye made from antimony, much as mascara is used today.

27. Whose daughter was Noah?

The daughter of Zelophehad, Numbers 27:1.—"Then came the daughters of Zelophehad, . . . and these are the names of his daughters; Mahlah, Noah, and Hoglah, and Milcah, and Tirzah."

28. What woman became a mineral?

Lot's wife, Genesis 19:26.—"But his wife looked back from behind him, and she became a pillar of salt." There is a ridge of rock salt in that region, which, under erosion, takes on strange shapes, a fact which easily explains the legend.

29. Whose daughter stole her father's idols and sat on
   them?

Rachel, Genesis 31:19, 34.—"And Laban went to shear
his sheep: and Rachel had stolen the images that were her
father's. . . . Now Rachel had taken the images, and put
them in the camel's furniture, and sat upon them. And Laban
searched all the tent, but found them not."

30. What woman perfumed her bed with cinnamon?

The harlot of Proverbs 7:6–23, especially verse 17.—"I
have perfumed my bed with myrrh, aloes, and cinnamon."

31. What widow was intimate with her brother-in-law and
   had twins by her father-in-law?

Tamar. Judah had three sons, Er, Onan, and Shelah. Er
married Tamar. Upon his death, Judah told Onan to go in
unto Tamar and raise up children for his deceased brother.
Onan mismanaged the affair and was punished by death.
Judah then promised Shelah to Tamar, but did not keep his
promise. Tamar then disguised herself as a harlot and seduced Judah. From the union twins were born to her. The
story is told at some length in Genesis 38.

32. What woman had five husbands?

The woman of Samaria, John 4:17–18.—"The woman answered and said, I have no husband. Jesus said unto her,
Thou hast well said, I have no husband: For thou hast had
five husbands; and he whom thou now hast is not thy husband: . . ."

33. Whose skull was broken by a stone cast by a woman?

Abimelech's, Judges 9:53 RV.—"And a certain woman
cast an upper millstone upon Abimelech's head, and brake
his skull."

34. What woman used a hammer effectively?

Jael, on Sisera, Judges 4:21.—"Then Jael Heber's wife
took a nail of the tent, and took an hammer in her hand,
and went softly unto him, and smote the nail into his temples, and fastened it into the ground: for he was fast asleep
and weary. So he died."

35. Was Delilah Samson's wife?

Evidently not. He had relations with three Philistine

women according to Judges, chapters 14 to 16, but was married to but one of them, the unnamed woman of Timnath. The second was the harlot of Gaza and the third the infamous Delilah of Sorek.

36. *What servant-girl, with child by the 86-year-old man of the house, was driven out by his wife?*

Hagar, Genesis 16:1, 2, 5, 6, 15, 16.—"Now Sarai Abram's wife bare him no children: and she had an handmaid, an Egyptian, whose name was Hagar. And Sarai said unto Abram, Behold now, the Lord hath restrained me from bearing: I pray thee, go in unto my maid; it may be that I may obtain children by her. And Abram hearkened to the voice of Sarai. . . . And Sarai said unto Abram, My wrong be upon thee: I have given my maid into thy bosom; and when she saw that she had conceived, I was despised in her eyes: the Lord judge between me and thee. But Abram said unto Sarai, Behold, thy maid is in thine hand; do to her as it pleaseth thee. And when Sarai dealt hardly with her, she fled from her face. . . . And Hagar bare Abram a son: and Abram called his son's name, which Hagar bare, Ishmael. And Abram was fourscore and six years old, when Hagar bare Ishmael to Abram."

37. *What was Eve's other name?*

Adam, Genesis 5:1–2.—". . . In the day that God created man, in the likeness of God made he him; Male and female created he them; and blessed them, and called their name Adam, in the day when they were created."

38. *What woman's advice was sought by five men?*

Huldah's, Second Kings 22:14.—"So Hilkiah the priest, and Ahikam, and Achbor, and Shaphan, and Asahiah, went unto Huldah the prophetess, the wife of Shallum the son of Tikvah, the son of Harhas, keeper of the wardrobe; (now she dwelt in Jerusalem in the college;) and they communed with her."

39. *What two women were the mothers of their half-brothers?*

The daughters of Lot, Genesis 19:36.—"Thus were both the daughters of Lot with child by their father."

40. *Who named his daughter after his beautiful sister?*

Absalom, after Tamar, Second Samuel 13:1 and 14:27.—

". . . Absalom the son of David had a fair sister, whose name was Tamar; . . . And unto Absalom there were born three sons, and one daughter, whose name was Tamar: she was a woman of fair countenance."

41. What man who had just killed 450 men fled from an angry woman?

Elijah, First Kings 18:22, 40; 19:2-3.—". . . but Baal's prophets are four hundred and fifty men . . . and Elijah brought them down to the brook Kishon, and slew them there. . . . Then Jezebel sent a messenger unto Elijah, saying, So let the gods do to me, and more also, if I make not thy life as the life of one of them by tomorrow about this time. And when he saw that, he arose, and went for his life, . . ."

42. To what did Solomon liken a woman of the sort now termed, "beautiful but dumb"?

Proverbs 11:22.—"As a jewel of gold in a swine's snout, so is a fair woman which is without discretion."

43. What women became masons?

The daughters of Shallum, Nehemiah 3:12.—"And next to him repaired Shallum the son of Halohesh, the ruler of the half part of Jerusalem, he and his daughters." This was in connection with the rebuilding of the walls of the city.

44. What girl dancer caused a murder?

The daughter of Herodias, Matthew 14:6-10.—"But when Herod's birthday was kept, the daughter of Herodias danced before them, and pleased Herod. Whereupon he promised with an oath to give her whatsoever she would ask. And she, being before instructed of her mother, said, Give me here John Baptist's head in a charger. And the king was sorry: nevertheless for the oath's sake, and them which sat with him at meat, he commanded it to be given her. And he sent, and beheaded John in the prison."

45. What did Salome do?

She witnessed the crucifixion of Jesus and visited the tomb, Mark 15:40 and 16:1-2.—"There were also women looking on afar off: among whom was Mary Magdalene, and Mary the mother of James the less and of Joses, and Salome; . . . And when the sabbath was past, Mary Magdalene, and Mary the mother of James, and Salome, had brought sweet spices, that they might come and anoint him. And very early in the morning the first day of the week, they came unto the sepulchre at the rising of the sun." This Salome is not to be confused with the somewhat more famous or infamous Salome, the daughter of Herodias, who appears in Matthew 14:1–12 and Mark 6:14–29, but who is not mentioned by name in the Bible.

46. Who said that if a girl's father had spit in her face, she should be ashamed seven days?

The Lord, to Moses, Numbers 12:14.—"And the Lord said unto Moses, If her father had but spit in her face, should she not be ashamed seven days? . . ."

XX

Angels and Demons

1. Who told angels to wash their feet?

2. Where is angels' food mentioned?

3. Did Jesus believe in a personal devil?

4. Where are dancing satyrs mentioned?

5. Who was Azazel?

6. What archangel debated with the devil?

7. What archangel fought the devil and defeated him?

8. What disciple was called "Satan" by Jesus?

9. Who prophesied that dragons would be in pleasant palaces?

10. What soldiers were scared of an angel?

11. What man and his nephew both entertained angels unawares?

12. What animal saw an angel?

13. Who transferred devils from men to animals?

14. When did an angel assist at a jail delivery of communists?

15. Who prophesied that the Lord would kill a sea-dragon "with his sore, and great, and strong sword"?

16. Who said he saw Satan fall from heaven?

ANSWERS TO QUESTIONS
ABOUT ANGELS AND DEMONS

1. Who told angels to wash their feet?

Lot, Genesis 19:1–2.—"And there came two angels to Sodom at even; . . . and Lot seeing them rose up to meet them; . . . And he said, Behold now, my lords, turn in, I pray you, into your servant's house, and tarry all night, and wash your feet. . . ."

2. Where is angels' food mentioned?

Psalm 78:24–25.—"And had rained down manna upon them to eat, and had given them of the corn of heaven. Man did eat angels' food: he sent them meat to the full."

3. Did Jesus believe in a personal devil?

Evidently, Matthew 25:41.—"Then shall he say also unto them on the left hand, Depart from me, ye cursed, into everlasting fire, prepared for the devil and his angels:" See also Matthew 4:1–11 and John 8:44.

4. Where are dancing satyrs mentioned?

Isaiah 13:21.—". . . and owls shall dwell there, and satyrs shall dance there." In Isaiah 34:14 crying satyrs are mentioned. A satyr was a goat-like demon.

5. Who was Azazel?

The wicked spirit or fallen angel, kept bound in the wilderness, to whom the Jews sent the scapegoat on the Day of Atonement, Leviticus 16:8 RV.—"And Aaron shall cast lots upon the two goats; one lot for Jehovah, and the other lot for Azazel." See also verses 10 and 26. According to the Book of Enoch (which was once in the Bible), Azazel was formerly the leader of the angels, or "sons of God," of Genesis 6:2, who married earthly women and begat giants.

6. What archangel debated with the devil?

Michael, Jude 1:9.—"Yet Michael the archangel, when contending with the devil he disputed about the body of Moses, . . ."

7. What archangel fought the devil and defeated him?

Michael, Revelation 12:7–9.—"And there was war in heaven: Michael and his angels fought against the dragon; and the dragon fought and his angels, And prevailed not; neither was their place found any more in heaven. And the great dragon was cast out, that old serpent, called the Devil, and Satan, which deceiveth the whole world: he was cast out into the earth, and his angels were cast out with him."

8. What disciple was called "Satan" by Jesus?

Peter, Matthew 16:23.—"But he turned and said unto Peter, Get thee behind me, Satan: thou art an offense unto me: ..."

9. Who prophesied that dragons would be in pleasant palaces?

Isaiah, Isaiah 13:22.—"And the wild beasts of the desert shall cry in their desolate houses, and dragons in their pleasant palaces: ..."

10. What soldiers were scared of an angel?

The guards at the tomb of Jesus, Matthew 28:2–4.—"... the angel of the Lord descended from heaven, ... And for fear of him the keepers did shake, and became as dead men." Also Cornelius, Acts 10:1–4.—"There was a certain man in Cesarea called Cornelius, a centurion. ... He saw in a vision evidently about the ninth hour of the day an angel of God coming in to him, and saying unto him, Cornelius. And when he looked on him, he was afraid, ..."

11. What man and his nephew both entertained angels unawares?

Abraham and Lot, see Genesis 18:1–22 and 19:1–26 for the detailed accounts, which are evidently referred to in Hebrews 13:2.—"Be not forgetful to entertain strangers: for thereby some have entertained angels unawares."

12. What animal saw an angel?

Balaam's ass, Numbers 22:23.—"And the ass saw the angel of the Lord standing in the way, and his sword drawn in his hand: and the ass turned aside out of the way, and went into the field: and Balaam smote the ass, to turn her into the way." It is a common belief that some animals can see spirits, ghosts, and fairies invisible to men.

13. Who transferred devils from men to animals?

Jesus, Matthew 8:31–32. "So the devils besought him, saying, If thou cast us out, suffer us to go away into the herd of swine. And he said unto them, Go."

14. When did an angel assist at a jail delivery of communists?

Acts 4:32, 5:17–19.—"And the multitude of them that believed were of one heart and of one soul: neither said any of them that ought of the things which he possessed was his own; but they had all things common. . . . Then the high priest rose up, and all they that were with him, . . . And laid their hands on the apostles, and put them in the common prison. But the angel of the Lord by night opened the prison doors, and brought them forth, . . ."

15. Who prophesied that the Lord would kill a sea-dragon "with his sore, and great, and strong sword"?

Isaiah, Isaiah 27:1.—"In that day the Lord with his sore and great and strong sword shall punish leviathan the piercing serpent, even leviathan that crooked serpent; and he shall slay the dragon that is in the sea."

16. Who said he saw Satan fall from heaven?

Jesus, Luke 10:17–18.—"And the seventy returned again with joy, saying, Lord, even the devils are subject unto us through thy name. And he said unto them, I beheld Satan as lightning fall from heaven." See also Revelation 12:7–9.

XXI

Names

1. How many different men named Jesus are mentioned in the Bible?

2. How many of Jesus' direct male ancestors were named Joseph?

3. How many Marys in the Bible?

4. How many Herods in the Bible?

5. Who was Apollyon?

6. What was Solomon's other name?

7. What was Daniel's other name?

8. Under what three other names was Peter known?

9. How many other Simons in the New Testament besides Simon Peter?

10. What four men and six women had the same name as a country?

11. What was Joseph's Egyptian name?

12. What was the name of Joseph's Egyptian wife?

13. To what Christian church did Julia, Persis, Rufus, and Narcissus belong?

14. What star was named Wormwood?

15. Who was Zipporah?

16. Who was Zaza?

17. Who or what were the Zuzim?

18. How many Bible characters were there whose names began with Z?

19. How many Bible men were named Dodo?

ANSWERS TO QUESTIONS
ABOUT NAMES

1. How many different men named Jesus are mentioned in the Bible?

Four in the New Testament:

1. Joshua, the son of Nun, is called Jesus in Acts 7:45 and Hebrews 4:8. The RV has Joshua.

2. An ancestor of Jesus Christ, Luke 3:29 RV. AV has Jose.

3. Jesus Christ, Matthew 1:1 and many places.

4. Jesus called Justus, Colossians 4:11.

There are three different men named Jesus mentioned in the Apocrypha:

1. Jesus the high-priest at the time of Zerubbabel, First Esdras 5:5.

2. Jesus the Levite, First Esdras 5:26.

3. Jesus the son of Sirach, author of Ecclesiasticus.

There are at least thirteen men named Jesus in the Old Testament, where the name appears as Joshua, Jeshua, Jeshuah, Jehoshua, Jehoshuah, and Oshea. Jesus is simply the Greek form. In the Greek translation of the Hebrew Old Testament, the book of Joshua is the book of Jesus. There are four different Joshuas and nine different Jeshuas in the Old Testament.

2. How many of Jesus' direct male ancestors were named Joseph?

Three, according to Luke 3:23, 24, 30. There are twelve different Josephs mentioned in the Bible, and three in the Apocrypha.

3. How many Marys in the Bible?

It can never be known exactly because of the difficulty in identifying them. Probably at least six, besides the two Miriams in the Old Testament (Exodus 15:20; First Chronicles 4:17) where Miriam is a form of Mary. Hastings' Dictionary of the Bible gives eight New Testament Marys: Mary the mother of James, the other Mary, Mary of Clopas, Mary the sister of Martha, Mary Magdalene, Mary the mother of

Mark, Mary saluted by Paul, and Mary the mother of Jesus, but states that the first three are usually identified as the same person.

4. How many Herods in the Bible?

Three:
1. Herod the Great, Matthew 2.
2. Herod Antipas, Matthew 14, Mark 6, Luke 3.
3. Herod Agrippa the First, Acts 12.

5. Who was Apollyon?

The angel of the abyss, who was the king of the locusts, Revelation 9:11.—"And they [the locusts] had a king over them, which is the angel of the bottomless pit, whose name in the Hebrew tongue is Abaddon, but in the Greek tongue hath his name Apollyon." The margin translates Apollyon as "A destroyer." Abaddon is usually translated "destruction" in Old Testament passages. Evidently destruction became personified into the angel of destruction, and locusts were so destructive that it was natural that the angel of destruction should be identified as the king of the locusts.

6. What was Solomon's other name?

Jedidiah, Second Samuel 12:24–25.—"And David comforted Bathsheba his wife, and went in unto her, and lay with her: and she bare a son, and he called his name Solomon: and the Lord loved him. And he sent by the hand of Nathan the prophet; and he called his name Jedidiah, because of the Lord." This is the only place where the name Jedidiah is used of Solomon.

7. What was Daniel's other name?

Belteshazzar, Daniel 1:7.—"Unto whom the prince of the eunuchs gave names: for he gave unto Daniel the name Belteshazzar; . . ."

8. Under what three other names was Peter known?

Cephas, John 1:42, Simon, Matthew 10:2; and Simeon, Acts 15:14.

9. How many other Simons in the New Testament besides Simon Peter?

Eight:
Simon the Canaanite, alias Simon Zelotes, Matthew 10:4, Mark 3:18, Luke 6:15, Acts 1:13.

Simon the brother of Jesus, Matthew 13:55, Mark 6:3.

Simon the leper, Matthew 26:6, Mark 14:3.

Simon the Cyrenian, Matthew 27:32, Mark 15:21, Luke 23:26.

Simon the Pharisee, Luke 7:40–44.

Simon the father (?) of Judas Iscariot, John 6:71, 12:4, 13:2.

Simon the sorcerer (Simon Magus), Acts 8:9–24.

Simon the tanner of Joppa, Acts 9:43, 10:6–32.

10. What four men and six women had the same name as a country?

The name is Maachah, sometimes Maacah. It was a small Aramean country east of the Sea of Galilee, mentioned in Second Samuel 10:8 and First Chronicles 19:6–7. The following four men and six women bore this same name:

The son of Nahor, Genesis 22:24.

The father of Achish, First Kings 2:39.

The father of Hanun, First Chronicles 11:43.

The father of Shephatiah, First Chronicles 27:16.

A wife of David and mother of Absalom, Second Samuel 3:3.

A wife of Rehoboam and mother of Abijah, First Kings 15:2.

The mother of Asa, Second Chronicles 15:16. This woman is by some scholars identified with the preceding, and reckoned as the grandmother of Asa.

A concubine of Caleb, First Chronicles 2:48.

A wife of Machir, First Chronicles 7:15–16.

A wife of Jehiel, First Chronicles 8:29, 9:35.

11. What was Joseph's Egyptian name?

Zaphnath-paaneah, Genesis 41:45.—"And Pharaoh called Joseph's name Zaphnath-paaneah; . . ."

12. What was the name of Joseph's Egyptian wife?

Asenath, Genesis 41:45.—". . . and he gave him to wife Asenath the daughter of Potipherah priest of On."

13. To what Christian church did Julia, Persis, Rufus, and Narcissus belong?

They were Roman Christians, listed among others in Romans 16:11–15.

14. What star was named Wormwood?

The great star of the Apocalypse, Revelation 8:10–11.—
"And the third angel sounded, and there fell a great star
from heaven, burning as it were a lamp, and it fell on the
third part of the rivers, and upon the fountains of waters;
And the name of the star is called Wormwood: and the
third part of the waters became wormwood; and many men
died of the waters, because they were made bitter." Wormwood, because of its bitter taste, was popularly but er-
roneously supposed by the Jews to be poisonous, hence it
became associated in their minds with dire calamity. (See
Proverbs 5:4, Lamentations 3:15, and Amos 5:7.) Hence the
star of destruction naturally is named Wormwood.

15. Who was Zipporah?

One of the wives of Moses, Exodus 2:21.—"And Moses
was content to dwell with the man: and he gave Moses
Zipporah his daughter."

16. Who was Zaza?

One of the sons of Jonathan son of Jada, First Chronicles
2:33.—"And the sons of Jonathan; Peleth, and Zaza."

17. Who or what were the Zuzim?

Evidently a prehistoric race in the land of Ham, which
may have been what was later known as the land of the
Ammonites. The AV of this passage has Zuzims, but "im"
is a Hebrew plural, and the "s" is unnecessary and is
omitted by the RV. The Zuzim are possibly the same race
as the Zamzummim of Deuteronomy 2:20, where they are
referred to as giants who dwelt therein in old time. The
Zuzim are mentioned only in Genesis 14:5, where it is
merely recorded that Chedorlaomer, king of Elam, smote
"the Zuzims in Ham" along with the "Rephaims" and
"Emims."

18. How many Bible characters were there whose names began with Z?

There are 87 different personal names in the Bible beginning with the letter "Z," representing 188 individuals,
including 27 Zechariahs, 12 Zichris, 9 Zebadiahs, 9 Zadoks,
7 Zabads, 7 Zaccurs, 7 Zerahs, and 5 Zedekiahs.

19. How many Bible men were named Dodo?

Three:
Dodo the grandfather of the judge Tola, Judges 10:1.—

"And after Abimelech there arose to defend Israel Tola the son of Puah, the son of Dodo, a man of Issachar; . . ."

Dodo the father of Eleazar, Second Samuel 23:9.—"And after him was Eleazar the son of Dodo the Alohite, . . ."

Dodo the father of Elhanan, Second Samuel 23:24.— "Elhanan the son of Dodo of Beth-lehem,"

XXII

Of Interest to Students of Comparative Religion

1. What ruler of Israel sacrificed his daughter as a burnt-offering to Jehovah?

2. What houses were "cleansed" by sprinkling with the blood of a bird killed over running water?

3. What king practised divination at the cross-roads by examining a liver?

4. What noted Hebrew had a magic cup for divination?

5. What Bible verse commands the execution of witches?

6. Who prophesied the abolition of witchcraft?

7. Who prayed for rain?

8. Who prayed that it might not rain?

9. What Hebrew kings offered their own children as burnt sacrifices?

10. What story marks the change from human sacrifice to animal sacrifice?

11. What gods did Solomon worship besides Jehovah?

12. How many centuries did the children of Israel worship the brass serpent which Moses made?

13. What Hebrew king worshiped the stars?

14. Who dedicated horses to the sun?

15. What Hebrew king's head was mounted in the temple of the Philistine fish-god?

16. Who discovered seventy men worshiping mural paintings of idols?

17. What king abolished fortune-tellers and then himself consulted four different kinds?

18. Who saw twenty-five men worshiping the sun?

19. Who staged a praying contest between two religions?

20. Who were the "keepers of the threshold"?

21. Why were the Hebrews so careful not to partake of blood?

ANSWERS TO QUESTIONS OF INTEREST TO STUDENTS OF COMPARATIVE RELIGION

1. What ruler of Israel sacrificed his daughter as a burnt-offering to Jehovah?

Jephthah, Judges 11:30-39.—"And Jephthah vowed a vow unto the Lord, and said, If thou shalt without fail deliver the children of Ammon into mine hands, Then it shall be, that whatsoever cometh forth of the doors of my house to meet me, when I return in peace from the children of Ammon, shall surely be the Lord's, and I will offer it up for a burnt offering. So Jephthah passed over unto the children of Ammon to fight against them; and the Lord delivered them into his hands. . . . And Jephthah came to Mispeh unto his house, and, behold, his daughter came out to meet him with timbrels and with dances: and she was his only child; beside her he had neither son nor daughter. . . . And he sent her away for two months: and she went with her companions, and bewailed her virginity upon the mountains. And it came to pass at the end of two months, that she returned unto her father, who did with her according to his vow which he had vowed: and she knew no man."

2. What houses were "cleansed" by sprinkling with the blood of a bird killed over running water?

The "leprous" houses, Leviticus 14:49-54.—"And he [the priest] shall take to cleanse the house two birds, and cedar wood, and scarlet, and hyssop: And he shall kill one of the birds in an earthen vessel over running water: And he shall take the cedar wood, and the hyssop, and the scarlet, and the living bird, and dip them in the blood of the slain bird, and in the running water, and sprinkle the house seven times: . . . But he shall let go the living bird out of the city into the open fields, and make an atonement for the house: and it shall be clean. This is the law for all manner of plague of leprosy, . . ."

3. What king practised divination at the cross-roads by examining a liver?

The king of Babylon, Ezekiel 21:21.—"For the king of Babylon stood at the parting of the way, at the head of the two ways, to use divination: he made his arrows bright, he consulted with images, he looked in the liver." Moffatt translates: "For the king of Babylon is standing at the crossroads, where the two paths fork, to practise divination; he is shaking the two arrows, consulting the oracle, and inspecting a beast's liver." In the beliefs of many races, cross-roads are especially sacred places, and the examination of entrails and organs of animals was devoutly relied on in ancient fortune-telling.

4. What noted Hebrew had a magic cup for divination?

Joseph, Genesis 44:1–5.—"And he commanded the steward of his house, saying, Fill the men's sacks with food, as much as they can carry, and put every man's money in his sack's mouth. And put my cup, the silver cup, in the sack's mouth of the youngest, and his corn money. And he did according to the word that Joseph had spoken. And as soon as the morning was light, the men were sent away, they and their asses. And when they were gone out of the city, and not yet far off, Joseph said unto his steward, Up, follow after the men; and when thou dost overtake them, say unto them, Wherefore have ye rewarded evil for good? Is not this it in which my lord drinketh, and whereby indeed he divineth? ye have done evil in so doing."

5. What Bible verse commands the execution of witches?

Exodus 22:18.—"Thou shalt not suffer a witch to live."

6. Who prophesied the abolition of witchcraft?

Micah, Micah 5:12.—"And I will cut off witchcrafts out of thine hand; and thou shalt have no more soothsayers:"

7. Who prayed for rain?

Elijah, First Kings 18:42–45.—". . . And Elijah went up

to the top of Carmel; and he cast himself down upon the earth, and put his face between his knees, And said to his servant, Go up now, look toward the sea. And he went up, and looked, and said, There is nothing. And he said, Go again seven times, And it came to pass at the seventh time, that he said, Behold, there ariseth a little cloud out of the sea, like a man's hand. And he said, Go up, say unto Ahab, Prepare thy chariot, and get thee down, that the rain stop thee not. And it came to pass in the mean while, that the heaven was black with clouds and wind, and there was a great rain. . . ."

8. Who prayed that it might not rain?

Elijah, First Kings 17:1.—"And Elijah the Tishbite . . . said unto Ahab, As the Lord God of Israel liveth, before whom I stand, there shall not be dew nor rain these years, but according to my word."

The effectiveness of Elijah's prayers for either rain or drought is recalled in the New Testament, James 5:16–18: ". . . The effectual fervent prayer of a righteous man availeth much. Elias [RV Elijah] was a man subject to like passions as we are, and he prayed earnestly that it might not rain: and it rained not on the earth by the space of three years and six months. And he prayed again, and the heaven gave rain, and the earth brought forth her fruit."

9. What Hebrew kings offered their own children as burnt sacrifices?

Ahaz, Second Chronicles 28:3.—"Moreover he [Ahaz] burnt incense in the valley of the son of Hinnom, and burnt his children in the fire, after the abominations of the heathen whom the Lord had cast out before the children of Israel." Manasseh, Second Kings 21:6.—"And he [Manasseh] made his son pass through the fire, . . ." Moffatt translates, "He burned his son alive, . . ."

10. What story marks the change from human sacrifice to animal sacrifice?

The story in Genesis 22 of Abraham's attempted sacrifice of his son Isaac, especially verse 13.—". . . and Abraham went and took the ram, and offered him up for a burnt offering in the stead of his son."

11. What gods did Solomon worship besides Jehovah?

Ashtoreth, Milcom, Chemosh, and Molech, First Kings

11:5, 7.—"For Solomon went after Ashtoreth the goddess of the Zidonians, and after Milcom the abomination of the Ammonites. . . . Then did Solomon build an high place for Chemosh, the abomination of Moab, in the hill that is before Jerusalem, and for Molech, the abomination of the children of Ammon." It is considered by most scholars that Milcom and Molech were two forms of the name of the same Ammonite god.

12. How many centuries did the children of Israel worship the brass serpent which Moses made?

At least five centuries, for Moses can hardly be dated later than the thirteenth century B.C., and Hezekiah lived in the late eighth and early seventh centuries B.C. Of the latter we read in Second Kings 18:4.—"He removed the high places, and brake the images, and cut down the groves, and brake in pieces the brasen serpent that Moses had made: for unto those days the children of Israel did burn incense to it: and he called it Nehushtan." (Margin, "i.e., a piece of brass.")

13. What Hebrew king worshiped the stars?

Manasseh, Second Chronicles 33:3.—"For he [Manasseh] built again the high places which Hezekiah his father had broken down, and he reared up altars of Baalim, and made groves, and worshipped all the host of heaven, and served them." According to Deuteronomy 17:2–7 this was a capital offense.

14. Who dedicated horses to the sun?

The Kings of Judah, Second Kings 23:11.—"And he [Josiah] took away the horses that the kings of Judah had given to the sun, at the entering in of the house of the Lord, by the chamber of Nathan-melech the chamberlain, which was in the suburbs, and burned the chariots of the sun with fire." Moffatt translates: "He removed the figures of horses set up for the sun. . . ."

15. What Hebrew king's head was mounted in the temple of the Philistine fish-god?

Saul's, First Chronicles 10:10.—"And they put his [Saul's] armour in the house of their gods, and fastened his head in the temple of Dagon." See also First Samuel 31:7–10. Dagon was the Philistine fish-god, and his image is somewhat described in First Samuel 5:1–5, which tells how it was mutilated until (verse 4) "only the stump of Dagon was left to him." The margin gives as an alternate to "the stump" the phrase "the fishy part."

16. Who discovered seventy men worshiping mural paintings of idols?

Ezekiel, Ezekiel 8:10–11.—"So I went in and saw; and behold every form of creeping things, and abominable beasts, and all the idols of the house of Israel, pourtrayed upon the wall round about. And there stood before them seventy men of the ancients of the house of Israel, and in the midst of them stood Jaazaniah the son of Shaphan, with every man his censer in his hand; and a thick cloud of incense went up."

17. What king abolished fortune-tellers and then himself consulted four different kinds?

Saul drove fortune-tellers out of the land and then consulted four kinds, dream interpreters, sacred lot casters, prophets, and a spiritistic medium, First Samuel 28:3–7. —". . . And Saul had put away those that had familiar spirits, and the wizards, out of the land. . . . And when Saul saw the host of the Philistines, he was afraid, and his heart greatly trembled. And when Saul enquired of the Lord, the Lord answered him not, neither by dreams, nor by Urim, nor by prophets. Then said Saul unto his servants, Seek me a woman that hath a familiar spirit, that I may go to her, and enquire of her . . ."

18. Who saw twenty-five men worshiping the sun?

Ezekiel, Ezekiel 8:16.—"And he brought me into the inner court of the Lord's house, and, behold, at the door of the temple of the Lord, between the porch and the altar, were about five and twenty men, with their backs toward the temple of the Lord, and their faces toward the east; and they worshipped the sun toward the east."

19. Who staged a praying contest between two religions?

Elijah, First Kings 18:20–40, especially verses 21 and 24.—"And Elijah came unto all the people, and said, How long halt ye between two opinions? if the Lord be God, follow him: but if Baal, then follow him. . . . And call ye on the name of your gods, and I will call on the name of the Lord: and the God that answereth by fire, let him be God. And all the people answered and said, It is well spoken."

20. Who were the "keepers of the threshold"?

The folklore of threshold superstitions is voluminous. Frazer in his *Folk-lore in the Old Testament* gives a whole chapter in volume three to the subject. The "keepers of the threshold" were guards part at least of whose duties was to prevent the threshold from being stepped on, which was considered bad luck, because the threshold was supposed to be haunted by spirits. In the Old Testament these guardians are usually called keepers of the door or keepers of the gates, but usually the margin gives "threshold." See Second Kings 12:9, 22:4, 23:4, 25:18, First Chronicles 9:19, Second Chronicles 34:9, Esther 2:21, 6:2, Psalm 84:10, Jeremiah 35:4, 52:24. All these passages refer to keepers of the threshold. The superstition about touching the threshold is obvious in two other passages, First Samuel 5:5: "Therefore neither the priests of Dagon, nor any that come into Dagon's house, tread on the threshold of Dagon in Ashdod unto this day." Zephaniah 1:9: "In the same day also will I punish all those that leap on the threshold, . . ."

21. Why were the Hebrews so careful not to partake of blood?

Because they believed that the blood was the life, and life was sacred: hence the blood must be drained from the meat and poured out to God on the ground or on the altar before the flesh was eaten, Deuteronomy 12:23, 24, 27.—"Only be sure that thou eat not the blood: for the blood is the life; and thou mayest not eat the life with the flesh. Thou shalt not eat it; thou shalt pour it upon the earth as water. . . . and the blood of thy sacrifices shall be poured out upon the altar of the Lord thy God, and thou shalt eat the flesh." This reverence for blood is found in many religions, sometimes shown by devoting the blood to God, as above, and sometimes by the opposite, the drinking of the blood, literally, or symbolically, as in Christianity.

XXIII

Cities

1. What city was built with two human sacrifices?

2. At the destruction of what city was a Negro promised rescue?

3. What Old Testament city had a waterworks system?

4. What hunter ruled four cities and built four more?

5. What city did Jehovah come down from heaven to see?

6. Who built the first city and what was its name?

7. What city was to become a camel-stable?

8. The dust of what city did Paul shake from his feet?

9. Who saw a city coming down out of heaven?

10. From what city did Paul escape in a basket?

11. What was the former name of Bethel?

12. Who said, "My cities shall yet overflow with prosperity"?

13. What was the "City of Palm Trees"?

14. What Old Testament city was the "City of David" and what New Testament city?

15. What city was noted for its horse-fairs and slave-markets?

16. Where was the first skyscraper started?

ANSWERS TO QUESTIONS
ABOUT CITIES

1. What city was built with two human sacrifices?

Jericho, First Kings 16:34.—"In his days did Hiel the Bethelite build Jericho: he laid the foundation thereof in Abiram his firstborn, and set up the gates thereof in his youngest son Segub, according to the word of the Lord, which he spake by Joshua the son of Nun." See Joshua 6:26.

2. At the destruction of what city was a Negro promised rescue?

Jerusalem, Jeremiah 39:15–17.—"Now the word of the Lord came unto Jeremiah, while he was shut up in the court of the prison, saying, Go and speak to Ebed-melech the Ethiopian, saying, Thus saith the Lord of hosts, the God of Israel; Behold, I will bring my words upon this city [Jerusalem] for evil, and not for good; and they shall be accomplished in that day before thee. But I will deliver thee in that day, saith the Lord: and thou shalt not be given into the hand of the men of whom thou art afraid."

3. What Old Testament city had a waterworks system?

Jerusalem, Second Kings 20:20.—"And the rest of the acts of Hezekiah, and all his might, and how he made a pool, and a conduit, and brought water into the city [Jerusalem], are they not written in the book of the chronicles of the kings of Judah?"

4. What hunter ruled four cities and built four more?

Nimrod, Genesis 10:9–12 RV.—"He was a mighty hunter before Jehovah: wherefore it is said, Like Nimrod a mighty hunter before Jehovah. And the beginning of his kingdom was Babel, and Erech, and Accad, and Calneh, in the land of Shinar. Out of that land he went forth into Assyria, and builded Nineveh, and Rehoboth-Ir, and Calah, and Resen between Nineveh and Calah (the same is the great city)."

5. What city did Jehovah come down from heaven to see?

Babel, Genesis 11:5.—"And the Lord came down to see the city [Babel] and the tower, which the children of men builded."

6. Who built the first city and what was its name?

Cain, Enoch, Genesis 4:17.—"And Cain knew his wife; and she conceived, and bare Enoch: and he builded a city, and called the name of the city, after the name of his son, Enoch." (The old query of the literalist as to where Cain got his wife has an equally difficult corollary, Where did he get the men to build and inhabit the city?)

7. What city was to become a camel-stable?

Rabbah, Ezekiel 25:5.—"And I will make Rabbah a stable for camels, and the Ammonites a couching place for flocks: . . ."

8. The dust of what city did Paul shake from his feet?

Antioch in Pisidia, Acts 13:14, 50, 51.—"But when they [Paul and his company] departed from Perga, they came to Antioch in Pisidia, and went into the synagogue on the sabbath day, and sat down. . . . But the Jews stirred up the devout and honorable women, and the chief men of the city, and raised persecution against Paul and Barnabas, and expelled them out of their coasts. But they shook off the dust of their feet against them, and came into Iconium." See also Matthew 10:14, Luke 9:5, 10:11, and Acts 22:23.

9. Who saw a city coming down out of heaven?

John, Revelation 21:2.—"And I John saw the holy city, new Jerusalem, coming down from God out of heaven, prepared as a bride adorned for her husband."

10. From what city did Paul escape in a basket?

Damascus, Second Corinthians 11:32-33.—"In Damascus the governor under Aretas the king kept the city of the Damascenes with a garrison, desirous to apprehend me: And through a window in a basket was I let down by the wall, and escaped his hands."

11. What was the former name of Bethel?

Luz, Judges 1:23.—"And the house of Joseph sent to descry Bethel. (Now the name of the city before was Luz.)"

12. Who said, "My cities shall yet overflow with prosperity"?

Jehovah, Zechariah 1:17 RV.—"Cry yet again, saying, Thus saith Jehovah of hosts: My cities shall yet overflow with prosperity; and Jehovah shall yet comfort Zion, and shall yet choose Jerusalem."

13. What was the "City of Palm Trees"?

Jericho, Deuteronomy 34:3.—"And the south, and the plain of the valley of Jericho, the city of palm trees, unto Zoar." See also Second Chronicles 28:15.

14. What Old Testament city was the "City of David" and what New Testament city?

In Old Testament times, Zion (part of Jerusalem), Second Samuel 5:7.—"Nevertheless David took the stronghold of Zion: the same is the city of David."

In New Testament times, Bethlehem, Luke 2:4.—"And Joseph also went up from Galilee, out of the city of Nazareth, into Judaea, unto the city of David, which is called Bethlehem; . . ."

15. What city was noted for its horse-fairs and slave-markets?

Tyre, Ezekiel 27. The entire chapter is a very interesting account of the business and commerce of this ancient city. Ezekiel 27:13–14.—". . . they traded the persons of men and vessels of brass in thy market. They of the house of Togarmah traded in thy fairs with horses and horsemen and mules."

16. Where was the first skyscraper started?

In the land of Shinar, Genesis 11:2–4.—"And it came to pass, as they journeyed from the east, that they found a plain in the land of Shinar; and they dwelt there. And they said one to another, Go to, let us make brick, and burn them thoroughly. And they had brick for stone, and slime had they for morter. And they said, Go to, let us build us a city and a tower, whose top may reach unto heaven; . . ."

XXIV

Of Scientific Interest

1. In what three places is astrology condemned in the Bible?

2. How do we know that Solomon was familiar with refrigeration?

3. Where is irrigation prophesied?

4. What evidence is there that the earth once reversed its motion?

5. Where are India and Spain mentioned?

6. What woman ninety years old gave birth to a child?

7. How did the serpent of Eden travel before it was condemned to crawl on its belly?

8. When was a rodent mistaken for a ruminant?

9. Where are some insects termed quadrupeds?

10. Who thought snails melted?

11. Who killed a giant having twelve fingers and twelve toes?

12. Who was the first biologist?

13. Who said he saw a man flying swiftly?

14. What prophet foretold an eclipse?

15. Who told the common signs for weather forecasting?

16. What stars and constellations are mentioned in the Bible?

17. Who improved a city's water supply by chemical treatment?

18. Was Noah's son Ham a Negro?

19. When were prayers for rain effective?

20. What Bible character, by a strange anachronism, is quoted as wishing that his words "were printed in a book"?

21. What Bible verses imply that the earth is flat?

22. What Bible verses imply that the earth does not move?

23. Who warned a preacher against "science falsely so called"?

24. Who was 500 years old when his sons were born?

25. What king became a father at the age of eleven?

26. Who was so thin he could count all his bones?

27. Who wrote his own obituary?

28. Who thought the sun went round the earth?

29. What Bible character lived the longest?

30. The victors in what battle believed that the stars helped them win?

ANSWERS TO QUESTIONS OF SCIENTIFIC INTEREST

1. In what three places is astrology condemned in the Bible?

Isaiah 47:13–14.—"Thou art wearied in the multitude of thy counsels. Let now the astrologers, the stargazers, the monthly prognosticators, stand up, and save thee from these things that shall come upon thee. Behold, they shall be as stubble; the fire shall burn them; they shall not deliver themselves from the power of the flame: . . ." Jeremiah 10:2.—"Thus said the Lord, Learn not the way of the heathen, and be not dismayed at the signs of heaven; for the heathen are dismayed at them." Daniel 1:19–20.— "And the king communed with them; and among them all was found none like Daniel, Hananiah, Mishael, and Azariah: therefore stood they before the king. And in all matters of wisdom and understanding, that the king enquired of them, he found them ten times better than all the magicians and astrologers that were in all his realm." See also Daniel 2:1–30, especially verse 9, where the predictions of astrologers are called "lying and corrupt words." See also Deuteronomy 18:9–12 and Second Kings 21:6.

2. How do we know that Solomon was familiar with refrigeration?

Proverbs 25:1, 13.—"These are also proverbs of Solomon, which the men of Hezekiah king of Judah copied out . . . As the cold of snow in the time of harvest, so is a faithful messenger to them that send him: for he refresheth the soul of his masters."

3. Where is irrigation prophesied?

Isaiah 43:19–20.—"Behold, I will do a new thing; now it shall spring forth; shall ye not know it? I will even make a way in the wilderness, and rivers in the desert. The beast of the field shall honour me, the dragons and the owls: because I give waters in the wilderness, and rivers in the desert, to give drink to my people, my chosen."

4. What evidence is there that the earth once reversed its motion?

When a sundial moved backward, Second Kings 20:11.— "And Isaiah the prophet cried unto the Lord: and he brought the shadow ten degrees backward, by which it had gone down in the dial of Ahaz." An interesting light is thrown on the naïveté of those who believed this story when we inquire why this cosmic catastrophe was arranged. It took place, according to the preceding verses, as a sign to Hezekiah that he would be cured of his boil!

5. Where are India and Spain mentioned?

Esther 1:1.—". . . this is Ahasuerus which reigned, from India even unto Ethiopia, . . ." See also Esther 8:9.

Romans 15:24.—"Whensoever I take my journey into Spain, I will come to you: . . ." See also Romans 15:28.

6. What woman ninety years old gave birth to a child?

Sarah, Genesis 17:17; 21:1–2.—"Then Abraham fell upon his face, and laughed, and said in his heart, . . . shall Sarah, that is ninety years old, bear? . . . And the Lord visited Sarah as he had said, and the Lord did unto Sarah as he had spoken. . . . For Sarah conceived, and bare Abraham a son in his old age, at the set time of which God had spoken to him."

7. How did the serpent of Eden travel before it was condemned to crawl on its belly?

Genesis 3:13-14.—"And the Lord God said unto the woman, What is this that thou hast done? And the woman said, The serpent beguiled me and I did eat. And the Lord God said unto the serpent, Because thou hast done this, thou art cursed above all cattle, and above every beast of the field; upon thy belly shalt thou go, and dust shalt thou eat all the days of thy life;" It is quite likely that in the original form of the story of Eve and the serpent the latter was a spirit, and was thought of as an angel or demon in human or semi-human form. Traces of that idea remain in the fact that the serpent shows great intelligence, and is quite a conversationalist. In the Book of Enoch, which was recognized as holy scripture by the early Christians, it is stated that it was a Satan named Gadreel who "led astray Eve," Enoch 69:6. The fact that snakes can raise a large part of their bodies may have given rise to the idea that they once walked erect.

8. When was a rodent mistaken for a ruminant?

Leviticus 11:6.—"And the hare, because he cheweth the cud, but divideth not the hoof; he is unclean unto you." Only a superficial observer would mistake a hare for a cud-chewing animal.

9. Where are some insects termed quadrupeds?

Leviticus 11:21-23.—"Yet these may ye eat of every flying creeping thing that goeth upon all four, which have legs above their feet, to leap withal upon the earth; Even these of them ye may eat; the locust after his kind, and the bald locust after his kind, and the beetle after his kind, and the grasshopper after his kind. But all other flying creeping things, which have four feet, shall be an abomination unto you." RV has "cricket" for "beetle." All of these insects, have, of course, six legs.

10. Who thought snails melted?

David, Psalm 58:8.—"As a snail which melteth, let every one of them pass away: . . ." The slimy track of a snail is not due, as David evidently thought, to the dissolution of its body.

11. Who killed a giant having twelve fingers and twelve toes?

Jonathan, son of Shimeah, Second Samuel 21:20–21.— "And there was yet a battle in Gath, where was a man of great stature, that had on every hand six fingers, and on every foot six toes, four and twenty in number; and he also was born to the giant. And when he defied Israel, Jonathan the son of Shimeah the brother of David slew him."

12. Who was the first biologist?

Solomon, First Kings 4:29, 33.—"And God gave Solomon wisdom and understanding exceeding much, and largeness of heart, even as the sand that is on the sea shore. . . . And he spake of trees, from the cedar tree that is in Lebanon even unto the hyssop that springeth out of the wall: he spake also of beasts, and of fowl, and of creeping things, and of fishes."

13. Who said he saw a man flying swiftly?

Daniel, Daniel 9:21.—"Yea, whiles I was speaking in prayer, even the man Gabriel, whom I had seen in the vision in the beginning, being caused to fly swiftly, touched me about the time of the evening oblation."

14. What prophet foretold an eclipse?

Amos, Amos 8:9.—"And it shall come to pass in that day, saith the Lord God, that I will cause the sun to go down at noon, and I will darken the earth in the clear day." It is interesting to note that a complete eclipse of the sun, visible at Jerusalem, occurred June 15, 763 B.C., which was during Amos' lifetime.

15. Who told the common signs for weather forecasting?

Jesus, Matthew 16:2–3.—"He [Jesus] answered and said unto them, When it is evening, ye say, It will be fair weather: for the sky is red. And in the morning, It will be foul weather today: for the sky is red and lowring. . . ."

16. What stars and constellations are mentioned in the Bible?

Arcturus, The Bear, Orion, The Pleiades, Saturn, The Serpent, The Twins, southern constellations, the planets, and the signs of the zodiac. Job 9:9.—"Which maketh Arcturus, Orion, and Pleiades, and the chambers of the south." RV has "the Bear" in place of "Arcturus." These "chambers of the south" must refer to southern constellations. Job 38:31–32.—"Canst thou bind the sweet influences of Pleiades, or loose the bands of Orion? Canst thou bring forth Mazzaroth in his season? or canst thou guide Arcturus with his sons?" RV has "the cluster of the Pleiades" and, instead of "Arcturus with his sons" has "the Bear with her train." The train is, of course, the three stars which form the tail of the Bear, or, as some know it, the handle of the Dipper. Mazzaroth is evidently the signs of the zodiac. Amos 5:8.—"Seek him that maketh the seven stars and Orion, . . ." RV has "the Pleiades" for "the seven stars." Amos 5:26.—"But ye have borne the tabernacle of your Moloch and Chiun your images, the star of your god, which ye made to yourselves." Several scholars have identified Chiun with Saturn, which was the star god of the Assyrians. Job 26:13.—"By his spirit he hath garnished the heavens; his hand hath formed the crooked serpent." This serpent has been identified by some scholars as the constellation between the Great Bear and the Little Bear, known as the Dragon, but the reference may be to the sea-serpent of Isaiah 27:1. Acts 28:11.—"And after three months we departed in a ship of Alexandria, which had wintered in the isle, whose sign was Castor and Pollux." Castor and Pollux is the name of a constellation sometimes known as the Gemini, or Twins. The "Planets" (margin, "twelve signs, or, constellations") are mentioned in Second Kings 23:5, and the "constellations" in Isaiah 13:10.

17. Who improved a city's water supply by chemical treatment?

Elisha, Second Kings 2:19–22.—"And the men of the city said unto Elisha, Behold, I pray thee, the situation of this city is pleasant, as my lord seeth: but the water is naught, and the ground barren. And he said, Bring me a new cruse, and put salt therein. And they brought it to him. And he went forth unto the spring of the waters, and cast the salt in there, . . . So the waters were healed. . . ." Moffatt has for "the spring of the waters," "the source of their water-supply."

18. Was Noah's son Ham a Negro?

The tenth chapter is a primitive attempt at ethnological

classification of the nations of the world. It ends, verse 32: "These are the families of the sons of Noah, after their generations, in their nations: and by these were the nations divided in the earth after the flood." It begins, verse 1, with the announcement: "Now these are the generations of the sons of Noah, Shem, Ham, and Japheth: and unto them were sons born after the flood." And when it comes to the sons of Ham, verse 6, it gives them as, "Cush, and Mizraim, and Phut, and Canaan." Now Cush and Mizraim are the Hebrew words for Ethiopia and Egypt.

The practical problem for the one who compiled this table of the nations was this: If Noah and his three sons were the only men left alive after the flood, from which of them did the black races descend? Ham was decided upon, evidently because the word Ham means swarthy or dark-colored. (Or that name may have been assigned to him by the compiler because the Negroes had to be accounted for.) But the problem still remained as to how a white couple, Noah and his wife, could have had a Negro son, and it will always trouble those who regard Genesis as a historical record.

19. When were prayers for rain effective?

In the times of Samuel and Elijah, according to the Bible books of Samuel and Kings. First Samuel 12:18.—"So Samuel called unto the Lord, and the Lord sent thunder and rain that day: and all the people greatly feared the Lord and Samuel." First Samuel 18:42–45.—". . . And Elijah went up to the top of Carmel; and he cast himself down upon the earth, and put his face between his knees, And said to his servant, Go up now, look toward the sea. . . . And it came to pass at the seventh time, that he said, Behold, there ariseth a little cloud out of the sea, like a man's hand. And he said, Go up, say unto Ahab, Prepare thy chariot, and get thee down, that the rain stop thee not. And it came to pass in the mean while, that the heaven was black with clouds and wind, and there was a great rain. . . ."

20. What Bible character, by a strange anachronism, is quoted as wishing that his words "were printed in a book"?

Job, Job 19:23.—"Oh that my words were now written! oh that they were printed in a book!" Printing was invented in China in the ninth century A.D., and in Europe about the middle of the fifteenth century.

21. What Bible verses imply that the earth is flat?

Isaiah 11:12.—". . . and gather together the dispersed of Judah from the four corners of the earth." Revelation 7:1. —"And after these things I saw four angels standing on the four corners of the earth, . . ." Matthew 4:8.—"Again, the devil taketh him up into an exceeding high mountain, and sheweth him all the kingdoms of the world, and the glory of them;" Isaiah 24:1.—"Behold, the Lord maketh the earth empty, and maketh it waste, and turneth it upside down, and scattereth abroad the inhabitants thereof."

22. What Bible verses imply that the earth does not move?

First Samuel 2:8.—". . . for the pillars of the earth are the Lord's, and he hath set the world upon them." First Chronicles 16:30 RV.—". . . The world also is established that it cannot be moved." Psalm 104:5.—"Who laid the foundations of the earth, that it should not be removed for ever." The margin notes that the Hebrew really reads,—"He hath founded the earth upon her bases." See also Job 38:4–6; Psalm 24:1–2; Hebrews 1:10.

23. Who warned a preacher against "science falsely so called"?

Paul warned Timothy, First Timothy 6:20–21.—"O Timothy, keep that which is committed to thy trust, avoiding profane and vain babblings, and oppositions of science falsely so called: Which some professing have erred concerning the faith. . . ."

24. Who was 500 years old when his sons were born?

Noah, Genesis 5:32.—"And Noah was five hundred years old: and Noah begat Shem, Ham, and Japheth."

25. What king became a father at the age of eleven?

Ahaz, Second Kings 16:2, 20; 18:2.—"Twenty years old was Ahaz when he began to reign, and reigned sixteen years in Jerusalem, . . . And Ahaz slept with his fathers, . . . and Hezekiah his son reigned in his stead. . . . Twenty and five years old was he [Hezekiah] when he began to reign; . . ." If Ahaz died at the age of thirty-six and was succeeded by a twenty-five-year-old son, then Ahaz must have been eleven when his son was born.

26. Who was so thin he could count all his bones?

The Psalmist, Psalm 22:17.—"I may tell all my bones; they look and stare upon me."

27. Who wrote his own obituary?

Deuteronomy is entitled "The Fifth Book of Moses" and is popularly believed to have been written by him, but the 34th chapter tells of his death and burial. Scholars date the writing of Deuteronomy, however, some six centuries later, during the Babylonian exile.

28. Who thought the sun went round the earth?

The author of Joshua 10:12–14, which records how Joshua commanded the sun to stand still so that the Israelites might have light to see to complete the slaughter of the Armorites.—"So the sun stood still in the midst of heaven, and hasted not to go down about a whole day."

29. What Bible character lived the longest?

Methuselah lived 969 years, according to Genesis 5:27, but Melchisedec is credited with even longer life. Genesis 14:18–20 tells how "Melchizedek king of Salem" and "priest of the most high God," met Abram, and Hebrews 7:1–3, written some two thousand years after the alleged date of Abram, states: "For this Melchisedec, king of Salem, priest of the most high God, who met Abraham returning from the slaughter of the kings, and blessed him; To whom also Abraham gave a tenth part of all; first being by interpretation King of righteousness, and after that also King of Salem, which is, King of peace; Without father, without mother, without descent, having neither beginning of days, nor end of life; but made like unto the son of God; abideth a priest continually."

30. The victors in what battle believed that the stars helped them win?

The Battle of Kishon, when Barak, at the call of the prophetess Deborah, led the Israelites against Sisera, captain of the host of Jabin, king of Canaan. The battle is described at great length in Judges 4 and 5. 5:20 states: "They fought from heaven; the stars in their courses fought against Sisera."

XXV

Athletics, Sports, and Prowess

1. Where is Jehovah likened to a ball pitcher?
2. When was fishing-tackle worshiped?
3. Where are fish-hooks mentioned?
4. Who caught 153 fishes?
5. When did a fish catch a man?
6. Where are different methods of fishing described?
7. What three Bible heroes slew lions?
8. Who shot an arrow through a man's body?
9. What indications are there that Paul was much interested in athletics?
10. Where is partridge hunting in the mountains mentioned?
11. What man captured single-handed an army that was seeking him?
12. Who "slew two lion-like men"?
13. Who killed 1,000 men with the jaw-bone of an ass?
14. Who killed 600 men with an ox-goad?
15. Who killed 800 men with a spear?
16. What man was known for his reckless driving?
17. What tribe had 700 expert left-handed slingers?
18. Where is breast-stroke swimming mentioned?
19. Where is God depicted as an archer?

20. Who won a contest with an Egyptian seven and a half feet tall?

21. Who was a hairy hunter?

22. Who was "a mighty hunter before the Lord"?

23. Who said he would send fishers and hunters to fish and hunt the Jews?

24. Who won a night wrestling contest with God himself?

ANSWERS TO QUESTIONS ABOUT ATHLETICS, SPORTS, AND PROWESS

1. Where is Jehovah likened to a ball pitcher?

Isaiah 22:17–18, RV.—"Behold, Jehovah, like a strong man, will hurl thee away violently; yea, he will wrap thee up closely [margin, "lay fast hold on thee"]. He will surely wind thee round and round, and toss thee like a ball into a large country; . . ." The AV has, "He will surely violently turn and toss thee like a ball into a large country:"

2. When was fishing-tackle worshiped?

In the days of Habakkuk, Habakkuk 1:15–16.—"They take up all of them with the angle, they catch them in their net, and gather them in their drag: therefore they rejoice and are glad. Therefore they sacrifice unto their net, and burn incense unto their drag; . . ."

3. Where are fish-hooks mentioned?

Amos 4:2.—"The Lord God hath sworn by his holiness, that, lo, the days shall come upon you, that he will take you away with hooks, and your posterity with fishhooks." See also Job 41:1 and Matthew 17:27.

4. Who caught 153 fishes?

Simon Peter, John 21:11.—"Simon Peter went up, and drew the net to land full of great fishes, an hundred and fifty and three: and for all there were so many, yet was not the net broken."

5. When did a fish catch a man?

Jonah 1:17.—"Now the Lord had prepared a great fish to swallow up Jonah. And Jonah was in the belly of the fish three days and three nights."

6. Where are different methods of fishing described?

Isaiah 19:8–10.—"The fishers also shall mourn, and all they that cast angle into the brooks shall lament, and they that spread nets upon the waters shall languish. Moreover they that work in fine flax, and they that weave networks, shall be confounded. And they shall be broken in the purposes [margin, "foundations"] thereof, all that make sluices and ponds for fish." See also Habakkuk 1:15–16.

7. What three Bible heroes slew lions?

Samson, Judges 14:5–6.—"Then went Samson down . . . to the vineyards of Timnath: and, behold, a young lion roared against him. And the Spirit of the Lord came mightily upon him, and he rent him as he would have rent a kid, and he had nothing in his hand: . . ."

David, First Samuel 17:34–36.—"And David said unto Saul, Thy servant kept his father's sheep, and there came a lion, and a bear, and took a lamb out of the flock: And I went out after him, and smote him, and delivereth it out of his mouth: and when he arose against me, I caught him by his beard, and smote him, and slew him. Thy servant slew both the lion and the bear: . . ."

Benaiah, Second Samuel 23:20.—"And Benaiah the son of Jehoiada, the son of a valiant man, of Kabzeel, who had done many acts, . . . he went down also and slew a lion in the midst of a pit in time of snow:"

8. Who shot an arrow through a man's body?

Jehu, Second Kings 9:24.—"And Jehu drew a bow with his full strength, and smote Jehoram between his arms, and the arrow went out at his heart, and he sunk down in his chariot."

9. What indications are there that Paul was much interested in athletics?

His illustrations are frequently drawn from athletic events. First Corinthians 9:24–27.—"Know ye not that they which run in a race run all, but one receiveth the prize? So run, that ye may obtain. And every man that striveth for the mastery is temperate in all things. Now they do it to obtain a corruptible crown; but we an incorruptible. I therefore so run, not as uncertainly; so fight I, not as one that beateth the air: But I keep under my body, and bring it into subjection: lest that by any means, when I have preached to others, I myself should be a castaway."

Moffatt's translation makes the point more evident: "Do you not know that in a race, though all run, only one man gains the prize? Run so as to win the prize. Every athlete practices self-restraint all round; but while they do it to win a fading wreath, we do it for an unfading. Well, I run without swerving; I do not plant my blows upon the empty air—no, I maul and master my body, in case, after preaching to other people, I am disqualified myself."

See also Philippians 3:14, Second Timothy 2:5, 4:7–8.

10. Where is partridge hunting in the mountains mentioned?

First Samuel 26:20.—". . . for the king of Israel is come out to seek a flea, as when one doth hunt a partridge in the mountains."

11. What man captured single-handed an army that was seeking him?

Elisha, Second Kings 6:8–23, especially verses 15, 18, and 19.—"And when the servant of the man of God was risen early, and gone forth, behold, an host compassed the city both with horses and chariots. And his servant said unto him, Alas, my master! how shall we do? . . . And when they came down to him, Elisha prayed unto the Lord, and said, Smite this people, I pray thee, with blindness. And he smote them with blindness according to the word of Elisha. And Elisha said unto them, This is not the way, neither is this the city: follow me, and I will bring you to the man whom ye seek. But he led them to Samaria."

12. Who "slew two lion-like men"?

Benaiah, Second Samuel 23:20.—"And Benaiah . . . slew two lionlike men of Moab: . . ."

13. Who killed 1,000 men with the jaw-bone of an ass?

Samson, Judges 15:15.—"And he [Samson] found a new jawbone of an ass, and put forth his hand, and took it, and slew a thousand men therewith."

14. Who killed 600 men with an ox-goad?

Shamgar, Judges 3:31.—"And after him was Shamgar the

son of Anath, which slew of the Philistines six hundred men with an ox goad: and he also delivered Israel."

15. Who killed 800 men with a spear?

Adino the Eznite, Second Samuel 23:8.—". . . the same was Adino the Eznite: he lift up his spear against eight hundred, whom he slew at one time."

16. What man was known for his reckless driving?

Jehu, Second Kings 9:20.—". . . and the driving is like the driving of Jehu the son of Nimshi; for he driveth furiously." The margin gives in place of furiously the literal translation from the Hebrew, "in madness."

17. What tribe had 700 expert left-handed slingers?

The tribe of Benjamin, Judges 20:16.—"Among all this people [the children of Benjamin] there were seven hundred chosen men left-handed; every one could sling stones at an hair breadth, and not miss."

18. Where is breast-stroke swimming mentioned?

Isaiah 25:11.—"And he shall spread forth his hands in the midst of them, as he that swimmeth spreadeth forth his hands to swim: . . ." For other mention of swimming, see Acts 27:42–43 and Ezekiel 32:6, 47:5.

19. Where is God depicted as an archer?

Psalm 7:11–13.—"God judgeth the righteous, and God is angry with the wicked every day. If he turn not, he will whet his sword; he hath bent his bow, and made it ready. He hath also prepared for him the instruments of death; he ordaineth his arrows against the persecutors." See also Habakkuk 3:8–11 and Genesis 9:8–17. This idea of God's bow and arrows was not so completely symbolic and figurative to the primitive Hebrews as it is to us. To them the flashes of lightning were God's arrows and the rainbow was his bow, hung up in the heavens after his storm of wrath was over. Similarly, to the Hindus, the rainbow was Indra's battle-bow, hung up after his battle with the demons. Professor Wellhausen states that the Arabs think, "Kuzah shoots arrows from his bow, and then hangs it up in the clouds."

20. Who won a contest with an Egyptian seven and a half feet tall?

Benaiah, First Chronicles 11:23–24.—"And he slew an

Egyptian, a man of great stature, five cubits high; and in the Egyptian's hand was a spear like a weaver's beam; and he went down to him with a staff, and plucked the spear out of the Egyptian's hand, and slew him with his own spear. These things did Benaiah the son of Jehoiada, and had the name among the three mighties." See also Second Samuel 23:21. A cubit was the distance from elbow to finger tips, about eighteen inches.

21. Who was a hairy hunter?

Esau, Genesis 25:25, 27.—"And the first came out red, all over like a hairy garment; and they called his name Esau . . . and Esau was a cunning hunter, a man of the field; . . ."

22. Who was "a mighty hunter before the Lord"?

Nimrod, Genesis 10:8–9.—"And Cush begat Nimrod: he began to be a mighty one in the earth. He was a mighty hunter before the Lord: wherefore it is said, Even as Nimrod the mighty hunter before the Lord."

23. Who said he would send fishers and hunters to fish and hunt the Jews?

The sixteenth chapter of Jeremiah is a prophecy of how God will bring utter ruin upon the Jews. In verse 16, the prophet indicates how they will be captured.—"Behold, I will send for many fishers, saith the Lord, and they shall fish them; and after I will send for many hunters, and they shall hunt them from every mountain, and from every hill, and out of the holes of the rocks."

24. Who won a night wrestling contest with God himself?

Jacob, Genesis 32:24–30.—"And Jacob was left alone; and there wrestled a man with him until the breaking of the day. And when he saw that he prevailed not against him, he touched the hollow of his thigh; and the hollow of Jacob's thigh was out of joint, as he wrestled with him. And he said, Let me go, for the day breaketh. And he said, I will not let thee go, except thou bless me. And he said unto him, What is thy name? And he said, Jacob. And he said, Thy name shall be called no more Jacob, but Israel: for as a prince hast thou power with God and with men, and hast prevailed. And Jacob asked him, and said, Tell me, I pray thee, thy name. And he said, Wherefore is it that thou dost ask after my name? And he blessed him there. And Jacob called the name of the place Peniel: for I have seen God face to face, and my life is preserved."

This story bears many marks of its very primitive origin, including the very anthropomorphic conception of God, the fact that the supernatural person had to leave at daybreak, as in so many folk-tales, and the fact that no opprobrium seems to attach to the heavenly wrestler for what seems to us very unsportsmanlike conduct.

XXVI

Of Interest to Preachers

1. Who stood in the only pulpit mentioned in the Bible?
2. When did one preacher hit another in the face?
3. What Negro lifted a preacher out of the mud?
4. How was a preacher's room furnished in Bible times?
5. What preacher was put on a bread-and-water diet by an angry hearer?
6. Who were the first seven deacons?
7. What preacher boiled a pot of bones to illustrate a sermon?
8. What was said to have been David's only sin?
9. Who protested at poor men being unwelcome in church?
10. Who was stoned to death for preaching a sermon?
11. How many of the Ten Commandments did Jesus recite when asked which of them should be kept?
12. When did priests work a "racket" with offering-money?
13. Where is the only mention of a vestry?
14. What preacher was angry when his preaching converted a city?
15. Who fell asleep during a long sermon?
16. What preacher broke a bottle at the climax of his sermon?
17. Who was the first preacher to get intoxicated?
18. Who instituted every-member weekly church offerings?

19. Who was the first Christian preacher to take wages from a church?

20. Where are Christians forbidden to permit heretics to enter their houses?

21. What man was made a priest for killing a pair of lovers?

ANSWERS TO QUESTIONS OF INTEREST TO PREACHERS

1. Who stood in the only pulpit mentioned in the Bible?

Ezra, Nehemiah 8:4–6.—"And Ezra the scribe stood upon a pulpit of wood, which they had made for the purpose; . . . And Ezra opened the book in the sight of all the people; (for he was above all the people;) and when he opened it, all the people stood up: And Ezra blessed the Lord, the great God. And all the people answered, Amen, Amen, with lifting up their hands: and they bowed their heads, and worshipped the Lord with their faces to the ground." Moffatt translates, "a wooden platform."

2. When did one preacher hit another in the face?

Zedekiah struck Micaiah, First Kings 22:24.—"But Zedekiah the son of Chenaanah went near, and smote Micaiah on the cheek, and said, Which way went the Spirit of the Lord from me to speak unto thee?" These two were rival prophets. Micaiah's answer (verse 25) was rather apt: "Behold, thou shalt see in that day, when thou shalt go into an inner chamber to hide thyself."

3. What Negro lifted a preacher out of the mud?

Ebed-melech, Jeremiah 38:6–13.—"Then took they Jeremiah, and cast him into the dungeon . . . And in the dungeon there was no water, but mire: so Jeremiah sunk in the mire. Now when Ebed-melech the Ethiopian, one of the eunuchs who was in the king's house, heard that they had put Jeremiah in the dungeon . . . [he] said unto Jeremiah, Put now these old cast clouts and rotten rags under thine armholes under the cords. And Jeremiah did so. So they drew up Jeremiah with cords, and took him up out of the dungeon: . . ."

4. How was a preacher's room furnished in Bible times?

With bed, table, stool, and candlestick, Second Kings 4:9–10.—"And she [the woman of Shunem] said unto her husband, Behold now, I perceive that this is an holy man of God, which passeth by us continually. Let us make a little chamber, I pray thee, on the wall; and let us set for him there a bed, and a table, and a stool, and a candlestick: and it shall be, when he cometh to us, that he shall turn in thither."

5. What preacher was put on a bread-and-water diet by an angry hearer?

Micaiah, First Kings 22:8, 26–28.—"And the king of Israel said unto Jehoshaphat, There is yet one man, Micaiah the son of Imlah, by whom we may enquire of the Lord: but I hate him; for he doth not prophesy good concerning me, but evil. . . . And the king of Israel said, Take Micaiah, and carry him back unto Amon the governor of the city, and to Joash the king's son; and say, Thus saith the king, Put this fellow in the prison, and feed him with bread of affliction and water of affliction, until I come in peace." Micaiah made another of his ready retorts, saying, verse 28: ". . . If thou return at all in peace, the Lord hath not spoken by me. . . ."

6. Who were the first seven deacons?

Stephen, Philip, Prochorus, Nicanor, Timon, Parmenas, and Nicolas, Acts 6:1–6.

7. What preacher boiled a pot of bones to illustrate a sermon?

Ezekiel, Ezekiel 24:1–14, especially verses 3–6.—"And utter a parable to the rebellious house, and say unto them, Thus saith the Lord God; Set on a pot, set it on, and also pour water into it: Gather the pieces thereof into it, even every good piece, the thigh, and the shoulder; fill it with the choice bones. Take the choice of the flock, and burn also the bones under it, and make it boil well, and let them seethe the bones of it therein. Wherefore thus saith the Lord God; Woe to the bloody city, to the pot whose scum is therein, . . ."

8. What was said to have been David's only sin?

The "matter of Uriah the Hittite," First Kings 15:5.— "Because David did that which was right in the eyes of the Lord, and turned not aside from anything that he commanded him all the days of his life, save only in the matter of Uriah the Hittite." David had had Uriah killed and took Uriah's wife Bathsheba as his wife. See Second Samuel 11 and 12. To say that David did right except in this matter is to let him off rather charitably, one thinks after reading the David cycle of stories in First and Second Samuel.

9. Who protested at poor men being unwelcome in church?

James, James 2:2–4.—". . . if there come into your assembly a man with a gold ring, in goodly apparel, and there come in also a poor man in vile raiment; And ye have respect to him that weareth the gay clothing, and say unto him, Sit thou here in a good place; and say to the poor, Stand thou there, or sit here under my footstool: Are ye not then partial in yourselves, and are become judges of evil thoughts?"

10. Who was stoned to death for preaching a sermon?

Stephen, Acts 6:8–7:60, especially 6:57–58.—"Then they cried out with a loud voice, and stopped their ears, and ran upon him with one accord, And cast him out of the city, and stoned him: . . ."

11. How many of the Ten Commandments did Jesus recite when asked which of them should be kept?

Five, Matthew 19:17–19.—". . . if thou wilt enter into life, keep the commandments. He [the rich young man] saith unto him, Which? Jesus said, Thou shalt do no murder, Thou shalt not commit adultery, Thou shalt not steal, Thou shalt not bear false witness, Honour thy father and thy mother: and, Thou shalt love thy neighbour as thyself." Note that the sixth one mentioned is not in the Ten Commandments (Exodus 20 or Deuteronomy 5) but is found in Leviticus 19:18. Both Mark's and Luke's account of this incident vary from Matthew's and from each other. In place of Matthew's sixth one, Mark 10:19 has a new one not found in the Ten Commandments, "Defraud not." Luke has only five, agreeing with the five common to Matthew and Mark. See Luke 18:20.

Note also that all three accounts record Jesus as quoting only commandments having to do with the relation of man to man.

12. When did priests work a "racket" with offering-money?

In the days of king Jehoash, Second Kings 12:4-7 (Moffatt's translation is preferable here).—"Jehoash had ordered the priests that 'all sacred monies paid into the temple of the Eternal, the money each man was assessed to pay, and the money which he contributed of his own accord, all must be taken by the priests, by each priest from his own customers, and devoted to the repair of any dilapidations to be found in the temple.' But even when king Jehoash had reached his twenty-third year, the priests had not repaired the dilapidations of the temple. So king Jehoash summoned Jehoiada and the other priests. 'Why have you not repaired the dilapidations of the temple?' he asked them. 'Instead of accepting money from your customers, hand it over for the repair of the temple.' "

13. Where is the only mention of a vestry?

Second Kings 10:22.—"And he said unto him that was over the vestry, Bring forth vestments for all the worshippers of Baal. And he brought them forth vestments."

14. What preacher was angry when his preaching converted a city?

Jonah, Jonah 3:1-5, 4:1.—"And the word of the Lord came unto Jonah the second time, saying, Arise, go unto Nineveh, that great city, and preach unto it the preaching that I bid thee. So Jonah arose, and went unto Nineveh, according unto the word of the Lord. . . . So the people of Nineveh believed God, and proclaimed a fast, and put on sackcloth, from the greatest of them even to the least of them. . . . But it displeased Jonah exceedingly, and he was very angry."

15. Who fell asleep during a long sermon?

Eutychus, Acts 20:9.—"And there sat in a window a certain young man named Eutychus, being fallen into a deep sleep: and as Paul was long preaching, he sunk down with sleep, and fell down from the third loft, and was taken up dead."

16. What preacher broke a bottle at the climax of his sermon?

Jeremiah, Jeremiah 19, especially verses 1, 2, 10, 11.—"Thus saith the Lord, Go and get a potter's earthen bottle, and take of the ancients of the people, and of the ancients of the priests; And go forth unto the valley of the son of Hinnom, which is by the entry of the east gate, and proclaim there the words that I shall tell thee. . . . Then shalt thou break the bottle in the sight of the men that go with thee, And shalt say unto them, Thus saith the Lord of hosts; Even so will I break this people and this city, as one breaketh a potter's vessel, that cannot be made whole again: and they shall bury them in Tophet, till there be no place to bury."

17. Who was the first preacher to get intoxicated?

Noah, Genesis 9:20–21.—"And Noah began to be an husbandman, and he planted a vineyard: And he drank of the wine, and was drunken: . . ." Second Peter 2:5: "And spared not the old world, but saved Noah the eighth person, a preacher of righteousness, bringing in the flood upon the world of the ungodly;"

18. Who instituted every-member weekly church offerings?

Paul, First Corinthians 16:1–2.—"Now concerning the collection for the saints, as I have given order to the churches of Galatia, even so do ye. Upon the first day of the week let every one of you lay by him in store, as God hath prospered him, that there be no gatherings when I come."

19. Who was the first Christian preacher to take wages from a church?

Paul, Second Corinthians 11:8.—"I robbed other churches, taking wages of them, to do you service."

20. Where are Christians forbidden to permit heretics to enter their houses?

Second John 1:9–11.—". . . He that abideth in the doctrine of Christ, he hath both the Father and the Son. If there come any unto you, and bring not this doctrine, receive him not into your house, neither bid him God speed: For he that biddeth him God speed is partaker of his evil deeds."

21. What man was made a priest for killing a pair of lovers?

Phinehas, for killing Zimri and Cozbi, Numbers 25.—

"And Israel abode in Shittim, and the people began to commit whoredom with the daughters of Moab. . . . And, behold, one of the children of Israel came and brought unto his brethren a Midianitish woman in the sight of Moses, and in the sight of all the congregation of the children of Israel, . . . And when Phinehas, the son of Eleazar, the son of Aaron the priest, saw it, he rose up from among the congregation, and took a javelin in his hand; And he went after the man of Israel into the tent, and thrust both of them through, the man of Israel, and the woman through her belly. So the plague was stayed from the children of Israel. And those that died in the plague were twenty and four thousand. And the Lord spake unto Moses, saying, Phinehas, the son of Eleazar, the son of Aaron the priest, hath turned my wrath away from the children of Israel, while he was zealous for my sake among them, that I consumed not the children of Israel in my jealousy. Wherefore say, Behold, I give unto him my covenant of peace: And he shall have it, and his seed after him, even the covenant of an everlasting priesthood; because he was zealous for his God, and made an atonement for the children of Israel. Now the name of the Israelite that was slain . . . was Zimri, . . . And the name of the Midianitish woman that was slain was Cozbi. . . ."

XXVII

Of Interest to Physicians

1. What are the first three recorded instances of artificial respiration?

2. What verse quotes Jesus as opposed to preventive medicine?

3. Where is described the ancient method of setting a fractured arm?

4. What congenital malformations are mentioned in the Bible?

5. Upon what Bible character was performed a surgical operation with use of an anesthetic?

6. What surgical operation was performed with a flint knife?

7. What hygienic measures were specifically commanded to prevent the spread of venereal disease?

8. Where are two methods of emasculation mentioned?

9. When did men have the pains of childbirth?

10. Where is a description of ancient obstetrical practice?

11. Where are labor-stools mentioned?

12. What city's drinking-water caused miscarriages?

13. What Bible record is there of a foetus hearing?

14. Who wished he had been an abortion?

15. In what four places is "medicine" mentioned in the Bible?

16. Who are the first physicians mentioned?

17. Who feigned insanity successfully?

18. Who said, "Is there no balm in Gilead; is there no physician there?"

19. Who "suffered many things of many physicians"?

20. Who said, "Physician, heal thyself"?

21. Who was "the beloved physician"?

22. With what diseases were the Jews threatened if they did not keep the commandments?

23. What evidence is there that the Bible theory of embryology was that of epigenesis?

24. What two long chapters are devoted to a description of a disease?

25. What sick man, bed-ridden for eight years, was told to get up and make his bed?

26. Who cured a boil with a fig poultice?

27. Who cured epilepsy, and how?

28. What verse indicates that the Jews feared moonstroke as well as sunstroke?

29. What was the greatest number of generations alive at one time?

30. What was the favorite part of the anatomy for stabbing victims?

31. Whose ear was amputated with a sword?

32. What king, suffering from a foot disease, excited comment because "in his disease he sought not to the Lord, but to the physicians"?

ANSWERS TO QUESTIONS OF INTEREST TO PHYSICIANS

1. What are the first three recorded instances of artificial respiration?

God and Adam, Genesis 2:7.—"And the Lord God formed

man of the dust of the ground, and breathed into his nostrils the breath of life; and man became a living soul."

Elijah and the son of the Widow of Zarephath, First Kings 17:17, 21, 22.—"And it came to pass after these things, that the son of the woman [of Zarephath], the mistress of the house, fell sick; and his sickness was so sore, that there was no breath left in him. . . . And he [Elijah] stretched himself upon the child three times, and cried unto the Lord, and said, O Lord my God, I pray thee, let this child's soul come into him again. And the Lord heard the voice of Elijah; and the soul of the child came into him again, and he revived."

Elisha and the son of the Shunammite woman, Second Kings 4:32–35.—"And when Elisha was come into the house, behold, the child was dead, and laid upon the bed. He went in therefore, and shut the door upon them twain, and prayed unto the Lord. And he went up, and lay upon the child, and put his mouth upon his mouth, and his eyes upon his eyes, and his hands upon his hands: and he stretched himself upon the child; and the flesh of the child waxed warm. Then he returned, and walked in the house to and fro; and went up, and stretched himself upon him: and the child sneezed seven times, and the child opened his eyes."

2. What verse quotes Jesus as opposed to preventive medicine?

Matthew 9:12.—"But when Jesus heard that, he said unto them, They that be whole need not a physician, but they that are sick." See also Mark 2:17.

3. Where is described the ancient method of setting a fractured arm?

Ezekiel 30:21.—"Son of man, I have broken the arm of Pharaoh king of Egypt; and, lo, it shall not be bound up to be healed, to put a roller to bind it, to make it strong to hold the sword." The Revised Version has: ". . . it hath not been bound up, to apply healing medicines, to put a bandage to bind it, . . ."

4. What congenital malformations are mentioned in the Bible?

Second Samuel 21:20.—"And there was yet a battle in Gath, where was a man of great stature, that had on every hand six fingers, and on every foot six toes, four and twenty in number; . . ." (See also First Chronicles 20:6.) Leviticus 21:18–21: "For whatsoever man he be that hath a blemish, he shall not approach: a blind man, or a lame, or he that hath a flat nose, or anything superfluous, Or a man that is brokenfooted, or brokenhanded, Or crookbackt, or a dwarf, or that hath a blemish in his eye, or be scurvy, or scabbed, or hath his stones broken; No man that hath a blemish of the seed of Aaron the priest shall come nigh to offer the offerings of the Lord made by fire: . . ." Moffatt's translation has: ". . . no blind man, no lame man, no one with a mutilated face, no one with a limb too long, no one with a broken foot or broken hand, no hunchback, no dwarf, no one with defective eyesight, no one suffering from itch or skin-disease, no one with broken testicles—. . ."

5. *Upon what Bible character was performed a surgical operation with use of an anesthetic?*

Adam, Genesis 2:21.—"And the Lord God caused a deep sleep to fall upon Adam, and he slept: and he took one of his ribs, and closed up the flesh instead thereof;"

6. *What surgical operation was performed with a flint knife?*

Circumcision, Joshua 5:2–3, RV.—"At that time Jehovah said unto Joshua, Make thee knives of flint, and circumcise again the children of Israel the second time. And Joshua made him knives of flint, and circumcised the children of Israel at the hill of the foreskins." AV has "sharp knives," but the margin gives "knives of flints."

See also Exodus 4:25, RV.—"Then Zipporah took a flint, and cut off the foreskin of her son, . . ." Here the AV has "a sharp stone."

The Septuagint version records in Joshua 24:30 that the flint knives were buried with Joshua. The use of flint knives points to the probable survival of the practice from the stone age.

7. *What hygienic measures were specifically commanded to prevent the spread of venereal disease?*

Leviticus 15 gives elaborate directions for the washing of every thing and every person coming in contact with a person who had "a running issue out of his flesh." The AV margin gives the alternate translation "running of the reins." Moffatt translates it "a discharge from his private parts." The Hebrew word used here is the one used for gonorrhea, and is also found in Leviticus 22:4; Numbers 5:2; and Second Samuel 3:29.

8. Where are two methods of emasculation mentioned?

Deuteronomy 23:1.—"He that is wounded in the stones, or hath his privy member cut off, shall not enter into the congregation of the Lord." Moffatt has: "No eunuch, no man sexually mutilated, . . ."

9. When did men have the pains of childbirth?

In the days of Jeremiah, Jeremiah 30:6.—". . . wherefore do I see every man with his hands on his loins, as a woman in travail, and all faces are turned into paleness?"

10. Where is a description of ancient obstetrical practice?

Ezekiel 16:4.—"And as for thy nativity, in the day thou wast born thy navel was not cut, neither wast thou washed with water to supple thee; thou wast not salted at all, nor swaddled at all."

11. Where are labor-stools mentioned?

Exodus 1:16.—"And he said, When ye do the office of a midwife to the Hebrew women, and see them upon the stools; if it be a son, then ye shall kill him: but if it be a daughter, then she shall live."

12. What city's drinking-water caused miscarriages?

Jericho's, Second Kings 2:19, Moffatt's translation.—"The townsmen said to Elisha, 'The situation of this town is delightful, as my lord sees, but the water is bad and it causes miscarriages.'" The AV has "but the water is naught, and the ground barren," but the margin admits that the Hebrew means, "causing to miscarry."

13. What Bible record is there of a foetus hearing?

Elisabeth was pregnant with the child later known as John the Baptist, which leaped in the womb at the sound of the voice of Mary who was to be the mother of Jesus. See Luke 1:41: "And it came to pass, that, when Elisabeth heard the salutation of Mary, the babe leaped in her womb; and Elisabeth was filled with the Holy Ghost:" Here, and in verse 44, it is implied that the unborn child recognized the presence of her who was to be the mother of Jesus, of whom John the Baptist was to be the forerunner or herald. This incident belongs to the class of myth in which a child gives very early precocious indication of his future life work.

14. Who wished he had been an abortion?

Job, Job 3:2, 3, 11, 16.—"And Job spake, and said, Let the day perish wherein I was born, and the night in which it was said, There is a man child conceived . . . Why died I not from the womb? Why did I not give up the ghost when I came out of the belly? . . . Or as an hidden untimely birth I had not been; as infants which never saw light." Moffatt translates verse 16: "Why was I not buried like an abortion, like still-born babies that never see the daylight?"

15. In what four places is "medicine" mentioned in the Bible?

Proverbs 17:22.—"A merry heart doeth good like a medicine: . . ."

Jeremiah 30:13.—". . . thou hast no healing medicines."

Jeremiah 46:11.—"Go up into Gilead, and take balm, O virgin, the daughter of Egypt: in vain shalt thou use many medicines; for thou shalt not be cured."

Ezekiel 47:12.—"And by the river upon the bank thereof, . . . shall grow all trees . . . and the fruit thereof shall be for meat, and the leaf thereof for medicine."

16. Who are the first physicians mentioned?

The Egyptians who embalmed Israel [Jacob], Genesis 50:2.—"And Joseph commanded his servants the physicians to embalm his father: and the physicians embalmed Israel." Instead of physicians Moffatt translates "embalmers," but the Hebrew word, rapha, used here, is the same as that used in Second Chronicles 16:12, where the healing of disease is obviously contemplated.

17. Who feigned insanity successfully?

David, First Samuel 21:12–15.—"And David . . . was sore afraid of Achish the king of Gath. And he changed his behavior before them, and feigned himself mad in their hands, and scrabbled on the doors of the gate, and let his spittle fall down upon his beard. Then said Achish unto his servants, Lo, ye see the man is mad: wherefore then have ye brought him to me? Have I need of mad men, that ye have brought this fellow to play the mad man in my presence? . . ."

18. Who said, "Is there no balm in Gilead; is there no physician there?"

Jeremiah, Jeremiah 8:22.—"Is there no balm in Gilead; is there no physician there? why then is not the health of the daughter of my people recovered?"

19. Who "suffered many things of many physicians"?

The woman of Mark 5:25–34 who had "an issue of blood," described in verses 25 and 26: "And a certain woman, which had an issue of blood twelve years, and had suffered many things of many physicians, and had spent all that she had, and was nothing bettered, but rather grew worse." Moffatt translates the issue of blood as a "hemorrhage." See also Luke 8:43.

20. Who said, "Physician, heal thyself"?

Jesus, quoting a proverb, Luke 4:23–24.—"And he [Jesus] said unto them, Ye will surely say unto me this proverb, Physician, heal thyself: whatsoever we have heard done in Capernaum, do also here in thy country. And he said, Verily I say unto you, No prophet is accepted in his own country." Dr. Alfred Plummer, commenting on this passage, notes that similar proverbs are found in the writings of Euripides, Sulspicius, Galen, Aeschylus, and Ovid.

21. Who was "the beloved physician"?

Luke, Colossians 4:14.—"Luke, the beloved physician, and Demas, greet you."

22. With what diseases were the Jews threatened if they did not keep the commandments?

Consumption, fever, inflammation, an extreme burning, the botch of Egypt, emerods, the scab, the itch, madness, and blindness, Deuteronomy 28:15, 22, 27, 28.—"But it shall come to pass, if thou wilt not hearken unto the voice of the Lord thy God, to observe to do all his commandments and his statutes which I command thee this day; that all these curses shall come upon thee, and overtake thee: . . . The Lord shall smite thee with a consumption, and with a fever, and with an inflammation, and with an extreme burning, . . . The Lord will smite thee with the botch of Egypt, and with the emerods, and with the scab, and with the itch, whereof thou canst not be healed. The Lord shall smite thee with madness, and blindness, and astonishment of heart:" Moffatt translates these diseases as "consumption, fever, ague, erysipelas, Egyptian boils, tumours, itch, madness and blindness."

23. What evidence is there that the Bible theory of embryology was that of epigenesis?

"The theory of generation" known as epigenesis is, according to Webster, the theory "holding that the germ or embryo is created entirely new, not merely expanded and unfolded by the procreative power." Psalm 139:13–16: ". . . thou hast covered me in my mother's womb. I will praise thee; for I am fearfully and wonderfully made: marvellous are thy works; and that my soul knoweth right well. My substance was not hid from thee, when I was made in secret, and curiously wrought in the lowest parts of the earth. Thine eyes did see my substance, yet being unperfect, and in thy book all my members were written, which in continuance were fashioned, when as yet there was none of them." See also Job 10:8–11.

24. What two long chapters are devoted to a description of a disease?

Leprosy, Leviticus, chapters 13 and 14.

25. What sick man, bed-ridden for eight years, was told to get up and make his bed?

Aeneas, Acts 9:33–34.—"And there he [Peter] found a certain man named Aeneas, which had kept his bed eight years, and was sick of the palsy. And Peter said unto him, Aeneas, Jesus Christ maketh thee whole; arise, and make thy bed. And he arose immediately." The "palsy" was paralysis.

26. Who cured a boil with a fig poultice?

Isaiah, Second Kings 20:7.—"And Isaiah said, Take a lump of figs. And they took, and laid it on the boil [of King Hezekiah], and he recovered." The same incident is referred to in Isaiah 38:21: "For Isaiah had said, Let them take a lump of figs, and lay it for a plaister upon the boil, and he shall recover."

27. Who cured epilepsy, and how?

Jesus by driving out a demon, according to Matthew 17:14–18.—". . . there came to him a certain man, kneeling down to him, and saying, Lord, have mercy on my son: for he is lunatick [RV has "epileptic"], and sore vexed: for ofttimes he falleth into the fire, and oft into the water. And I brought him to thy disciples, and they could not cure him. Then Jesus answered and said, O faithless and perverse generation, how long shall I be with you? how long shall I suffer you? bring him hither to me. And Jesus rebuked the devil; and he departed out of him: and the child was cured from that very hour."

28. What verse indicates that the Jews feared moonstroke as well as sunstroke?

Psalm 121:6.—"The sun shall not smite thee by day, nor the moon by night."

29. What was the greatest number of generations alive at one time?

Nine, according to Genesis, chapter 5, where it is easily to be figured that Adam's great-great-great-great-great-great-grandson, Lamech, was 56 years old when Adam died at the age of 930 years. The nine men alive at once were Adam, Seth, Enos, Cainan, Mahalaleel, Jared, Enoch, Methuselah, and Lamech.

30. What was the favorite part of the anatomy for stabbing victims?

Evidently "under the fifth rib," where Asahel was stabbed by Abner (Second Samuel 2:23), Abner in his turn by Joab (Second Samuel 3:27), Ishbosheth by Rechab and Baanah (Second Samuel 4:6), and Amasa by Joab (Second Samuel 20:10).

31. Whose ear was amputated with a sword?

Malchus's, John 18:10.—"Then Simon Peter having a sword drew it, and smote the high priest's servant, and cut off his right ear. The servant's name was Malchus." See also Mark 14:47.

32. What king, suffering from a foot disease, excited comment because "in his disease he sought not to the Lord, but to the physicians"?

Asa, Second Chronicles 16:12.—"And Asa in the thirty and ninth year of his reign was diseased in his feet, until his disease was exceeding great; yet in his disease he sought not to the Lord, but to the physicians." See also First Kings 15:23.

XXVIII

Naïve Ideas About God

1. What giants were God's grandsons?
2. Who fed God butter, milk, and veal?
3. At what did God wink?
4. When did God change his mind?
5. Who said that God would hiss for a fly and a bee?
6. What color was God's hair?
7. When did God get tired?
8. When did God walk in a garden?
9. Where is God's face mentioned?
10. Who tells of God's lips?
11. Who mentions God's eyelids?
12. Who tells of God exhaling smoke from his nostrils?
13. Who describes God's tongue?
14. Who mentions God's mouth?
15. Where are God's fingers mentioned?
16. Who thought God had wings?
17. Where does it speak of God shaving someone from head to foot with a borrowed razor?
18. Where does it speak of God giving a bill of divorce?
19. How did God travel through the sky?
20. Who saw God's back but not his face?
21. When did God smell a sweet odor?

22. Who said that God had a glorious voice?

23. Where does it state that God controls a game of chance?

24. When did God kindle a bonfire with his breath?

25. What other passage implies that God's breath was hot?

26. When was God a tailor?

27. Where does it say that the Lord went sight-seeing?

28. When did God say that he was jealous?

29. With whom was God angry?

30. Who said that God was a man of war?

31. When did God make bare his arm?

32. Who said that God was as strong as a unicorn?

ANSWERS TO QUESTIONS ON NAIVE IDEAS ABOUT GOD

1. What giants were God's grandsons?

The children of the sons of God and the daughters of men, Genesis 6:1, 2, 4.—"And it came to pass, when men began to multiply on the face of the earth, and daughters were born unto them, That the sons of God saw the daughters of men that they were fair; and they took them wives of all which they chose. . . . There were giants in the earth in those days; and also after that, when the sons of God came in unto the daughters of men, and they bare children to them, the same became mighty men which were of old, men of renown." Similar beliefs, i.e., that primitive men were of large size, and that gods and other supernatural beings mated with human beings, are found in the folklore of many races, and are reflected in many virgin birth stories.

2. Who fed God butter, milk, and veal?

Abraham, Genesis 18, especially verses 1, 2, 7, 8.—"And the Lord appeared unto him [Abraham] in the plains of Mamre: and he sat in the tent door in the heat of the day;

And he lift up his eyes and looked, and, lo, three men stood by him: and when he saw them, he ran to meet them from the tent door, and bowed himself toward the ground. . . . And Abraham ran unto the herd, and fetcht a calf tender and good, and gave it unto a young man; and he hasted to dress it. And he took butter, and milk, and the calf which he had dressed, and set it before them; and he stood by them under the tree, and they did eat." This chapter has many resemblances to the story of Philemon and Baucis and the gods they entertained. .

3. At what did God wink?

At ignorance, according to Acts 17:30.—"And the times of this ignorance God winked at; but now commandeth all men every where to repent:"

4. When did God change his mind?

Genesis 6:5–7.—"And God saw that the wickedness of man was great in the earth, and that every imagination of the thoughts of his heart was only evil continually. And it repented the Lord that he had made man on the earth, and it grieved him at his heart. And the Lord said, I will destroy man whom I have created from the face of the earth; both man, and beast, and the creeping thing, and the fowls of the air; for it repenteth me that I have made them." See also Exodus 32:14.

5. Who said that God would hiss for a fly and a bee?

Isaiah, Isaiah 7:18.—"And it shall come to pass in that day, that the Lord shall hiss for the fly that is in the uttermost part of the rivers of Egypt, and for the bee that is in the land of Assyria."

6. What color was God's hair?

White, Daniel 7:9–14, especially verse 9.—". . . and the Ancient of days did sit, whose garment was white as snow, and the hair of his head like the pure wool: his throne was like the fiery flame, . . ." Revelation 1:10–20, especially verse 14: "His head and his hairs were white like wool, as white as snow; and his eyes were as a flame of fire;"

7. When did God get tired?

After his work of creation, Genesis 2:2.—"And on the seventh day God ended his work which he had made; and he rested on the seventh day from all his work which he had made."

8. When did God walk in a garden?

Genesis 3:8.—"And they heard the voice of the Lord God walking in the garden in the cool of the day: . . ."

9. Where is God's face mentioned?

Psalm 17 is a prayer of David to God, and concludes as follows: "As for me, I will behold thy face in righteousness: I shall be satisfied, when I awake, with thy likeness."

10. Who tells of God's lips?

Psalm 17:4.—". . . by the word of thy lips I have kept me from the paths of the destroyer." Isaiah 30:27.—"Behold, the name of the Lord cometh from far, burning with his anger, and the burden thereof is heavy: his lips are full of indignation, . . ."

11. Who mentions God's eyelids?

The Psalmist, Psalm 11:4.—"The Lord is in his holy temple, the Lord's throne is in heaven: his eyes behold, his eyelids try, the children of men."

12. Who tells of God exhaling smoke from his nostrils?

The Psalmist, Psalm 18:8.—"There went up a smoke out of his [God's] nostrils, and fire out of his mouth devoured: . . ."

13. Who describes God's tongue?

Isaiah, Isaiah 30:27.—"Behold, the name of the Lord cometh from far, . . . and his tongue as a devouring fire."

14. Who mentions God's mouth?

Isaiah, Isaiah 1:20.—". . . for the mouth of the Lord hath spoken it." Also very many other places.

15. Where are God's fingers mentioned?

Psalm 8:3.—"When I consider thy heavens, the work of thy fingers, the moon and the stars, which thou hast ordained;"

16. Who thought God had wings?

The Psalmist, Psalm 18:10.—"And he [God] rode upon

a cherub, and did fly: yea, he did fly upon the wings of the wind."

17. Where does it speak of God shaving someone from head to foot with a borrowed razor?

Isaiah 7:20.—"In the same day shall the Lord shave with a razor that is hired, namely, by them beyond the river, by the king of Assyria, the head, and the hair of the feet: and it shall also consume the beard." Assyria is the razor, and Judah the victim.

18. Where does it speak of God giving a bill of divorce?

Jeremiah 3:6-8.—"The Lord said also unto me in the days of Josiah the king, Hast thou seen that which backsliding Israel hath done? she is gone up on every high mountain and under every green tree, and there hath played the harlot. And I said after she had done all these things, Turn thou unto me. But she returned not. And her treacherous sister Judah saw it. And I saw, when for all the causes whereby backsliding Israel committed adultery I had put her away, and given her a bill of divorce; yet her treacherous sister Judah feared not, but went and played the harlot also."

19. How did God travel through the sky?

He rode on the cherubim, fabulous winged creatures, Ezekiel 10, especially verses 18-21.—"Then the glory of the Lord departed from off the threshold of the house, and stood over the cherubims. And the cherubims lifted up their wings, and mounted up from the earth in my sight: when they went out, the wheels also were beside them, . . . and the glory of the God of Israel was over them above. This is the living creature that I saw under the God of Israel by the river of Chebar; and I knew that they were the cherubims. Every one had four faces apiece, and every one four wings; and the likeness of the hands of a man was under their wings."

20. Who saw God's back but not his face?

Moses, Exodus 33:17-23.—"And the Lord said unto Moses, I will do this thing also that thou hast spoken: for thou hast found grace in my sight, and I know thee by name. And he said, I beseech thee, shew me thy glory. . . . And he said, Thou canst not see my face: for there shall no man see me and live. And the Lord said, Behold, there is a place by me, and thou shalt stand upon a rock: And it shall come to pass, while my glory passeth by, that I will put thee in a clift of a rock, and will cover thee with my hand while I pass by: And I will take away mine hand, and thou shalt see my back parts: but my face shall not be seen."

21. When did God smell a sweet odor?

When Noah offered burnt beasts and fowl, Genesis 8:20–21.—"And Noah builded an altar unto the Lord; and took of every clean beast, and of every clean fowl, and offered burnt offerings on the altar. And the Lord smelled a sweet savour; and the Lord said in his heart, I will not again curse the ground any more for man's sake; . . ."

22. Who said that God had a glorious voice?

Isaiah, Isaiah 30:30.—"And the Lord shall cause his glorious voice to be heard, . . ." See also Revelation 1:15: ". . . and his voice as the sound of many waters."

23. Where does it state that God controls a game of chance?

Proverbs 16:33.—"The lot is cast into the lap; but the whole disposing thereof is of the Lord." See also Joshua 18:6–10, Joel 3:3, Obadiah 1:11, Jonah 1:7, Nahum 3:10.

24. When did God kindle a bonfire with his breath?

Isaiah 30:33.—"For Tophet is ordained of old; yea, for the king it is prepared; he hath made it deep and large: the pile thereof is fire and much wood; the breath of the Lord, like a stream of brimstone, doth kindle it." See also Psalm 18:8.

25. What other passage implies that God's breath was hot?

Isaiah 40:7.—"The grass withereth, the flower fadeth: because the spirit (RV "breath") of the Lord bloweth upon it: . . ."

26. When was God a tailor?

When he made coats for Adam and Eve, Genesis 3:21.—"Unto Adam also and to his wife did the Lord God make coats of skins, and clothed them."

27. Where does it say that the Lord went sight-seeing?

Genesis 11:5.—"And the Lord came down to see the city and the tower, which the children of men builded."

28. When did God say that he was jealous?

In the Ten Commandments, Exodus 20:5.—"Thou shalt not bow down thyself to them, nor serve them: for I the Lord thy God am a jealous God, visiting the iniquity of the fathers upon the children . . ." See also Exodus 34:14, Deuteronomy 4:24, 5:9, 6:15, Joshua 24:19, Nahum 1:2.

29. With whom was God angry?

Solomon, First Kings 11:9.—"And the Lord was angry with Solomon, because his heart was turned from the Lord God of Israel, . . ." See also Exodus 22:24, Numbers 11:1, 10, 33, 12:9, 25:3, and many other places.

30. Who said that God was a man of war?

Moses, Exodus 15:3.—"The Lord is a man of war: the Lord is his name."

31. When did God make bare his arm?

Isaiah 52:10.—"The Lord hath made bare his holy arm in the eyes of all the nations; . . ."

32. Who said that God was as strong as a unicorn?

Balaam, Numbers 23:22.—"God brought them out of Egypt; he hath as it were the strength of an unicorn." Also Exodus 24:8.

XXIX

Of General Human Interest

1. Where in the Bible is Lilith, the legendary first wife of Adam, mentioned?

2. What famous Bible character had halitosis, "B. O.," and pyorrhea?

3. What Negro led an army of a million men?

4. How many brothers and sisters did Jesus have?

5. In what invasion did the Hebrews cut down all the trees and fill up the wells?

6. What Hebrew hocked horses?

7. What two Old Testament men loved each other "passing the love of women"?

8. Who commanded Christians to kiss each other?

9. What two men hid in a well?

10. What Biblical precedent is there for the college prank of stealing gates?

11. What men did not dare to come home until their beards had grown?

12. Where are atheists classed as fools?

13. Where is putting money out at interest condemned?

14. Where is the only mention of mortgages in the Bible?

15. Who stole money from his mother?

16. What son fell on his father's neck, and what father on his son's neck?

17. Who walked naked and barefoot three years as a publicity "stunt"?

18. Where is Ben-Hur mentioned in the Bible?

19. What was the unforgivable sin?

20. How large was Solomon's Temple?

21. How large was Solomon's own house?

22. Whose lips were touched with a live coal?

23. Who kissed calves?

24. What prophet was swept away by a whirlwind?

25. Who lost a borrowed axe?

26. When did an all-day prayer-meeting of 450 fail?

27. Who comforted a man by sitting silently beside him for a week?

28. How old was Noah at the time of the flood?

29. How long did Noah live after the flood?

30. For what were "boiling places" used?

31. Who had to shave his eyebrows?

32. Who longed for a drink of well-water and refused it when it was brought?

33. When did the Hebrews have a navy?

34. Where is a paper shortage prophesied?

35. Why was Daniel cast into the den of lions?

36. When was 120 years set as the normal life-span?

37. Who disguised himself successfully from his own brothers?

38. What are the three most famous heads of hair in the Bible?

39. What princess went bathing in a river?

40. Who behaved like a stubborn heifer?

41. Who advised a man not to trust a neighbor, a friend, nor even a wife?

42. Whose purse had holes in it?

43. Who prophesied that ten men of all nations would take hold of the skirt of a Jew?

44. Who asked for reserved seats in heaven?

45. Were the apostles sent by Jesus to anyone but Jews?

46. Who set up the first silent policeman?

47. What disciple had a Jewess for mother and a Greek for father?

48. Who said that whoever called another a fool was in danger of hell fire?

49. Whom did God strike dead because they would not practise communism?

50. Who escaped from Damascus in a basket?

51. What two fat men are mentioned in the Bible?

52. What pit was so smoky that the sun was darkened?

53. How soon did Jesus say he would return to earth?

54. Who thought Jesus was John Baptist risen from the dead?

55. Where is an Italian band mentioned in the Bible?

56. Of what nationality did Paul say that they were always liars?

57. What was done with Judas' thirty pieces of silver?

58. What does "Marana tha" mean?

59. What apostle was shipwrecked three times?

60. What were the oldest Christian denominations?

61. Who called the two leading religious sects of his time sons of snakes?

62. What was the penalty for copying a holy perfume?

63. Who charged that young widows are prone to gossip?

64. Who sat down under a juniper tree and prayed to die?

65. What Jew called himself greater than Solomon?

66. Of whom did Jesus say no man was greater?

67. How much older was John Baptist than Jesus?

68. Who or what was Antichrist?

69. Did Jesus believe in defending a lawsuit?

70. Who bought a field and a wife in the same transaction?

71. What is the Bible origin of the idea of Peter as gate-keeper of heaven?

72. What two birthday parties are described in the Bible?

73. How often did Jesus say one should forgive?

74. What apostle hinted that he had a cross branded on his body?

75. Who hid rings under an oak?

76. What two men cursed their own birthdays?

77. What rich man was a disciple of Jesus?

78. What is the only place in the Bible where a vampire is mentioned?

79. Who shook his lap?

80. Who dreamed of a tree which reached to heaven?

81. Who said God scared him with dreams and nightmares?

82. What dream was prohibited under penalty of death?

83. Who saw men as trees walking?

84. In what battle did the forest devour more than the sword?

85. What nation first discriminated against the Hebrews socially?

86. Who trampled naked sheikhs among thorns and this-tles?

ANSWERS TO QUESTIONS OF GENERAL HUMAN INTEREST

1. Where in the Bible is Lilith, the legendary first wife of Adam, mentioned?

Isaiah 34:14 RV margin only.—"And the wild beasts of the desert shall meet with the wolves, and the wild goat shall cry to his fellow; yea, the night-monster [margin, Hebrew Lilith] shall settle there, and shall find her a place of rest." The AV has "screech-owl," for which there is no excuse. The Hebrew has plainly, "Lilith" and Lilith was a well known figure in Jewish demonology and folk-lore. She was a female demon who hated children. "She was said to have been the first wife of Adam and to have flown away from him and to have become a demon." Hastings' Dictionary of the Bible, vol. 3:122. The word is related to the Hebrew word for "night," and Lilith was supposed to be abroad only at night, like a vampire.

2. What famous Bible character had halitosis, "B. O.," and pyorrhea?

Job, Job 19:17-20, especially Moffatt's translation.—"my breath is loathsome to my very wife, my smell is hateful to my children; even young lads despise me, when I draw near they run away; all my intimates detest me, men I love turn against me. My skin is clinging to my bones, my teeth are falling out."

3. What Negro led an army of a million men?

Zerah the Ethiopian, Second Chronicles 14:9.—"And there came out against them Zerah the Ethiopian with a host of a thousand thousand, . . ."

4. How many brothers and sisters did Jesus have?

Four brothers and at least two sisters, Mark 6:3.—"Is not this the carpenter, the son of Mary, the brother of James, and Joses, and of Juda, and Simon? and are not his sisters here with us? . . ."

5. In what invasion did the Hebrews cut down all the trees and fill up the wells?

The invasion of Moab, Second Kings 3:24-25.—". . . the Israelites rose up and smote the Moabites. . . . And they beat down the cities, and on every good piece of land cast every man his stone, and filled it; and they stopped all the wells of water, and felled all the good trees: . . ."

6. What Hebrew hocked horses?

David, First Chronicles 18:3-4.—"And David smote Hadarezer king of Zobah . . . And David took from him a thousand chariots, and seven thousand horsemen, and twenty thousand footmen: David also houghed all the chariot horses, but reserved of them an hundred chariots." RV has "hocked"; Moffatt has "hamstrung."

7. What two Old Testament men loved each other "passing the love of women"?

David and Jonathan, Second Samuel 1:26.—"I am distressed for thee, my brother Jonathan: very pleasant hast thou been unto me: thy love to me was wonderful, passing the love of women." See also First Samuel 20:17.

8. Who commanded Christians to kiss each other?

Paul, Romans 16:16.—"Salute one another with an holy kiss. . . ." See also First Corinthians 16:20, Second Corinthians 13:12, and First Thessalonians 5:26.

The author of First Peter gives similar advice in 5:14: "Greet ye one another with a kiss of charity. . . ." RV has "kiss of love."

9. What two men hid in a well?

Jonathan and Ahimaaz, Second Samuel 17:17-19.—"Now Jonathan and Ahimaaz stayed by En-rogel; for they might not be seen to come into the city: and a wench went and told them; and they went and told king David. Nevertheless a lad saw them, and told Absalom: but they went both of them away quickly, and came to a man's house in Bahurim, which had a well in his court; whither they went down. And the woman took and spread a covering over the well's mouth, and spread ground corn thereon; and the thing was not known."

10. What Biblical precedent is there for the college prank of stealing gates?

Samson at Gaza, Judges 16:1-3.—"Then went Samson to Gaza, and saw there an harlot, and went in unto her. . . . And they [the Gazites] compassed him in, and laid wait for him all night in the gate of the city. . . . And Samson lay till midnight, and arose at midnight, and took the doors of the gate of the city, and the two posts, and went away with them, bar and all, and put them upon his shoulders, and carried them up to the top of an hill that is before Hebron."

11. What men did not dare to come home until their beards had grown?

The servants of David, First Chronicles 19:4–5.—"Wherefore Hanun took David's servants, and shaved them, and cut off their garments in the midst hard by their buttocks, and sent them away. Then there went certain, and told David how the men were served. And he sent to meet them: for the men were greatly ashamed. And the king said, Tarry at Jericho until your beards be grown, and then return."

12. Where are atheists classed as fools?

Psalm 14:1.—"The fool hath said in his heart, There is no God. . . ."

13. Where is putting money out at interest condemned?

In many places, but especially Psalm 15:5.—"He that putteth not out his money to usury, nor taketh reward against the innocent. He that doeth these things shall never be moved."

14. Where is the only mention of mortgages in the Bible?

Nehemiah 5:3.—"Some also there were that said, We have mortgaged our lands, vineyards, and houses, that we might buy corn, because of the dearth."

15. Who stole money from his mother?

Micah, Judges 17:1–2.—"And there was a man of mount Ephraim, whose name was Micah. And he said unto his mother, The eleven hundred shekels of silver that were taken from thee, about which thou cursedst, and spakest of also in mine ears, behold, the silver is with me; I took it. And his mother said, Blessed be thou of the Lord, my son."

16. What son fell on his father's neck, and what father on his son's neck?

Joseph fell on his father's neck, Genesis 46:29.—"And Joseph made ready his chariot, and went up to meet Israel his father, to Goshen, and presented himself unto him; and he fell on his neck, and wept on his neck a good while."

The father fell on the prodigal son's neck, Luke 15:20.—"And he arose, and came to his father. But when he was yet a great way off, his father saw him, and had compassion, and ran, and fell on his neck, and kissed him."

17. Who walked naked and barefoot three years as a publicity "stunt"?

Isaiah, Isaiah 20:3.—"And the Lord said, Like as my

servant Isaiah hath walked naked and barefoot three years for a sign and wonder upon Egypt and upon Ethiopia;"

18. Where is Ben-Hur mentioned in the Bible?

A Ben-hur was an officer in Solomon's household, First Kings 4:7-8, RV.—"And Solomon had twelve officers over all Israel, who provided victuals for the king and his household: each man had to make provision for a month in a year. And these are their names: Ben-hur, in the hill-country of Ephraim; . . ."

19. What was the unforgivable sin?

Blasphemy against the Holy Ghost, according to Jesus, Mark 3:28-29.—"Verily I say unto you, All sins shall be forgiven unto the sons of men, and blasphemies wheresoever they shall blaspheme: But he that shall blaspheme against the Holy Ghost hath never forgiveness, but is in danger of eternal damnation:"

20. How large was Solomon's Temple?

Ninety feet long, thirty feet wide, and forty-five feet high, First Kings 6:2.—"And the house which king Solomon built for the Lord, the length thereof was threescore cubits, and the breadth thereof twenty cubits, and the height thereof thirty cubits." A cubit was approximately 18 inches. The Chronicler calls this temple, "exceeding magnifical" (First Chronicles 22:5), but it would hardly seem so to us today.

21. How large was Solomon's own house?

One hundred fifty feet long, seventy-five feet wide, and forty-five feet high, First Kings 7:1-2.—"But Solomon was building his own house thirteen years, . . . the length thereof was an hundred cubits, and the breadth thereof fifty cubits, and the height thereof thirty cubits, . . ." It is interesting to note that his own house was over four times the cubic capacity of the temple. It would have to be larger, in order to accommodate his seven hundred wives and three hundred concubines, who, if they had ever been permitted to enter the sacred temple at one time, would hardly have left room for anyone else.

22. Whose lips were touched with a live coal?

Isaiah's, Isaiah 6:6-7.—"Then flew one of the seraphims unto me, having a live coal in his hand, which he had taken with the tongs from off the altar: And he laid it upon my mouth, and said, Lo, this hath touched thy lips; and thine iniquity is taken away, and thy sin purged."

23. Who kissed calves?

The idolaters of Hosea 13:2.—"And now they sin more and more, and have made them molten images of their silver, and idols according to their own understanding, all of it the work of the craftsmen: they say of them, Let the men that sacrifice kiss the calves."

24. What prophet was swept away by a whirlwind?

Elijah, Second Kings 2:11.—"And it came to pass, as they still went on, and talked, that, behold, there appeared a chariot of fire, and horses of fire, and parted them both asunder; and Elijah went up by a whirlwind into heaven."

25. Who lost a borrowed axe?

A son of the prophets, Second Kings 6:5.—"But as one [of the sons of the prophet, see verse 1] was felling a beam, the ax head fell into the water: and he cried, and said, Alas, master! for it was borrowed."

26. When did an all-day prayer-meeting of 450 fail?

First Kings 18:26, 29.—"And they [the 450 prophets of Baal] took the bullock which was given them, and they dressed it, and called on the name of Baal from morning even until noon, saying, O Baal, hear us. But there was no voice, nor any that answered. And they leaped upon the altar which was made. And it came to pass, when midday was past, and they prophesied until the time of the offering of the evening sacrifice, that there was neither voice, nor any to answer, nor any that regarded."

27. Who comforted a man by sitting silently beside him for a week?

Job's three friends, Job 2:11, 13.—"Now when Job's three friends heard of all this evil that was come upon him, they came every one from his own place; . . . for they had made an appointment together to come to mourn with him and to comfort him. . . . So they sat down with him upon the ground seven days and seven nights, and none spake a word unto him: for they saw that his grief was very great."

28. How old was Noah at the time of the flood?

Six hundred years, Genesis 7:6.—"And Noah was six hundred years old when the flood of waters was upon the earth."

29. How long did Noah live after the flood?

Three hundred fifty years, Genesis 9:28.—"And Noah lived after the flood three hundred and fifty years."

30. For what were "boiling places" used?

For sacrifices, Ezekiel 46:23–24.—"And there was a row of building round about in them, round about them four, and it was made with boiling places under the rows round about. Then said he unto me, These are the places of them that boil, where the ministers of the house shall boil the sacrifice of the people." In verse 24, RV has "boiling-houses."

31. Who had to shave his eyebrows?

The leper, Leviticus 14:9.—"But it shall be on the seventh day, that he [the leper] shall shave all the hair off his beard and his eyebrows, even all his hair he shall shave off: ..."

32. Who longed for a drink of well-water and refused it when it was brought?

David, Second Samuel 23:15–17.—"And David longed, and said, Oh that one would give me drink of the water of the well of Bethlehem, which is by the gate! And the three mighty men brake through the host of the Philistines, and drew water out of the well of Bethlehem, that was by the gate, and took it, and brought it to David: nevertheless he would not drink thereof, but poured it out unto the Lord. And he said, Be it far from me, O Lord, that I should do this: is not this the blood of the men that went in jeopardy of their lives? therefore he would not drink it. ..."

33. When did the Hebrews have a navy?

In Solomon's time, First Kings 9:26.—"And king Solomon made a navy of ships in Ezion-geber, which is beside Eloth, on the shore of the Red Sea, in the land of Edom."

34. Where is a paper shortage prophesied?

Isaiah 19. This chapter is a prediction of dire calamity to be visited on Egypt. Among other troubles would be the drying up of their source of paper, the papyrus reed, Isaiah 19:7.—"The paper reeds by the brooks, by the mouth of the brooks, and everything sown by the brooks, shall wither, be driven away, and be no more."

35. Why was Daniel cast into the den of lions?

Because he was "framed" by his enemies, who succeeded in getting a law passed which they knew Daniel's religion would cause him to break. See at length in Daniel 6.

36. When was 120 years set as the normal life-span?

In antediluvian days, Genesis 6:3.—"And the Lord said, My spirit shall not always strive with man, for that he also is flesh: yet his days shall be an hundred and twenty years." Contrast this with Psalm 90:10.

37. Who disguised himself successfully from his own brothers?

Joseph, Genesis 42:7–8.—"And Joseph saw his brethren, and he knew them, but made himself strange unto them, and spake roughly unto them; and he said unto them, Whence come ye? And they said, From the land of Canaan to buy food. And Joseph knew his brethren, but they knew not him."

38. What are the three most famous heads of hair in the Bible?

Samson's, Judges 16:17.—"That he [Samson] told her [Delilah] all his heart, and said unto her, There hath not come a razor upon mine head; for I have been a Nazarite unto God from my mother's womb: if I be shaven, then my strength will go from me, and I shall become weak, and be like any other man."

Absalom's, Second Samuel 14:25–26.—"But in all Israel there was none to be so much praised as Absalom for his beauty: from the sole of his foot even to the crown of his head there was no blemish in him. And when he polled his head, (for it was at every year's end that he polled it:) he weighed the hair of his head at two hundred shekels after the king's weight."

The woman's who anointed Jesus, Luke 7:44.—"And he turned to the woman and said unto Simon, Seest thou this woman? I entered into thine house, thou gavest me no water for my feet: but she hath washed my feet with tears, and wiped them with the hairs of her head."

39. What princess went bathing in a river?

Pharaoh's daughter, Exodus 2:5.—"And the daughter of Pharaoh came down to wash herself at the river; . . ."

40. Who behaved like a stubborn heifer?

Israel (The Hebrew people personified), Hosea 4:16 RV. —"For Israel hath behaved himself stubbornly, like a stubborn heifer: . . ." AV has "backsliding."

41. Who advised a man not to trust a neighbor, a friend, nor even a wife?

Micah, Micah 7:5 RV.—"Trust ye not in a neighbor; put ye not confidence in a friend; keep the doors of thy mouth from her that lieth in thy bosom."

42. Whose purse had holes in it?

The wage earner's, Haggai 1:6.—". . . and he that earneth wages earneth wages to put it into a bag with holes."

43. Who prophesied that ten men of all nations would take hold of the skirt of a Jew?

Zechariah, Zechariah 8:23.—". . . In those days it shall come to pass, that ten men shall take hold out of all languages of the nations, even shall take hold of the skirt of him that is a Jew, saying, We will go with you: for we have heard that God is with you."

44. Who asked for reserved seats in heaven?

James and John, Mark 10:35, 37.—"And James and John, the sons of Zebedee, come unto him, saying, . . . Grant unto us that we may sit, one on thy right hand, and the other on thy left hand, in thy glory." In Matthew 20:20–23 it is their mother who asks.

45. Were the apostles sent by Jesus to anyone but Jews?

At first, no, Matthew 10:5–6.—"These twelve Jesus sent forth, and commanded them, saying, Go not into the way of the Gentiles, and into any city of the Samaritans enter ye not: But go rather to the lost sheep of the house of Israel."

But later, yes, Matthew 28:19.—"Go ye therefore, and teach all nations, baptizing them in the name of the Father, and of the Son, and of the Holy Ghost:" The authenticity of this passage has been questioned, partly because the triune baptismal formula has been held to belong to a later period. Mark 13:10, however, represents Jesus as saying:

"And the gospel must first be published among all nations."

46. Who set up the first silent policeman?

Jacob and Laban, Genesis 31:43–55, especially 45, 48, 49, 52.—"And Jacob took a stone, and set it up for a pillar. . . . And Laban said, This heap is a witness between me and thee this day. Therefore was the name of it called Galeed; And Mizpah; for he said, The Lord watch between me and thee, when we are absent one from another. . . . This heap be witness, and this pillar be witness, that I will not pass over this heap to thee, and that thou shalt not pass over this heap and this pillar unto me, for harm."

47. What disciple had a Jewess for mother and a Greek for father?

Timothy, Acts 16:1.—". . . a certain disciple was there, named Timotheus, the son of a certain woman, which was a Jewess, and believed; but his father was a Greek:"

48. Who said that whoever called another a fool was in danger of hell fire?

Jesus, Matthew 5:22.—". . . but whosoever shall say, Thou fool, shall be in danger of hell fire."

49. Whom did God strike dead because they would not practise communism?

Ananias and Sapphira, Acts 4:32 to 5:11.—"And the multitude of them that believed were of one heart and of one soul: neither said any of them that ought of the things which he possessed was his own; but they had all things common. . . . But a certain man named Ananias, with Sapphira his wife, sold a possession, And kept back part of the price, his wife also being privy to it, and brought a certain part, and laid it at the apostles' feet. But Peter said, Ananias, why hath Satan filled thine heart to lie to the Holy Ghost, and to keep back part of the price of the land? . . . And Ananias hearing these words fell down, and gave up the ghost." Verses 7–11 tell of the same fate befalling his wife.

50. Who escaped from Damascus in a basket?

Saul (Paul), Acts 9:23–25.—"And after that many days were fulfilled, the Jews took counsel to kill him: But their laying await was known of Saul. And they watched the gates day and night to kill him. Then the disciples took him by night, and let him down by the wall in a basket."

51. What two fat men are mentioned in the Bible?

Jeshurun and Eglon. Deuteronomy 32:15.—"But Jeshurun waxed fat, and kicked: thou art waxen fat, thou art grown thick, thou art covered with fatness; then he forsook God which made him, and lightly esteemed the Rock of his salvation." Judges 3:17: "And he brought the present unto Eglon king of Moab: and Eglon was a very fat man."

52. What pit was so smoky that the sun was darkened?

The bottomless pit of Revelation 9:2.—"And he opened the bottomless pit; and there arose a smoke out of the pit, as the smoke of a great furnace; and the sun and the air were darkened by reason of the smoke of the pit."

53. How soon did Jesus say he would return to the earth?

During the lifetime of his disciples, Matthew 16:28.— "Verily I say unto you, There be some standing here, which shall not taste of death, till they see the Son of man coming in his kingdom." See also Matthew 10:23, 24:34, Mark 8:38–9:1, 13:30, and Luke 21:32.

54. Who thought Jesus was John Baptist risen from the dead?

Herod, Matthew 14:1–2.—"At that time Herod the tetrarch heard of the fame of Jesus, And said unto his servants, This is John the Baptist; he is risen from the dead; and therefore mighty works do shew forth themselves in him."

55. Where is an Italian band mentioned in the Bible?

Acts 10:1.—"There was a certain man in Caesarea called Cornelius, a centurion of the band called the Italian band."

56. Of what nationality did Paul say that they were always liars?

The Cretians, Titus 1:12–13.—"One of themselves, even a prophet of their own, said, The Cretians are always liars, evil beasts, slow bellies. This witness is true. . . ."

57. What was done with Judas' thirty pieces of silver?

The potter's field was purchased, Matthew 27:7.—"And they took counsel, and bought with them the potter's field, to bury strangers in."

58. What does "Marana tha" mean?

"O Lord, come!" First Corinthians 16:22 RV margin.—
"If any man loveth not the Lord, let him be anathema.
Marana tha." Margin, "That is, O (or Our) Lord, come!"

59. What apostle was shipwrecked three times?

Paul, Second Corinthians 11:25.—"Thrice was I beaten
with rods, once was I stoned, thrice I suffered ship-
wreck, ..."

60. What were the oldest Christian denominations?

Partisans of Paul, Apollos, Cephas, and Christ, First Corinthians 1:10–15.—"Now I beseech you, brethren, by the
name of our Lord Jesus Christ, that ye all speak the same
thing, and that there be no divisions among you; ... Now
this I say, that every one of you saith, I am of Paul; and I
of Apollos; and I of Cephas; and I of Christ."

61. Who called the two leading religious sects of his time
    sons of snakes?

John Baptist, Matthew 3:7.—"But when he [John Bap-
tist] saw many of the Pharisees and Sadducees come to
his baptism, he said unto them, O generation of vipers, who
hath warned you to flee from the wrath to come?"
Jesus, Matthew 23:27, 33.—"Woe unto you, scribes and
Pharisees, hypocrites! ... Ye serpents, ye generation of vipers, how can ye escape the damnation of hell?" In both passages the RV has, "offspring of vipers."

62. What was the penalty for copying a holy perfume?

Exile, Exodus 30:34–38, especially 37–38.—"And as for
the perfume which thou shalt make, ye shall not make to
yourselves according to the composition thereof: it shall be
unto thee holy for the Lord. Whosoever shall make like
unto that, to smell thereto, shall even be cut off from his
people."

63. Who charged that young widows are prone to gossip?

Paul, First Timothy 5:11–13.—"But the younger widows
... withal they learn to be idle, wandering about from house
to house; and not only idle, but tattlers also and busybodies,
speaking things which they ought not."

64. Who sat down under a juniper tree and prayed to die?

Elijah, First Kings 19:4.—"But he himself [Elijah] went
a day's journey into the wilderness, and came and sat down

under a juniper tree: and he requested for himself that he might die; and said, it is enough; now, O Lord, take away my life; for I am not better than my fathers."

65. *What Jew called himself greater than Solomon?*

Jesus, Matthew 12:42.—". . . and, behold, a greater than Solomon is here."

66. *Of whom did Jesus say no man was greater?*

John the Baptist, Matthew 11:11.—"Verily I say unto you, Among them that are born of women there hath not risen a greater than John the Baptist: . . ." Then Jesus added, rather enigmatically, "notwithstanding he that is least in the kingdom of heaven is greater than he."

67. *How much older was John Baptist than Jesus?*

A comparison of Luke 1:24–26, 36, and 56–57 would indicate that John Baptist was about six months older than Jesus.

68. *Who or what was Antichrist?*

There is a little confusion about the matter. First John 2:22 states: ". . . He is antichrist, that denieth the Father and the Son." But First John 4:3 and Second John 1:7 state that an antichrist is anyone who "confesseth not that Jesus Christ is come in the flesh."

69. *Did Jesus believe in defending a lawsuit?*

Evidently not, Matthew 5:40.—"And if any man will sue thee at the law, and take away thy coat, let him have thy cloke also."

70. *Who bought a field and a wife in the same transaction?*

Boaz, Ruth 4, especially verses 9–10.—"And Boaz said unto the elders, and unto all the people, Ye are witnesses this day, that I have bought all that was Elimelech's, and all that was Chilion's and Mahlon's, of the hand of Naomi. Moreover Ruth the Moabitess, the wife of Mahlon, have I purchased to be my wife, to raise up the name of the dead upon his inheritance, . . ."

71. *What is the Bible origin of the idea of Peter as gate-keeper of heaven?*

Matthew 16:17–19.—"And Jesus answered and said unto him, Blessed art thou, Simon Barjona: for flesh and blood hath not revealed it unto thee, but my Father which is in heaven. And I say also unto thee, That thou art Peter, and upon this rock I will build my church; and the gates of hell shall not prevail against it. And I will give unto thee the keys of the kingdom of heaven: and whatsoever thou shalt bind on earth shall be bound in heaven: and whatsoever thou shalt loose on earth shall be loosed in heaven."

72. What two birthday parties are described in the Bible?

Pharaoh's, Genesis 40:20.—"And it came to pass the third day, which was Pharaoh's birthday, that he made a feast unto all his servants: . . ."

Herod's, Matthew 14:6.—"But when Herod's birthday was kept, the daughter of Herodias danced before them, and pleased Herod."

73. How often did Jesus say one should forgive?

Four hundred and ninety times, Matthew 18:21–22.— "Then came Peter to him, and said, Lord, how oft shall my brother sin against me, and I forgive him? till seven times? Jesus saith unto him, I say not unto thee, Until seven times: but, Until seventy times seven."

74. What apostle hinted that he had a cross branded on his body?

Paul, Second Corinthians 4:10.—"Always bearing about in the body the dying of the Lord Jesus, . . ." Galatians 6:17: ". . . for I bear in my body the marks of the Lord Jesus."

75. Who hid rings under an oak?

Jacob, Genesis 35:4.—"And they gave unto Jacob all the strange gods which were in their hand, and all their earrings which were in their ears; and Jacob hid them under the oak which was by Shechem."

76. What two men cursed their own birthdays?

Job, Job 3:1–3.—"After this opened Job his mouth, and cursed his day. And Job spake, and said, Let the day perish wherein I was born, and the night in which it was said, There is a man child conceived." Jeremiah, Jeremiah 20:14–15: "Cursed be the day wherein I was born: let not the day wherein my mother bare me be blessed. Cursed be the man who brought tidings to my father, saying, A man child is born unto thee; making him very glad."

77. What rich man was a disciple of Jesus?

Joseph of Arimathea, Matthew 27:57.—"When the even was come, there came a rich man of Arimathea, named Joseph, who also himself was Jesus' disciple:"

78. What is the only place in the Bible where a vampire is mentioned?

Only in the margin of the Revised Version of Proverbs 30:15.—"The horseleach [margin, "or vampire"] hath two daughters, crying, Give, give. . . ." Whether the Hebrew word, alukah, here has affinity with the Arabic, alakah, leech, or with aluk, vampire, is difficult to determine.

79. Who shook his lap?

Nehemiah, Nehemiah 5:13.—"Also I shook my lap, and said, So God shake out every man from his house, and from his labour, that performeth not this promise, even thus shall he be shaken out, and emptied. . . ."

80. Who dreamed of a tree which reached to heaven?

Nebuchadnezzar, Daniel 4:4, 5, 10, 11.—"I Nebuchadnezzar was at rest in mine house, and flourishing in my palace: I saw a dream which made me afraid, . . . I saw, and, behold, a tree in the midst of the earth, and the height thereof was great. The tree grew, and was strong, and the height thereof reached unto heaven, and the sight thereof to the end of all the earth:"

81. Who said God scared him with dreams and nightmares?

Job, Job 7:14-15, especially in Moffatt's translation.—"Then thou scarest me with dreams, thou appallest me with nightmares, till I would fain be strangled, I would prefer death to my pains."

82. What dream was prohibited under penalty of death?

Rebellion against Jehovah, Deuteronomy 13:1-5 RV.—"If there arise in the midst of thee a prophet, or a dreamer of dreams, and he give thee a sign or a wonder, and the sign or the wonder come to pass, whereof he spake unto thee saying, Let us go after other gods, . . . that prophet, or that dreamer of dreams, shall be put to death, because he hath spoken rebellion against Jehovah."

83. Who saw men as trees walking?

The blind man of Bethsaida, Mark 8:22-24.—"And he

cometh to Bethsaida; and they bring a blind man unto him, and besought him to touch him. And he took the blind man by the hand, and led him out of the town; and when he had spit on his eyes, and put his hands upon him, he asked him if he saw ought. And he looked up, and said, I see men as trees, walking."

84. In what battle did the forest devour more than the sword?

The Battle of the Forest of Ephraim, Second Samuel 18:6–8.—". . . and the battle was in the wood of Ephraim; Where the people of Israel were slain before the servants of David, and there was there a great slaughter that day of twenty thousand men. For the battle was there scattered over the face of all the country: and the wood devoured more people that day than the sword devoured."

85. What nation first discriminated against the Hebrews socially?

The Egyptians, Genesis 43:32.—". . . because the Egyptians might not eat bread with the Hebrews; for that is an abomination unto the Egyptians."

86. Who trampled naked sheikhs among thorns and thistles?

Gideon, Judges 8:4–16, especially Moffatt's translation.— "When Gideon reached the Jordan and crossed it, he and his three hundred men, they were worn out and famishing. So he asked the men of Sukkoth, 'Pray give my followers some loaves of bread, for they are worn out; we are in pursuit of Zebah and Zalmunna, the Midianite kings.' 'Give bread to your forces?' said the headmen of Sukkoth. 'Are Zebah and Zalmunna already in your hands?' Gideon answered, 'Very well, as soon as the Eternal has put Zebah and Zalmunna into my hands, I will trample you naked among thorns of the desert and thistles!' . . . Then Gideon the son of Joash returned from the battle, from the pass of Heres. . . . Whereupon he laid the sheikhs of the town upon thorns of the desert and thistles, and trampled down these men of Sukkoth."

XXX

Folk Questions with a Catch to Them

Author's Note:—These have been picked up here and there in America, and form probably the first collection of the sort. Some of them are atrocious puns, and others are very farfetched. They are inaccurate and unscholarly, but they are astonishingly popular and widely circulated. I have not been able to trace the authorship of any of them, and some are evidently ancient in America's oral tradition. They have come to me from farm folk, Sunday-school scholars, men at noontime luncheon clubs, one from a college professor, and three from a United States Congressman's wife. There must be many more current, and if readers will send me any others of interest, I will include them in the next edition. Some of the most popular, however, must needs abide in the oral tradition.

1. Who was the shortest man in the Bible?

2. Who was the smallest man?

3. Who was the straightest man?

4. Who was the first electrician?

5. Is the book of Hezekiah in the Old Testament or the New?

6. Why didn't the lions eat Daniel?

7. Who is the first woman mentioned in the Bible?

8. Who is the first man mentioned in the Bible?

9. Who is the first king mentioned in the Bible?

10. When was tennis played in Bible times?

11. Why was Paul like a horse?

12. What eight men milked a bear?

13. What verse makes children afraid?

14. Where is baseball referred to in the Bible?

15. Why did Moses not take any bees into the ark?

16. What game of cards is mentioned in the Bible?

17. What Bible character and his wife were golfers?

18. Who slept five in a bed?

19. What was the first mention of money?

20. Who, beside Melchizedek, had neither father nor mother?

21. At what time of day was Adam created?

22. What man was presented with a walking-stick?

23. Who stopped Adam and Eve from gambling?

24. What did Adam and Eve do when they were driven out of Eden?

25. What day of Adam's life was the longest?

26. Why was Eve made?

27. Who introduced salt meat into the navy?

28. Why was Noah like a hungry cat?

29. When was a rooster's crow heard by every living creature on earth?

30. Who ran the first canning factory?

31. Who had his seat changed in a theatre?

32. Why was Moses the wickedest man?

33. Who was the greatest orator?

34. Who was the most ambitious man?

35. What are the two smallest insects mentioned in the Bible?

ANSWERS TO FOLK QUESTIONS
WITH A CATCH TO THEM

1. Who was the shortest man in the Bible?

This question has three answers. In Massachusetts, they say, "Knee-high Miah" (Nehemiah); in New York, "Bildad the Shuhite" (shoe height); but when I quoted these at a Kiwanis luncheon in Ohio, they said their version was much better than either, for Simon Peter was obviously the shortest man, for he said, "Silver and gold have I none," and no one could be shorter than that.

For references, Nehemiah 1:1: "The words of Nehemiah the son of Hachaliah . . ." Bildad the Shuhite was one of Job's three comforters, Job 2:11: "Now when Job's three friends heard of all this evil that was come upon him, they came every one from his own place; Eliphaz the Temanite, and Bildad the Shuhite, and Zophar the Naamathite: for they had made an appointment together to come to mourn with him and to comfort him." The Simon Peter reference is Acts 3:6.

2. Who was the smallest man?

Peter, the disciple who slept on his watch, Matthew 26:40. —"And he cometh unto his disciples and findeth them asleep, and saith unto Peter, What, could ye not watch with me one hour?"

3. Who was the straightest man?

Joseph, because Pharaoh made a ruler of him, Genesis 41:42–43.—"And Pharaoh took his ring from his hand, and put it upon Joseph's hand, . . . and he made him ruler over all the land of Egypt."

4. Who was the first electrician?

Noah, when he took his family and the animals out of the ark, and thus made the ark light (arclight), Genesis 8:18–19.—"And Noah went forth, and his sons, and his wife, and his sons' wives with him: Every beast, every creeping thing, and every fowl, and whatsoever creepeth upon the earth, after their kinds, went forth out of the ark."

5. *Is the book of Hezekiah in the Old Testament or the New?*

Neither; there is no such book in the Bible.

6. *Why didn't the lions eat Daniel?*

Because he was mostly grit and backbone. See Daniel, chapters 1, 2, 4, 5, and especially 6.

7. *Who is the first woman mentioned in the Bible?*

Genesis (Jenny's sis-ter).

8. *Who is the first man mentioned in the Bible?*

Chap. 1 (Chapter One).

9. *Who is the first king mentioned in the Bible?*

King James, if you have the King James or Authorized Version, because of the dedication by the translators: "To the most high and mighty prince James, by the grace of God, King of Great Britain, etc."

10. *When was tennis played in Bible times?*

When Joseph served in Pharaoh's courts. There is no place in the Bible where this is definitely stated, but it is implied in Genesis 41:38–46 and the chapters following.

11. *Why was Paul like a horse?*

Because he liked Timothy ("timothy" is a kind of grass, named for one Timothy Hanson who brought the seed from New England to Maryland in the early 18th century). In Second Timothy 1:2, Paul addresses the epistle "To Timothy, my dearly beloved son: . . ." This incredibly simple joke is very popular in rural America, and is tried out on every new preacher in country churches by some one of his flock.

12. *What eight men milked a bear?*

Huz, Buz, Kemuel, Chesed, Hazo, Pildash, Jidlaph, and Bethuel, the eight sons of Abraham's brother Nahor, by his wife, Milcah. Genesis 22:23 RV states ". . . these eight did Milcah bear to Nahor, Abraham's brother."

13. *What verse makes children afraid?*

Psalm 69:9.—"For the zeal of thine house hath eaten me up; . . ." Children have actually been reported as afraid to go to church for fear of being eaten up by the "zeal," evidently thought of as an animal, perhaps a "seal."

14. Where is baseball referred to in the Bible?

In many places, according to the jokesters, including among the ones most frequently heard:

Genesis 1:1: "In the beginning . . ." (in the big inning).

Genesis 3:6: "And when the woman saw that the tree was good for food, and that it was pleasant to the eyes, and a tree to be desired to make one wise, she took of the fruit thereof, and did eat, and gave also unto her husband with her; and he did eat." This is interpreted as when Eve "stole first" and Adam "stole second."

Genesis 22:1–18, the account of Abraham preparing to slay his son Isaac and being prevented, is quoted as when Abraham tried to make a "sacrifice" hit.

Genesis 24:15–16: ". . . behold Rebekah came out, . . . and she went down to the well, and filled her pitcher, and came up." This is known as when Rebekah went to the well with a "pitcher."

Luke 15:11–32, the well known account of the return of the prodigal, is called when the prodigal son made a "home-run."

Luke 17:17: ". . . but where are the nine?"

The following are occasionally heard, and the connection with baseball will be obvious to anyone who knows the game:—

Genesis 4:8: ". . . when they [Cain and Abel] were in the field, . . ."

Genesis 43:26: "And when Joseph came home, . . ."

Exodus 4:4: ". . . And he put forth his hand, and caught it, . . ."

Numbers 11:32: "ten homers."

Second Kings 16:17: "And king Ahaz cut off the borders of the bases, . . ."

Second Kings 25:16: ". . . and the bases which Solomon had made . . ."

Psalm 19:12: "Who can understand his errors? . . ."

Psalm 26:1: "Judge me, O Lord; for I have walked in mine integrity: I have trusted also in the Lord; therefore I shall not slide."

Proverbs 18:10: ". . . the righteous runneth into it, and is safe."

Isaiah 41:16: "Thou shalt fan them, . . ."

Jeremiah 15:7: "And I will fan them. . . ."

Ezekiel 36:12: "Yea, I will cause men to walk. . . ."

Acts 14:14: ". . . Barnabas and Paul . . . ran in . . ."
Galatians 5:7: "Ye did run well; . . ."

15. *Why did Moses not take any bees into the ark?*

Because he hadn't yet been born: it was Noah who took
the various living things into the ark.

16. *What game of cards is mentioned in the Bible?*

When Neb euchred Nezzar (Nebuchadnezzar), Daniel 1:1.

17. *What Bible character and his wife were golfers?*

Ananias and Sapphira, Acts 5:1–11. This famous Bible
story of how Ananias told his memorable lie, was seconded
by his wife, and both were buried in the same grave, is interpreted as follows in golfing language: He was caught in a
bad lie, and she followed. Both, however, holed out in one.

18. *Who slept five in a bed?*

David, when he slept with his forefathers, First Kings
2:10: "So David slept with his fathers, . . ." The Hebrew
word, "aboth," here translated "fathers," means also "ancestors," and would be better translated in this passage as
"forefathers."

19. *What was the first mention of money?*

Genesis 8:10–11.—". . . he [Noah] sent forth the dove
out of the ark; And the dove came in to him in the evening;
and, lo, in her mouth was an olive leaf plukt off: . . ." This
becomes, forsooth, Noah's dove had a bill and went out
and brought a green back (green-back)!

20. *Who, beside Melchizedek, had neither father nor
mother?*

Melchizedek, in Hebrews 7:3, is said to have been "without father, without mother, . . ." Exodus 33:11 mentions
"Joshua, the son of Nun, . . ."

21. *At what time of day was Adam created?*

A little before Eve, Genesis 2:7, 21, 22.

22. *What man was presented with a walking-stick?*

Adam, when Eve presented him with a little Cain, Genesis 4:1.

23. *Who stopped Adam and Eve from gambling?*

God, when he took their Paradise (pair o' dice) away from them, Genesis 3:23.

24. What did Adam and Eve do when they were driven out of Eden?

They raised Cain, Genesis 3:23; 4:1.

25. What day of Adam's life was the longest?

The first, because it had no Eve, Genesis 2:18.

26. Why was Eve made?

For Adam's Express Company, Genesis 2:18–24. This quip is very popular in districts served by that company.

27. Who introduced salt meat into the navy?

Noah, when he took Ham into the ark, Genesis 7:13.

28. Why was Noah like a hungry cat?

Because he went 150 days and nights without finding Ararat (e'er a rat), Genesis 8:3–4.

29. When was a rooster's crow heard by every living creature on earth?

In Noah's ark, Genesis 7:13–23.

30. Who ran the first canning factory?

Noah, who filled a whole boat with preserved pairs, Genesis 7:7–9.

31. Who had his seat changed in a theatre?

Joseph, who was taken from the family circle and put in the pit, Genesis 37:3–24.

32. Why was Moses the wickedest man?

Because he broke all the Ten Commandments at once, Exodus 32:15–19.

33. Who was the greatest orator?

Samson, because he brought down the house although it was filled with his enemies, Judges 16:27–30.

34. Who was the most ambitious man?

Jonah, because even a whale couldn't keep him down, Jonah 2:10.

35. What are the two smallest insects mentioned in the
    Bible?

The widow's mite and the wicked flea. These are both
plays upon the double meanings of words. The "mite" which
the widow of Mark 12:42 contributed was a lepton, or a
half-farthing, but the word also means a tiny insect infest-
ing animals. Proverbs 28:1 gives a good opportunity for pun-
sters: "The wicked flee when no man pursueth: . . ."